Crazy Talk:
The Stories Jesus Told
(about himself)

Praise for *Crazy Talk: Stories Jesus Told (about himself)*

"Jesus got killed for the outrageous, irresponsible, and offensive stories he told. Read Crazy Talk from the posse at the Crackers and Grape Juice podcast and you will be reminded of what it's like to want to kill somebody because of his preaching."

> Rev. Dr. Will Willimon, United Methodist Bishop, Professor of the Practice of Christian Ministry at Duke Divinity

"Christianity is both a 2,000-year-old argument and an adventure during which you discover friends you would not have found apart from Jesus Christ. Here you will surely find either preachers with whom you want to argue or preachers whom you will want as friends. Perhaps you will find both."

> Dr. Stanley Hauerwas, Professor Emeritus of Christian Ethics at Duke Divinity

"Like the parables of Jesus, the sermons collected here are earthy, humorous, and connect with our most hidden, secret self. Like the preaching of the prophets, they manage to afflict the comfortable, comfort the afflicted, and never sound preachy. Not since Balaam's ass has the Word of the Lord been delivered in such an entertaining package!"

> The Rev. Dr. Rubén Rosario Rodríguez, Professor of Systematic Theology, Saint Louis University

"The Church has done more damage to the power of the parables than any other category of scripture. We have moralized them and purposed them for our own agendas. We have foisted them onto children and told them to "be good." We have called ourselves Good Samaritans and Eldest Brothers like a Biblically uneducated clown parade. They were never intended for any of that nonsense.

The Parables are intended to be void of morality and only consumed with the agenda of Jesus, who came *only* to save us. Buy this book. Jason, Teer, and the other yahoos at Crackers and Grape Juice will remind you just how bizarre, compelling, and truly unfair the parables really are. Thank God."

> Rev. Sarah Condon, *Churchy: The Real Life Adventures of a Wife, Mom, and Priest*

"I couldn't have said it better myself."

> Jesus of Nazareth, Carpenter & CEO of the Universe

A Publication by the Crackers & Grape Juice Podcast:

Taylor Mertins
David King (our minion)
Tommie Marshall
Dr. Johanna Hartelius
Teer Hardy
Jason Micheli

You can find us at www.crackersandgrapejuice.com

For Robert Capon:

Without whom we could not have written this book.

For Richard Bass (Master):

We're grateful to you for helping us to talk faith with and without stained glass language.

Table of Contents

Introduction
Dr. Johanna Hartelius

I wonder what would happen if anytime a pastor was about to preach on one of Jesus's parables, she started out saying, "The story you're about to hear is not about you. So, just listen." Would we in the pews feel relief or disappointment? I wonder, because the parables are so eminently invitational, almost irresistibly personal. How can we *not* think about how hard it would be to squeeze ourselves through the eye of a needle? (Luke 18:24-27) How can I not mutter under my breath, "If I had been working in that vineyard all day and those lazy bums got the same wage as me, I'd be pissed.'"? (Matthew 20:1–16) And how great is it to think of myself as a good Samaritan? (Luke 10:25-37). When I hear the one about the sower, I can secretly pat myself on the back for being such good soil. (Mark 4:1-20) I mean, I work out. I eat right. I donate to GoFundMe projects. My soil is the best.

In *Crazy Talk: Stories Jesus Told*, you'll find pastors doing what pastors do, which is trying to get congregations to laugh. Only professors are thirstier for giggly affirmation from students than clergy from churchgoers. No, but seriously, folks, the excellent sermons collected here Teer Hardy, Taylor Mertins, Jason Micheli and his minion David King walk us through the unrelenting message of the gospel parables: that Jesus Christ the Risen Lord is here and in charge. We humans are here, too, but we mess everything up. Not to mention, we cannot understand Jesus to save our lives. Literally. In "Inescapable," Taylor works through the first ten verses of Luke 17 to help us distinguish between the Good News of salvation and the really terrible news, or prospect, of getting what we all deserve, which is a millstone around our necks.

In "God in the Hands of Angry Sinners," Jason shows us that the post-resurrection narrative of Jesus visiting those who betrayed him pivots on the greeting, "Peace!" Just like the disciples, we fear our own infinite shittiness, but Christ shows up at the door (that we are cowering behind) and imposes a love that brings me to tears even as I write this. In "We're the Ones in the Ditch," Teer pulls off an almost M. Night Shyamalanesque plot-twist, disabusing us of the smug notion that we're the Samaritan who extends mercy; when really, mercy is all we can hope for – extravagant and unmerited. In "Extracting the Truth," David finds the simplest yet potent reading of one of Luke's parables: Lazarus doesn't do anything. And from this, David proclaims the justification of God.

One of my favorite passages has always been when Jesus calls the first disciples, saying, "Come and follow me, and I will make you fishers of men." I don't know exactly why I like it so much. It's in my ear most of the time. I'm not a fisher by any stretch of the imagination. I'm not a pastor, or a social justice advocate, or even a do-gooder. I am an academic introvert, so the idea that this parable is somehow resonant with me is ridiculous. But the great thing is, I don't have to figure out why the parable moves me. It is not about me. It is a revelation, not an allegorical or analytical hermeneutic or teaching method. It is a form through which Jesus reflects himself into light that I can see, but just for a moment. And so, when I hear a parable, it is sufficient for me to listen. And what a relief – Thanks be to God!

Every Last Loser
Matthew 20:1-16
Jason Micheli

I'm sorry if you've been led to believe that Jesus should mind his own business and stay out of the public square.

"I don't want to hear about politics at church!"

It's maybe the only surviving bipartisan sentiment. Church folks always want the Church to stay out of politics, which for most of us—let's be honest now—usually means we don't want the Church to challenge our particular hue of politics.

I remember—

One Sunday back in my very first church just outside of Princeton, after I preached an allegedly "political" sermon against state-sponsored torture, which both of America's political parties supported at the time (this was right after September 11), this ruddy-faced church member assaulted me in the narthex and, sticking his finger in my chest, hollered at me, "Just where do you get off preaching like that, preacher?!"

I stammered.

So, he pressed me.

"If Jesus were still alive, do you honestly think he'd having anything to say about torture and the government?!"

"Um, well, uh...I mean, he was crucified, I think...um...maybe he would have..." I started to say.

He shook his head and waved me off.

"Jesus would be rolling over in his grave if knew you'd brought politics into *our* church!"

Of course, that's the rub.

It's not our church. It's not my church. It's not your church. It's not *our* church. It's his Church. *We* can insist that the Church keep out of politics—that's fine, I'm not a sadist. It makes my life easier—but notice how such insistence assumes that we're in charge of the Church.

Though we spent three long years plotting to kill him, unfortunately for us Jesus Christ is not dead.

With Gestapo officers standing in the back of his lecture hall, spying on him, Karl Barth said:

> If Jesus Christ is only a pleasing religious memory, there will be nothing left of the church but a human community which is puffed up with the illusion that it has inherited the kingdom task all to itself—an illusion that works its own revenge upon the church.

Most of the time, there, I think Barth's describing the United Methodist Church, but Barth's point is that Jesus Christ—God's only chosen one—is not dead.

And the God we serve is Living God, a God who speaks and acts, a God who calls and conscripts. The God we serve is a Living God, a God on the move, a God who is able—able to do more than answer the items on your prayer list.

The God we serve is a Living God who is able to push and pull and prod and provoke his Church to go where it wants not to go.

In our sin, we can do our damnedest to keep politics out of the church, but can we, in our finitude, keep the Living God from dropping politics into our laps if God so elects? Are we able to resist the Risen Lord who persists in recruiting undeserving sinners like us into his labor?

I'm not being speculative here.

Having returned from vacation last Sunday, I arrived here at church on Tuesday morning, bright and early, with a long To Do list and my whole work week meticulously laid out.

Then our Lord, as he's wont to do, messed up all my preconceived plans. He dragged politics into his church, and he strong-armed us into doing his work.

We were in the middle of a staff meeting.

A visitor buzzed the security intercom at Door #2.

"I need help," she shouted into the speaker in hesitant, broken English.

Dottie, our secretary, buzzed her inside and showed her to my office to wait while we finished our work at the staff meeting. I figured if her request was illegitimate then she'd grow impatient with waiting and would move on to the next easy mark.

When we were finished with our work, I walked back to my office and discovered a woman about my age, neatly but simply dressed, with her black hair pulled back taut. Three children sat across the same sofa as her.

Their names, she told me, were Scarlett, Edward, and Denis—6, 12, and 14 years old respectively.

I offered her my hand and introduced myself in my broken Spanish.

She introduced herself as Carolina.

"I was a teacher," she said out of the blue and looking like she was struggling to get the English right.

I must've looked confused because she went on to explain, and what she told me wasn't what I was expecting nor was it what I wanted to hear with such a busy week before me.

"We just arrived here," she said, "last night. From Nicaragua."

I still wasn't processing her situation and it must've showed because she quickly added: "We left Nicaragua fifty days ago."

"Por qué?"

"My community very dangerous," she said and wiped away tears, "I left—my home, my work—for them, for my children."

And then, as best as she could, she told me about their journey, first by bus, then on foot, and finally stowed away in the back of a delivery truck.

Seeking asylum, they'd been separated and detained at the border and then eventually reunited and released on her own recognizance to report back at a later date.

She pulled a cell phone out of her back pocket and showed me the documents that corroborated her story, the first one stamped with her mug shot.

They arrived here on Monday and are now living in the basement of an acquaintance less than a minute's walk from here.

Literally, a stone's throw.

God apparently isn't all that concerned with our concerns about keeping politics out of his Church.

"Do you have any food?" I asked her.

"No."

"Do you have a job lined up?"

"No."

"Do you have a lawyer—an abogado?"

"No."

"What about your children—are they registered for school?"

She shook her head and appeared overwhelmed.

"What are you going to do?"

This time she had an answer.

"I prayed and I prayed all last night," she said, and she'd suddenly stopped crying and looked both serious and euphoric. "I prayed and finally God spoke. He answered me, and God said to me to come here."

"Here?"

She nodded.

"God said to me that he'd make you help us."

"He did, did he?"

And she smiled and shook her head and said "Yes."

She said "Yes" emphatically, like she'd just witnessed a miracle.

"Isn't that just like God," I muttered under my breath, "he knows I don't have time for one more thing and so he sends you my way."

"Como?" she asked, confused by my mumbling to myself.

"Nevermind," I said, "it sounds like Jesus is determined for us to help you so what choice do I have?"

"None," she said matter-of-factly, "no choice," like it had been a serious question.

As though God had made me her hired hand.

Check out this parable.

Jesus would've known it. It was taught by the ancient rabbis before getting recorded and canonized in the Jewish Talmud.

A king had a vineyard for which he engaged many laborers, one of whom was especially apt and skillful. What did the king do? He took his laborer from his work and walked through the garden conversing with him.

When the laborers came for their wage in the evening, the skillful laborer also appeared among them and received a full day's wage from the king. The other laborers were angry at this and said, "We have toiled all day long while this man has worked but two hours; why does the king give him the full wage even as to us?"

The king said to them: "Why are you angry? Through his skill he has produced more in two hours than all of you have done all the day long.

Notice—

In the Jewish Talmudic parable, the emphasis falls on the exceptional worker's economic productivity, but in Jesus' remix of the parable, the stress is not on the laborer but on the landowner.

The focus is not on the worker's activity but the owner's activity, going out, again and again, seeking and summoning. The focus isn't on the laborer's contributions but on the landowner's character, "Are you envious because I am generous?"

Actually, in Matthew's Greek, the landowner asks the grumbling laborers, "Is your eye evil because I am good?"

Because I am good—that's the money line; that's the clue.

Right before Jesus spins his version of this parable, Jesus chastises a wealthy honor roll student for calling him good. "Good teacher," the rich young man says to Jesus, "what must I do to have salvation?"

And rather than answer him outright, Jesus takes him to task for his salutation. "Why do you call me good? No one is good but God alone."

No one is good, Jesus has just said, *but God.*

If you want salvation, Jesus then tells him, *you've got to be free for it. Freed for it. Go, offload all your stuff on Craigslist and then come follow me.*

In other words, whatever that word *salvation* includes it cannot exclude following and obeying Jesus Christ.

Follow me, Jesus invites the rich kid with the perfect resume.

But, Matthew reports (this was centuries before Marie Kondo), the rich young man had too much stuff in the way of following after Jesus so he turns around and turns away from Jesus and returns home.

He is the only person recorded in the Gospels who's invited by Jesus to become a disciple but refuses.

And looking on the rich kid walking back home, Jesus says, "It's hard for rich folks like him to follow me, about as hard as camel squeezing its humps and luggage through the eye of a needle."

And the disciples, knowing they have more in common with the overachieving do-gooder than with the unemployed, homeless carpenter from Nazareth, throw up their hands, chagrined.

"Then there's no hope for any of us!" they gripe, "If a success story like him can't follow you and following you is salvation, then who can be saved?"

Jesus responds, "For mortals, it's impossible. But for God, all things are possible," which offends Peter, who gave up his fishing business—all on his own—to come work for the Lord and here Jesus is saying "Well, God will get even losers like this rich guy to 'Yes.' Watch, God will make followers of them too."

"That's not fair" Peter grumbles, and I get it. Trust me, no one has a beef with Christ's poor taste in Christians quite like a pastor.

"That's not fair," Peter gripes.

So, then Jesus doubles down with a redacted version of a familiar parable.

The denarius, which the landowner pays all the laborers, was the daily subsistence pay required by the Torah.

It's prescribed in the Book of Leviticus. It's minimum wage. It's the equivalent of pulling a shift at Wendy's. So, the workers who show up just before quitting time—their pay is unearned, yes, but it's not extravagant by any means. It's not gratuitous; it's what the Law requires.

This is not a parable of God's grace as opposed to our works.

This is a parable about God's gracious and determined work to enlist every last loser to his work. Like a lot of the parables, this one is misnamed.

It's not the Parable of the Laborers in the Vineyard. Heck, the laborers don't do any labor onstage that we see at all. The laborers don't so much as speak until they grumble at the very end.

No, this is the Parable of the Land Owner and his prodigal labor of summoning workers to his vineyard.

Nearly all the verbs in the story belong to him. He goes out—five times he goes out; he even goes out after there's hardly anything left to be done—seeking laborers for his vineyard.

Jesus tells you the takeaway at the very top of the story.

"The Kingdom of God," Jesus says, "is like a landowner who went out to find laborers..."

For his what?

For his vineyard.

Jesus assumes you know the Book of Isaiah where God's self-chosen image for Israel and her vocation—her vocation to be a light to the world, to be a peculiar, set-apart, pilgrim people, to be a holy people, to be a nation within and among the nations, to be a people who embody—unlike the nations—*God's* justice and righteousness—God's image for his elect People and their vocation in the world is a vineyard.

It's Isaiah chapter five.

God is the landowner who labors in this parable.

It's about God's work to find workers.

The primary difference between a Living God and a dead god, an idol, is that the latter will never shock or surprise you, never offend you or inconvenience you, and never call you to do something you wouldn't have done apart from conversion and worship.

This parable—

It's about this vocative God of ours.

This God who refuses to accommodate our apathy and functional atheism by remaining comfortably distant and idle but is instead always on the move, going out, inviting and enlisting, calling and conscripting, seeking and finding and arm-twisting Kingdom accomplices in a world that knows not that Jesus is Lord.

We can argue whether or not there's any work we *must* do as Christians who are justified by grace alone, but the reality is that Jesus Christ is not dead and if he's got a work for you to do, by God, he's going to give it to you and he's going to get you to do it.

I remember—

There was a young woman in one of the congregations I once served. Her name was Ann. She was a straight-A student at an Ivy League school.

She was nearing graduation, and her parents couldn't have been more excited about what lay in her future: maybe a graduate degree at another prestigious school; maybe a career and no less than a six-figure salary.

Instead Ann threw them all for a loop and one day, out of the blue, announced to her parents that rather than doing anything they wanted, she was going to work in a clinic in some poor village in Venezuela.

I only found out about this when Ann's mother burst into my office one day, clearly assuming I was the one who put the idea in her daughter's head.

Red-faced and furious, she said: "Preacher, you've got to talk to her. You've got to convince her to change her mind. You've got to show her she's throwing her life away."

Ever the obedient minister, I met with Ann and communicated all her mother's fears: she was being naive, she was being irresponsible, she was being idealistic, her education should come first, she shouldn't jeopardize her career.

The Gospel's about grace not works, I told her.

Ann looked back at me liked I'd disappointed her in some way. "Didn't Jesus tell the young man to give up all his stuff and follow him?" she asked.

"Uh, well, yeah but...I mean...Jewish hyperbole and all...he couldn't have been serious...that would've been irresponsible. At least tell me why you're doing this."

"Why do you think?" she asked like there could be only possible answer and it should be obvious. "Jesus sorta came to me and he spoke to me and he told me to go and do it."

"He did, did he?"

And her eyes narrowed, like she was about lay a straight flush down on the table.

"Are you telling me, pastor, that I should listen to you instead of him."

"Um, uh...okay, I think we're done here. Just leave me out of it when you talk to your parents."

I know you want to keep politics out of the Church.

I get it.

But the problem is, it's not your Church and the Risen Christ, the Living God, he's on the move. He's always going out, calling and conscripting.

And he is free to drop whatever work he chooses into your lap whether or not it obeys our boundaries of what's acceptable.

The Lord is no respecter of propiety. With pictures of asylum seekers all over the newspapers, God this week brought politics into his church here.

And just like that, God got us to working.

Meredith, our Children's Director, found games to occupy the kids while they waited. Peter put down what he was doing and left to stuff his trunk with food for them. And I stared at the fourteen items I had on my To Do list for the day as I waited on hold, making calls all day long for Carolina, connecting her with the county, finding her a lawyer, locating services, resourcing her three kids.

When we drove them home later, I carried bags of food inside and I gave her my cell number and I told her that if there was anything else she needed to call me. It was the sort of compassionate gesture you make to someone when you don't really expect them to take you up on the offer.

Later that night I got a text from a number I didn't recognize.

"This is Carolina," it said, "thank you to you and your church."

"De nada."

And then I watched the text bubbles roll up and down as she texted another message. "The school say I need to go to Central Office to register my children."

"How are you going to get there?" I texted back.

"I prayed," she replied, "and God said you should take me."

"He did, did he?"

"Si."

And then the next text quickly followed.

"God say to tell you that I'm baptized. You have an obligation to me. As a brother. In Christ."

"That's the annoying inconvenience of worshipping a Living God," I typed but didn't send.

And so, thanks to Jesus, I spent most of the next day driving her and her children to Merrifield to get her kids registered and tested and immunized. And then the next day, Jesus apparently summoned my wife and son to go purchase school supplies for all of them.

At the end of the week, I mentioned all the details to Dottie, our secretary and she replied, "In order to be a pastor, you must have to really enjoy helping people in need."

"Enjoy?" I asked, "Do you know many people in need? Most of them aren't that enjoyable."

"Then why did you choose to do it?"

"Choose? I didn't choose it at all. I got summoned."

All Is Lost
Matthew 18.10-14
Taylor Mertins

I was sitting around a table with a bunch of adults who had agreed to give up a week of their summer to take a group of youth on a mission trip to Raleigh, North Carolina. We had successfully made it to our site and as the kids were preparing to sleep, or at least pretending to, the adults had to figure out where each kid would be working during the week and what project they would focus on.

We ultimately decidedly to do it via a random lottery so that every person had a fair chance at any of the missional opportunities. One group would be spending most of the week working in a nursing home providing fellowship and entertainment for the residents. Another group would be doing simple carpentry for low-income housing on the economically challenged side of town. And still yet another group would be responsible for keeping tabs on a group of younger kids through a very inexpensive summer camp program.

It took thirty minutes to separate all of the children appropriately, and as we prepared to leave the room the director informed us that we had omitted one important step in the process—we, the adults, had to sign up for sites as well.

I, being the remarkably gifted, faithful, and holy pastor that I am, elected to pick last and was stuck with the glorified babysitting opportunity.

So the following morning I drove a large fan full of hormonal teenagers to meet with the program at a local museum. We were given very little instruction other than go inside, don't lose anybody, and come back to the main entrance at 3:00 p.m. I decided to separate the more responsible teenagers and assigned groups of the camp participants to them, and then ended by striking the fear of God into them, "Do not lose any of your kids."

And then I let them go.

Which, admittedly, was a big mistake.

Hours went by, I kept an eye on my little group and kept stepping on my tiptoes through all of the exhibits to see if I could see any of the other kids, many of whom I barely recognized from our brief encounter in the morning. And sure enough, when 3:00 rolled around, a group of sweaty kids congregated by the main entrance, and I started a head count.

After I tapped every single head, I decided to start over again, just to be safe, and it was only after the third count that I had to admit the truth.

We were missing one kid.

I immediately interrogated all of the students on the mission trip and berated them for losing a child in their care, but the clock kept ticking, and we needed to get the kids back to their families, and we were still missing one kid.

I had a few choices:

Send all the kids back through the museum with the charge to find the one who was missing, at the risk of losing more.

Cut my losses and pretend like I didn't know one was missing.

Or leave everyone behind to find the kid by myself.

Jesus predicts his passion for the second time, the Son of Man must be handed over, killed, and in three days rise again. And in response to the Lord's declaration, the disciples enter into a lively discussion, what we might otherwise call a fight, about who will be the greatest in the kingdom of God.

And why do they respond this way?

Because they're idiots.

Jesus has just told them that he, the Lord of Lords, Son of Man and Son of God, is going to die.

And they, apparently, can't stand the idea of it, so they jump quickly to, "that's fine and all, but how about we talk about who will be your next-in-command when you finally get the throne…"

Jesus then gives them one of the all-time great theological punches: "Whoever wishes to be first among you must be last, whoever is the least among you will be the greatest."

It's like Jesus just wants these disciples to get it through their thick skulls that the work of God in the world is done by losing and not by winning. God loves taking the least likely and making them the objects of transformation. God has a knack for making something out of nothing.

Which, if we're honest with ourselves, we hate.

Maybe hate is too strong of a word. We can be on board with Jesus' project of being with and for the last, the least, the lost, the little, and the dead. But then we struggle with the idea of labeling ourselves in any of those categories.

We, like the disciples before us, would rather be part of the first, the great, the found, the big, and the alive.

Think about it, even the way we practice religion is all about the myth of progress. We preach and teach a religion of "doing" and "earning" and "finding."

We are consumed by what we consume, and what we consume most of all are these fabricated versions of our possible future selves.

There's a reason that self-help books are always at the top of the best-seller lists.

We are, constantly, works in progress.

Now, there's nothing necessarily wrong with wanting to be better—it's just that in spite of our desires for approval and change and growth, the work of the Lord remains steadfast.

Jesus saves losers and only losers.

He raises the dead and only the dead.

He finds the lost and only the lost.

The last, least, lost, little, and dead receive more of Jesus' joy than all of the winners in the world.

And we can't stand it.

And now we arrive at the parable.

What do you think? If a shepherd has a hundred sheep, and one of them has gone astray, does he not leave the ninety-nine on the mountains and go in search of the one that went astray?

I stood by the main entrance of the museum with a cacophony of kids when I, reluctantly, decided to head back into the museum by myself to find the one who was lost. I strictly ordered the youth from the church to keep an eye on the rest of the group and prayed under my breath with every step that nothing would go wrong.

Within ten minutes I had combed most of the museum—I flew through all of the exhibits and the kid was nowhere. I started shouting his name and even asked a few strangers to help me look. I was honestly starting to lose hope when I passed by the gift shop and I saw the kid sitting on the floor in the corner flipping through a picture book.

I promptly picked him up and prepared to march back triumphantly toward the entrance, and that's precisely when the fire alarm went off.

So, we ran, along with everyone else, to the nearest exist, on the opposite side of the museum and we walked around the building looking for the rest of our people and they were all gone.

That's the thing about going off in pursuit of the one lost sheep—the only real result will be ninety-nine more lost sheep.

Ultimately, going off for the one is pretty bad advice. It puts everyone else at risk, and there's no guarantee that any of them will be found in the end.

For me, it took the better part of another hour to round up everyone as they had dispersed in different directions when the fire alarm sounded. We were almost two hours late in terms of returning home, and I made a vow to leave the sheep finding business to Jesus.

This story, this parable, just like the rest of them, is strange—it points at something greater than the sum of its parts. The lost sheep declares, oddly enough, that we are saved in our lostness.

Unlike a novice pastor, even if a hundred sheep get lost it will not be a problem for our wonderfully weird Good Shepherd. Our Lord rejoices and is in the business of finding the lost.

And here's maybe the craziest thing of all—the lost sheep does nothing to be found. No amount of good works, or faithful prayers, or money offerings, brings the Shepherd out into the wilderness. The sheep does nothing except hang around in its own lostness.

And to make things all the more prescient—a lost sheep, in all reality, is a dead sheep. Without the shepherd, the sheep has not a chance in the world.

We might love the idea of always doing more, of finding that one right book or list or program that will finally enable us to be who we are supposed to be. But the parable of the lost sheep is a deadly reminder for us that we need not do anything to get God to love us, or find us, or even forgive us.

God is determined to move before we do. Christ died for us while we were yet sinners.

It is our lostness that is our ticket into the dinner party of the Lamb.

The parables of Jesus, though they greatly vary in form and even in function, they do point again and again to the fact that God acts first and God acts definitively without conditions.

Well, there might be one condition, and if there is one it is this: we need only admit we are lost.

We're all lost.

We're lost in our ambitions, in our sins, we're even lost in our faith. Last Saturday, a young man walked into a synagogue and started shooting. He killed one and injured three others. And when these things happen, and they happen all too often, we are quick to point out how isolated the attacker was, or how damaging the ideology was that led to the violence. But this particular young man was a faithful Christian, he attended a Presbyterian church nearly every week.

His manifesto in defense of his actions against the Jews came from some of the theology he acquired in his church.

His is a radical example of lostness. It is extreme. And yet, all of us here, whether we want to admit it or not, are lost as well.

Which, paradoxically, is Good News. It is Good News because when God is given a world full of losers, a world full of people lost in our own journeys, lost in our own sins, that's just fine. Lostness is what God is all about.

We may be determined to do whatever we do—we can try all we want to save ourselves—but it will largely only result in us becoming more lost. Thanks be to God then that the Lord's determination will always exceed our own.

God is determined with an unshakable fervor, to raise the dead, to find the lost.

We can all be better, of course. And I don't mean to knock self-help programs and books so much. But we are a people who have fallen for the greatest trap in the world and we believe, foolishly, that God is going to close the door in our faces unless we do enough.

We are a people moved by guilt.

When the truth is entirely different.

God isn't waiting around for us to become the most perfect sheep.

If God is waiting for anything it's for us to admit our lostness, that we are dead in our sins. Because when can see the condition of our condition, we can begin to experience the joy of having no power to save ourselves or to convince anyone else that we are worth finding.

And even if we can't admit how lost we are, the shepherd will look for and find us anyway. That's kind of the whole point.

This beloved parable, and the image of Jesus returning to the fold with the one lost sheep over his shoulders, is but another reminder that our whole lives are forever out of our hands, that we really are dead, and that if we are to ever live again, it will only be because of the grace of a Shepherd named Jesus.

Who will never stop looking for us. Amen.

The Way of the Son in the Far Country
Luke 15.1-32
Jason Micheli

St. Luke reports the motive.

The Pharisees and the scribes were grumbling, Luke writes at the top of chapter fifteen. They were outraged: "This Jesus welcomes sinners—tax collectors, even, Jewish enablers of Israel's imperial enemy. This rabbi welcomes the very worst sinners among us."

So, Jesus, Luke says, told them three parables. The first about a lost sheep. The second about a lost coin. And then, a parable about a family.

The father said his son had wandered far off from how he'd been raised.

He'd wandered far from home.

That's what the father had told the tipline after the Charleston Police Department released Dylan Roof's picture to the press just after six in the morning on June 18, already four years ago. The father called the hotline to identify the suspect as his son. The father warned them that Dylan owned a .45 caliber pistol, a gift he'd given his son for his twenty-first birthday.

But the son had taken the father's gift and left home and was now living out of his black Hyundai, the father told the tipline, adding that they could identify the nondescript car by the confederate flag on it.

"My son's gotten himself lost," the father said, "obsessing over segregation and another civil war coming. I keep hoping he'll come to his senses."

He'd wandered and gotten himself lost.

The night before, aiming to ignite a nationwide race war, the father's son crept into the fellowship hall of Emmanuel AME, an historically black church in Charleston. The pastor and eleven church members gathered there for Wednesday night Bible Study welcomed him and invited him to join them.

Seeing the stranger, Polly Sheppard, one of the leaders of the Bible Study, declared that "if our guest has come to Emmanuel in search of God, we will guide him to God." She didn't know he carried hidden in his knapsack a Glock and eighty-eighty bullets— the number symbolic for "Heil Hitler."

The class members pulled up a chair for him. They gave him a Bible. They offered him a spare copy of the study guide.

They prepared table in the presence of their enemy.

He joined them in turning to the Gospel of Mark, chapter four. They were in the middle of a Bible Study on the parables of Jesus. And he sat next to them and studied with them the Parable of the Sower as Mark tells it.

After an hour, a class leader named Myra read from their study guide: "In like manner, the seed of God's word, falling upon a heart rendered callous by the custom of sinning, is straightaway snatched away by the "Evil One.""

Given their hospitality towards him, he almost changed his mind. But, while they all bowed their heads and closed their eyes to pray, he pulled his gun, quickly, as he'd practiced.

And then he wandered out, even more lost than when he'd come, as Felicia Sanders, one of the three survivors, wept Jesus' name over and again.

————————————-

You know the story.

Two days later Dylan Roof appeared before a magistrate in Charleston County's bond court. Reporters, photographers, and cameramen filled the courtroom to cover the bail hearing. Cable news stations showed Dylan Roof as he entered escorted by a sheriff, wearing shackles and a gray striped jumpsuit.

As the black-robed and silver-haired judge announced the case, on the other side of the world, in Dubai, Steve Hurd, whose wife had been a victim and who was desperately trying to make his way home, stood up in an airport bar and pointed at the television screen and shouted: "That! That thing killed my wife!"

Before the bond hearing concluded, Judge James Gosnell read the names of the victims, carefully, one at a time. Having finished, he invited their family members to come forward to speak.

Nadine Collier, the youngest daughter of Ethel Lance, sat in the back and hadn't planned to say anything.

Yet, when her mother's name was read, she later said she felt herself rise. Something moved her to the front of the packed room, she said. And as she walked forward, she said she heard her mother's voice warning her, "I don't want any fast talking out of you today. Don't be a smart-ass today."

Nadine's Mother, Ethel, had been the church's custodian. Ethel had chided Nadine for her stubbornness and incendiary sense of humor, but in the courtroom, Nadine was determined that her words would be her mother's words and her mother's words had always been disciplined by the Gospel Word.

Nadine was so overcome by the Holy Spirit that when she stepped the microphone, at first, she couldn't remember her name.

"You can talk to me," the judge told her, "I'm listening to you."

Instead Nadine looked at the lost son and summoned what she knew her mother would've said to him:

"I just want everybody to know, to you, I forgive you! You took something very precious away from me. I will never talk to her ever again. I will never be able to hold her again. But I forgive you! And have mercy on your soul. You. Hurt. Me! You hurt a lot of people. But God forgives you. And I forgive you."

And then she turned away from him and returned to her seat.

Next, a pastor, Anthony Thompson, came forward on behalf of his dead wife, Myra. A retired probation officer, he knew the bond hearing was only a formality, so he hadn't planned to say anything.

Like Nadine, the Spirit compelled him, he said later. He stood at the lectern, staring at Roof. In his mind, he said, it was as if everyone else had vanished and he was sitting alone with the killer in his jail cell.

In fact, Reverend Thompson spoke so softly the judge had to ask him to speak up.

"I forgive you," the pastor whispered to him, "and my family forgives you, and we invite you to give your life to the one who matters the most; so that, he can change it, change you, no matter what happens to you."

When Felicia Sanders heard her son, Tywanza's, name read by the judge, she said she felt God nudge her forward.

As she walked to the microphone, clutching a ball of folded-up tissues, she said she'd thought about how her baby boy was in heaven now and how Jesus says the Kingdom of Heaven is like a father who forgives his son who'd wished him dead. Therefore, she figured, forgiveness was the way she'd see her son again.

And so she said to the lost son who'd killed her son:

> "We welcomed you Wednesday night in our Bible Study with open arms. You have killed some of the most beautifullest people that I know. Every fiber in my body hurts! And I'll never be the same. Tywanza Sanders is my son, but he was also my hero! As we say in Bible Study: We enjoyed you, but may God have grace and mercy on you."

Other family members spoke too. All of them echoed the same themes of God's unmerited grace and forgiveness in Jesus Christ.

If you read Luke's parable closely, it's the gratuity of the grace that sets him off.

Whatever resentments the older brother was harboring, whatever anger lay buried inside him already—it's the singing and the dancing and the feasting and the rejoicing that send him over the edge. Why shouldn't it?

Ancient Judaism had clear guidelines for the return of a penitent.

Ancient Judaism was clear about how to handle a prodigal's homecoming.

There was nothing ambiguous in Ancient Judaism about how to treat someone who'd abandoned and disgraced his family.

It was called a *kezazah* ritual, a cutting off ritual.

Just as they would have done when the prodigal left for the far country, when he returned home members of his community and members of his family would have filled a barrel with parched corn and nuts.

And then in front of everyone, including the children—to teach them an example—they would smash the barrel and declare, "This disgrace is cut off from us."

Having returned home, thus would begin his shame and his penance.

So you see, by all means, let the prodigal return, but to bread and water not to fatted calf.

By all means, let him come back, but dress him in sackcloth not in a new robe. Sure, let him come back, but make him wear ashes not a new ring.

By all means let the prodigal return, but in tears not in merriment, with his head hung down not with his spirits lifted up. Bring him to his knees before you bring him home.

Celebration comes after contrition not as soon as the sinner heads home. Repentance is more than saying "I'm sorry" and forgiveness cannot be without justice.

It's the outrageousness of the forgiveness that outrages him off.

Here's the thing: the eldest, he's absolutely *right*.

It's as if, in this parable, Jesus is after something different—something bigger—than what's *right*.

One of the children of the Emmanuel Nine stood on the outside, looking in on their outrageous Gospel celebration.

Sharon Risher is Nadine Collier's sister.

Of church custodian Ethel Lance's five children, Sharon is the oldest.

30

She is the one who'd helped their mother care for her deaf brother. She is the one who showed up and did whatever needed to be done when Ethel's second child, Terrie, struggled in a fatal battle with cervical cancer. She is the one who made their mother proud by being ordained and working as a trauma chaplain in Dallas.

Resentments still lingered between Sharon, the eldest, and Nadine, the youngest, from the fight that exploded between them at their sister Terrie's funeral.

Sharon was still in Dallas, packing for a late flight to South Carolina, when the bail hearing came on the network news. Pacing her apartment and chain-smoking cigarettes, she heard her youngest sister, Nadine, mention their Mother—Ethel's faith in the Gospel of Jesus Christ—before announcing in a quavering voice, "I just want everybody to know, to you, I forgive you!"

With her black horn-rimmed glasses pointed at the TV screen, Sharon watched from afar as other victim's family members echoed her sister's outrageous sentiments.

"What is going on?" she asked the television.

Nadine hadn't told her about any bond hearing much less anything about any plans to offer up forgiveness for him—the police hadn't even contacted her. While busy juggling her work and now her responsibilities as the family's eldest, she just stumbled upon it on the TV.

"Why didn't anyone tell me?" she wondered aloud.

When the news coverage of the hearing ended and the anchors marveled at the extravagant display of grace, Sharon felt infuriated. Not two days had passed. They hadn't even buried their mother. She still hardly knew any details of what he had done.

Seeing their outrageous display of forgiveness on the TV screen, Sharon, Ethel Lance's eldest, refused ever to join in.

"I'm the one who knows what should be done. How can you forgive this man?!" Sharon screamed the television.

When Sharon finally arrived in Charleston, she and her sister Nadine embraced, but the latter didn't feel any warmth from the former.

None was intended, the eldest said.

Colloquial wisdom says that Jesus taught in parables so that the everyday rabble would better understand him. Clearly, whoever first made that argument hadn't read many of Christ's parables.

Surely the members of the Bible Study at Emmanuel knew better. Likely, in their study guide on the parables of Jesus, they'd already encountered Jesus explaining to his disciples that the reason he taught in parables was so that the crowds would *not* understand him.

Jesus taught in parables—according to Jesus—not to make his teaching clear for the eavesdropping crowds but to confuse them. "To you," Jesus says to his disciples, "it has been given to know the secrets of the Kingdom of God, but to them it has not been given."

Jesus teaches in parables because the offensive, upside-down nature of the Kingdom of God is not for everybody to know.

Just anyone (who knows not Jesus) cannot possibly understand such a counterintuitive Kingdom.

You've got to see such a Kingdom before you can believe it—you've got to catch a glimpse of it. The words need to find flesh.

Jesus teaches in parables because the parables aren't for everyone. Jesus teaches in parables because the parables are for the new family constituted by his call to baptism and discipleship.

Jesus teaches in parables that are unintelligible to the world so that Jesus' disciples might then live lives that make intelligible the Kingdom disclosed in those parables.

That is, the parable Jesus gives to the unbelieving world is the parable that the Church tells by its becoming a parable—by exemplifying *for* the world what Jesus deliberately obscures *from* the world.

This parable at the end of Luke 15– it's not a picture of a generalized, universal principle of forgiveness to which anyone can aspire.

As Stanley Hauerwas says, a God who forgives sinners without giving them something to do is a God of sentimentality.

This is why the lectionary always pairs Christ's parable of the family with St. Paul's second letter to the Corinthians:

"If anyone is in Christ [by baptism] there is a new creation: everything old has passed away; see, everything has become new! All this is from God, who reconciled us to himself through Christ, and has given us the ministry of reconciliation."

Christ has given the ministry of reconciliation to us—not to Congress, not to POTUS OR SCOTUS, not to Democrats, not to Republicans, to us. Christ has given us—the new family of the Father and the Son, created by baptism—Christ's own ministry of reconciliation.

Christ has given it to us; therefore, it's not simply something we should do or ought to do in order to get to Christ. We're already in Christ. And Christ has given us his ministry of reconciliation; therefore, it's something we can do—it's something we get to do.

Karl Barth said one of the ways we're hostile to God's grace, one of the ways we contend against God's grace, is by not doing what we may and can do, for grace not only pardons; grace empowers.

Grace empowers us to live lives that make no sense if the one who told this parable of the family is not Lord.

Grace not only pardons. Grace empowers us to live lives that corroborate the Gospel. Grace empowers us to live lives that corroborate the Gospel because what God wants is not just your life but the whole world.

We are, as St. Paul says in that same passage, "ambassadors of Christ."

The Living God, the apostle Paul writes, is determined to make his appeal through us, the particular, peculiar people called Church.

We're the parable Christ communicates to the wider, watching world.

At the end of their testimony at Dylan Roof's bond hearing, the Charleston police chief, Greg Mullen, said he was in awe of how, with the world watching, God's Church had rendered every reporter in the courtroom speechless, their jaws all hanging open, dumbfounded, amazed at grace.

Be Unprepared
Luke 11.1-13
Taylor Mertins

Be prepared.

It's the Boy Scout motto, drilled into my brain over years of camping trips, patrol meetings, merit badge requirements.

I loved being a Boy Scout. I joined as a Tiger Cub when I was in Kindergarten and I continued all the way through until I earned my Eagle Scout. To this day I can still recite the Boy Scout Law and Oath, I can remember how to tie countless knots, and I still hear that incessant reminder in my head all the time: Be prepared.

When I was 13 years old, we met at the church to organize our caravan before heading off into the woods for two nights of camping. We had meticulously gone through all of our gear to make sure we had everything we needed, we had checked the weather forecast in order to bring the appropriate clothing, and we had even planned out all of the activities we would be doing until it was time to return home.

By the time we got to our campsite that night it was dark. But we were prepared for that eventuality and we hung up our flashlights in order to tie down the tarp and pull out the camping stove. The adults were always very good about giving the boys their space as we navigated the necessary survival techniques, and when we went to open the cooler to begin cooking dinner, we were glad that they were far away.

We were glad because the one boy who was responsible for bringing all of our food that weekend had forgotten that it was his responsibility.

We were prepared for everything, except for not having food.

So, we did what any reasonable scouts would do, we kept the information to ourselves and went without food the entire weekend.

It was only on the ride home, when one of the boys let it slip how absolutely famished he was that the driver of our vehicle, our scoutmaster, said, "I hope you boys learned your lesson." We all grumbled about how we knew we were supposed to be prepared. And he waved that off and said, "No. We all could tell that you forgot to bring food and we had plenty to share, we were only waiting for you to come ask for help. I hope you learned that you can't be prepared for everything, but that you can always ask for help."

"Hey Jesus!" shouts one of the disciples. "When are you going to teach us to pray like John taught his followers?"

Jesus, reluctantly says, "When you pray, pray like this: Father, you are great. Do what you need to do. Give us some bread. Forgives us, because we are trying to forgive everyone indebted to us. And keep us away from evil."

Hopefully, the first thing you noticed as the scripture was being read this morning was how similar it sounded, but maybe not too similar. Its familiarity stems precisely from the fact that this is Luke's version of the Lord's prayer—the prayer we pray every week in this place.

And, if you recognized it, then you no doubt noticed it's quite a bit shorter than Matthew's version, the one we pray in church. In fact, it dispenses with some of the elevated language that we so often use and instead cuts right to the heart of the matter.

No fuss, no muss.

And even though we say something close to it every week we can't help but wrestle with how strange of a prayer it really is. Particularly when considering this is how Jesus taught his disciples how to pray in response to them wanting to be educated in the way John the Baptist educated his disciples.

John, unlike Jesus, was living by a different paradigm, one in which people could enter into what we might call the program of salvation. You start here, and make your way here, and eventually you get over there. You confess and repent of your sins, you start engaging in works of piety and social justice, and then you earn your heavenly reward.

36

In John's worldview, redemption was all about having the right ethical, religious, moral, and political beliefs in order to make something new happen in the world.

Jesus, on the other hand, sees things differently. In fact, to the Lord of lords, the new thing has already happened in him, and it has happened for everyone. There's no 12-step program to get God to do anything.

Jesus doesn't come just to show the disciples, and us, a new way of life but is, himself, the new way.

This can be rather frustrating for the many of us who want Jesus to just be clear about what we should and shouldn't do. Contrary to what we often hear from the church, Jesus does not call for perfect lives, but simply says the time has come for us to recognize how last, lost, least, little, and dead we all are.

And we are, all of us. Make no mistake: even those of us who look perfectly beautiful and wonderful and happy right now are but shells of people whose real lives are actually pulling at the seams.

The disciples, people like us, we want a program. We want it to be laid out nice and clear as to what we are supposed to do, say, and believe. We like little trite and memorable zingers like, do a good turn daily, or be prepared.

But then Jesus responds to the disciples' request for a prayer with something that's so simple, perhaps too simple, that it's a prayer in which we don't have to do much of anything. In fact the only thing we can do, according to the prayer, is forgive. Which, as we have said in nearly every week of this parable series, it intricately connected with our own willingness to die.

From the king forgiving the debt of his servant, to the father forgiving the prodigal son, to cancel someone's debt, to really forgive, is only possible for someone who dies to their own version of what life could've been.

This so-called Lord's Prayer rejects all of our contemporary understandings of what it means to pray. It does not contain giant and lofty ideals that are often present in our own prayers. There's not even a hint of ethical perfection, or moral equivocation. It just about the bare necessities to keep us together and fed so that we can get to the best part of life which comes through the realization that we have already died with Christ.

And we haven't even gotten to the parable yet.

Jesus teaches the disciples how to pray, and without being asked he starts rambling on with another one of his crazy stories.

Imagine you have a friend who is at home in bed at midnight, and you go knocking on her door because someone just showed up at your house and you don't have anything to offer them. You aren't prepared. And when you start banging on the door, she says, "Leave me alone!" However, even though she brushes you aside, you know that she will eventually give you what you need.

What kind of story is that?

Jesus has his friends imagine that God is like a sleepy friend. Someone who experiences the closest thing to death while we are still alive, sleep. And then Jesus has them picture this whole scene in which they break in upon the drowsy God with a battering ram of requests.

In other words, "I need you to wake up for me."

We could, of course, explore why we/the disciples don't have anything to entertain our untimely friends in the first place, but we will get there in due time.

First, Jesus calls the disciples to see that the sleeping friend is their only hope. That they are a people in need and the only one who can provide is the one who has something better to do.

And, to make matters all the more complicated, the figure of God in the story gives them the cold shoulder.

In other words, "Let me sleep!"

This is not the God we are often called to imagine in our minds. Don't we all think and believe that God will drop everything for us should we only must the courage to knock on the door and ask?

It is certainly strange, but part of the parable functions in such a way to tell us, particularly with the language of sleeping and rising, that God rises to our prayers out of death.

But if we were good people, if we were prepared for friends showing up at strange times, we would never need to intrude upon the privacy of someone else in the middle of night. Many of us would never dare dream of knocking on a friend's door let alone and neighbor in the middle of night. And why not? Because if we did so, it would show how in need we are of other people.

And we hate the idea of needing other people.

We hate that idea because we have all been fed a lie since the time, we were kids that we have to get through whatever our lives are on our own—that we can't trust or expect anyone to do anything for us. Otherwise we come off looking like beggars who haven't worked hard enough to figure out our lives.

And yet, if we were dead to those judgments (most of the time self-inflicted), then we could show up at a friend's house in the dark of the night with nothing more than a confession of our unpreparedness, and it would be the beautiful admission of our inability to be what we thought we were supposed to be, namely perfect.

Being unprepared, therefore, would raise us out of that death into something far greater than we can even imagine.

And yet, today, more often than not, this prayer and parable from Jesus get whittled down to some version of "you have to be persistent in prayer." Which is another way of saying, "If we nag God enough, God will come through with what we need."

When all of us know that's simply untrue.

Of course, we should be relentless with our prayers, with our needs, but if that's all Jesus is saying with the parable then all of us will eventually be disappointed.

We will be disappointed because God does not answer our prayers the more, we ask them. Far too often people (like me) tell people (like you) that if your prayers are unanswered then it's because you don't have enough faith.

Which is terrible.

Tell that to the mother whose child stops responding to chemotherapy.

Tell that to the husband who has to make the decision about unplugging his wife from the respirator.

Tell that to the son who studies night after night only to bring in Ds and Fs.

This might be the most confounding thing about the parable—God rises from death, awakens from sleep, not to satisfy our requests, reasonable or unreasonable, but to raise us from our own deaths.

Therefore, if we walk away from today thinking that we can keep praying until we can con God into giving us something we really want or even need, then we have failed to see the gospel for what it really is. However, if we can take the story in all of its weirdness for what it is really saying, then we can constantly bring our death to the death bed of the Lord and rejoice.

Jesus concludes this particular parabolic encounter with a statement that we might rather ignore, but we are compelled to approach it head on. "If you then, who are *evil*, know how to give good gifts to your children, how much more will the heavenly Father give the Holy Spirit to those who ask him!"

We don't like being called evil.

It's as if Jesus is saying, you, who can never seem to do enough, who avoids doing the right thing, who hangs your head among all the wrong things, who turns a blind eye toward the relentless injustices of the world, who believes that things will always get better if you just try harder, who struggles to be prepared for a world of unpredictability, if even you know what a good gift is, then how much more will God give to you!

Thanks be to God that the Lord will resurrect us from the death of our own foolishness.

There is no greater gift than this.

We can't make it through life on our own—and that, dear friends, is why we pray. Not to get some things done for us, but to celebrate the greatest work of all that has already been done for us, in spite of us.

We can rejoice knowing that we have a friend at midnight and that, even in our death, that friend is there for us no matter what.

We can't be prepared for everything, but we can always ask for help. In fact, it is the asking that sets us free. Amen.

Simply Put... We're Living on a Prayer
Luke 11:1-13
Teer Hardy

Like many of you, my earliest memories in church center on prayer. I can remember back to Mrs. Frank's Sunday school class at Calvary United Methodist Church and cutting prepared words out of construction paper and then gluing the words onto a paper plate. Either the lesson was to teach us that our prayers are connected to one another in a circular pattern, moving around the plate or the Sunday school department had run out of card stock.

I can remember sitting in youth group in the church basement and waiting anxiously as our youth director would call on someone to pray. Oh, the anxiety! Not only was I trying to navigate being cool around the girls at the table, but I had to also balance my coolness so that the older kids would think I at the least was not weird as they thought I was. Our youth director would call on someone to pray and in that moment of youth group Russian roulette it felt as though my heart was going to jump out of my chest and into the chaffing dish holding whatever pasta dish had been prepared for us that week.

In seminary, of all the places, finding someone to pray at the beginning of class was a difficult task. Perhaps, it was having your professor staring you down while you attempted to muddle through the organizing of words into a prayer that made a small bit of sense or maybe it was thinking that your classmates were critiquing your prayer, word for word, as you spoke.

Prayer causes the anxiety of many people to rise, I know this and you know it, because in any church meeting or to open/close a Sunday school gathering when it comes time to pray it is a though someone pulled the pin on a hand grenade and everyone in the room in running for cover. I have found the best way to get out of praying is to pretend I am one step ahead of the class leader by folding my hands, bowing my head, and closing my eyes. We forget that as Thomas Merton put it, prayer acts as the communion of our freedom in Christ with God's ultimate freedom.

42

Jesus, turned and now making his way to Jerusalem, is asked to teach the disciples how to pray. They have been following him for 11 chapters now and this is the first and only time the disciples ask Jesus to teach them a specific task. The disciples have seen Jesus prayer over and over again as they followed him.

Jesus prayed as he escaped the gathering crowds who had come to hear him teach after he healed "a man covered with leprosy."

Jesus prayed, through an entire night while on a mountainside, before he called the twelve disciples.

The disciples had seen Jesus pray and they wanted to learn from their teacher how to as well.

And now in a crucial piece of what Jesus will teach his disciples, Jesus instructs the disciples that prayer is an indispensable act as it places the one praying in touch with the generosity of God. Prayer, Jesus tells his disciples, offers the one praying and those being prayed over the opportunity to be placed into an intimate encounter with our Creator.

"When you pray, say:
Father, hallowed be your name.
Your kingdom come.
Give us each day our daily bread.
And forgive us our sins,
for we ourselves forgive everyone indebted to us.
And do not bring us to the time of trial."

Luke's accounting of what Jesus taught the disciples to pray includes less detail than the version from Matthew's gospel—the version we pray weekly whether attached to our prayers of the people or as part of our communion liturgy.

I first learned the Lord's Prayer when I was in third grade. I say I learned it because that was the first time in my formal Sunday school curriculum, I can remember having someone explain to me what the words meant and more importantly we got to place stickers next to our names on the attendance chart.

This attendance chart was conspicuously placed on the door as you walked into the classroom for all to see, and for each part of the prayer we memorized we earned a gold star. The student with the most gold stars at the end of the year won a prize. We stood in front of the class and recited the Lord's Prayer, the version from Matthew's gospel not the Readers' Digest version offered to us in our reading this morning.

There, in front of the classroom, praying this memorized prayer, while my real prayer was that I would get through this and add more gold star hardware to the door, my anxiety rose. My hands became sweaty, I'm sure my voice was pitchy, and I looked around the room for any classroom decorations that might aid me in reciting this prayer.

And I wish I could say that as I've gotten older praying has become easier, but you all know as well as I do that prayer is difficult. A recent Pew research study found that 54 percent of Mainline Protestants pray on a daily basis while another 23 percent pray on a weekly basis. If the Lord's Prayer is truly a gift, as Stanley Hauerwas and Will Willimon suggest, then why do nearly half of Mainline Protestants not pray daily?

After all, if we cannot find the words to pray we have these words from Jesus, given to disciples who wanted learn what to say when they themselves did not have the words. Words that for many of us were etched into our brains way back when we were still breaking in the spine on our first Bibles.

The difficulty we have with prayer is corrected by the words Jesus gave to us to pray. The answer is right in front of us, but we are blinded by our anxiety and we fail to see that the purpose of what Jesus told the disciples was to aid them and thus aiding us when we do not have the words to pray.

Jesus has not let us on our own to figure out our relationship with God. Every step of the way Jesus spelled out to the disciples just what his ministry was doing and who it was glorifying.

What seems to be a habit we just muddle through was actually designed to aid us when we either don't know the words to pray or we are unsure of what we even need to pray for.

The words Jesus gave his disciples to pray and the prayer we use today serves is a habit the Church has been living on since the resurrection. Habits can either be harmful or healthy. Smoking we all know is a bad habit. Running and exercising are good habits. You know this. Prayer is the habit that connects us with the one who breathed the breath of life into our lungs while we were being knitted in our mother's wombs. But the problem with a habit is that often the action becomes a process of going through the motions rather than something meant to build up the body.

There are Sundays where I know there are some of you who just want to get through the service (and I'm not just talking about during the sermon). You have somewhere else to be later in the day or later in the week and while you are sitting on the wooden pew your mind is already in that other place. I know this is true because, believe it or not, clergy go through the same experience. There are days, not when we do not know the words to say, rather we do not even know we need to say them, and like the liturgy that does not change from week to week, the prayer taught to us by Christ serves as the habit we lean into when it feels as though we are bending away from God.

So, pray is meant to be a habit. Jesus' prayer frees us from the need to make everything new and novel and spontaneous. This prayer eliminates the socialite assumption that prayer needs to be genuine and spontaneous which is indicative of our bondage to a culture that does not want us shaped by a particular Jew from a place like Nazareth.

Simply put... Bon Jovi is right; we are a community living on a prayer. A prayer mind you, that lacks $15 seminary words and is not longwinded. The prayer Jesus taught to his disciples is sufficient witness to God, made truthful by worshipers, through the One who taught is to be prayed.

The unsureness we feel in our prayers is precisely the reassurance Jesus offered his disciples in the parable he told.

The knocking on the door from a friend who is unable to feed his unexpected guests sounds like a silly story to tell. Of course, we think, it would be unreasonable for the man in bed to get up. After all it is late into the night or early into the morning. Just go to the gas station or 24-hour grocery store. But the man knocking on the door, seeking help from his friend for a friend knows that the custom of the day was to welcome traveling family, friends, and friends of friends because as Jesus reminded us in the parable of the Good Samaritan, travel during this day was dangerous. The man knocking on the door knows his friend will get out of bed, providing for his need because the man does not want to receive the glares of his neighbors in the morning when they find out he did not come to the aid of a friend.

"How much more then, will our Creator provide," is the rationale Jesus moves to. If the neighbor is asking for bread, then how much more will our Creator give us when we petition our need for "our daily bread?"

Jesus offers us, through this prayer and all prayer to God, sufficient grace and compassion to ensure our needs, our daily bread is made available. The response we receive from God to the need we present may not match the desires we have. The daily bread or the healing we request from God may not mirror what we desire, and this is where the difficult work of seeking God's will through prayerful dialogue with our Creator begins. This is when we begin to lean into the Lord, bending even further towards God so that we can catch a glimpse, we pray, of what God's will is for our lives and for the new creation inaugurated by Christ's death and resurrection.

As we pray and make the words of Christ not only our prayer but a post by which we build our faith—knowing we were created by a God who desires to provide for our needs—know that when you do not feel like speaking the words or that you do not have the faith to do so in the moment, not only is this community praying the words for you, but the church universal is as well. In a world full of division among the church, Christ is still the head of the church, and through prayer we are still connected to Christ and one another.

Forgiven, Don't Forget
Matthew 18:21-35
Jason Micheli

I presided over a wedding yesterday here in the sanctuary.

The bride and the groom, both of whom were in their sixties, said "I do" and when we were all done, I went up to Starbucks to write my sermon.

I had my clergy collar still strapped around my neck. I sat down at a little round table with my notes and my Bible, and before I could get very far a woman crept up to me and said: "Um, excuse me Father....could I?"

She gestured to the empty seat across from me.

"Well, I'm not exactly a Fa_____" I started to say but she just looked confused.

"Never mind" I said. "Sit down."

She looked to be somewhere in her fifties. She had long, dark hair and hip, horn-rimmed glasses and pale skin that had started to blush red.

No sooner had she sat down than she started having second thoughts.

"Maybe this is a mistake. I just saw you over here and I haven't been to church in years..."

She fussed with the button on her shirt while she rambled, embarrassed.

"It's just. . .. I've been carrying this around for years and I can't put it down."

"Put what down?" I asked.

"Where do I start? You don't even know me, which is probably why I'm sitting here in the first place." She fussed with her hair.

"Beginning at the beginning usually works," I said.

"Yeah," she said absent-minded, she was already rehearsing her story in her head.

And then she told it to me.

About her husband and their marriage.

48

About his drinking, the years of it.

About his lies, the years of it.

She told me about how he's sober now.

And then she told me about how *now* the addiction in their family is her anger and resentment over how she'll never get back what she gave out, how she'll never be paid back what she spent.

Then she bit her lip and paused.

And so I asked her: "Are you asking me if you're supposed to forgive him?'

"No, I know I ought to forgive him" she said. "Our priest told me years ago —he said I should forgive but not forget."

"He told you to forgive but not forget?" I asked.

She nodded.

"Well, that's why God gave us the Reformation," I said under my breath.

"What was that?"

"Never mind—what's your question then if it's not about forgiveness?" I asked.

"I've forgiven him—at least, I've tried, I've told him I have—but ... why can't I just wipe this from my slate and move on?"

And when she said that ("Why can't I just wipe this from my slate?") I excused myself and I walked to the restroom and I closed the door and I threw my hands in the air and I shouted:

"Thank you, Jesus, for, as reliably as Papa John's, you have delivered unto me this perfect anecdote for tomorrow's parable!"

Just kidding.

But without her realizing it, I did tell her about the slave in today's text, who even before you get to the parable's grim finale is in a cage he cannot see.

When Peter asks Jesus if forgiving someone seven times is sufficient, Peter must've thought it was a good answer.

Peter's a hand-raiser and a rear-kisser. Peter wouldn't have volunteered if he thought it was the wrong answer.

After all, the Jewish Law commanded God's people to forgive a wrongdoer three times. Seven times no doubt struck Peter as a generous, Jesusy amount of forgiveness.

Not only does Peter double the amount of forgiveness prescribed by the Law, he adds one, rounding the total to seven.

Because God had spoken creation into being in seven days, the number seven was the Jewish number for completeness and perfection.

Peter might be an idiot, but he's not stupid.

Peter knew seven times—that's a divine amount of forgiveness.

Think about it—seven times:

Imagine someone sins against you. Say, a church member gossips about you behind your back. I'm not suggesting anyone in this church would do that, just take it as a for instance.

Imagine someone gossips about you.

And you confront them about it.

1. And they say: "I'm sorry." So, you say to them: "I forgive you."
2. And then they do it again. And you forgive them.
3. And then they do it again. And you forgive them.
4. And then they do it again. And you forgive them.
5. And then they do it again. And you forgive them.
6. And then they do it again for sixth time. And you forgive them.

I mean...fool me once shame on you.

Fool me 2, 3 ,4, 5, 6 times...how many times does it take until its shame on me?

It's got to stop somewhere, right?

"What's the limit, Jesus? Where's the boundary?"

And remember, Matthew 18 is all one scene.

It's Jesus' yarn about the Good Shepherd, who all but abandons the well-behaved ninety-nine to search out the single sheep too stupid to stay with the flock, that prompts Peter's question and the parable that answers Peter's question.

How many times should the lost sheep be sought and brought back, Jesus?

How many fatted calves does the father have to slaughter for his kid?

How many times do we have to forgive, Jesus?

And Peter suggests drawing the line at seven times.

Whether we're talking about gossip or anger or adultery or synagogue shooters, *seven is a whole lot of forgiveness.*

Probably Peter expected a pat on the back and a gold star from Jesus. But he doesn't get one.

Notice what Jesus doesn't do with Peter's question.

Notice—Jesus doesn't respond to Peter's question with another question. Jesus doesn't ask Peter *"What'd they do?"* Jesus doesn't say *"Well, you know, it depends—the forgiveness has to fit the crime. Roseanne Barr and racist tweets, maybe four times forgiveness. But Trysten Terrell at UNC-Charlotte..."*

No, Jesus takes it in the other direction: "Not seven times, but, seventy-seven times."

Seventy-seven times—pay attention, now, this is important.

Jesus didn't pull that number out of his incarnate keister.

By telling Peter seventy-seven times forgiveness for those who sin against you, Jesus hearkens back to the mark of Cain and the sin of all of us in Adam.

In Genesis 4, after Cain murders his brother Abel, in order to prevent a cycle of bloodshed, God—in God's mercy—places a mark on Cain, and God warns humanity that whoever harms Cain will suffer a sevenfold vengeance. *They will receive seven times vengeance,* God warns.

Later in Genesis 4, after civilization is founded east of Eden on the blood of Abel, Lamech, Cain's grandson, murders a man.

And in telling his two wives about the murder, Lamech plagiarizes God's promise for himself and Lamech declares that if anyone should harm Lamech then vengeance will be visited upon them—guess how many times—seventy times.

If you don't get this, you won't get it.

When Jesus tells Peter, he owes another seventy-seven times forgiveness, Jesus is not fixing a boundary, albeit a gracious and superabundant boundary.

No, Jesus is saying here that in him there is no limit to God's forgiveness because his is a pardon powerful to unwind all of our sin as far back as Adam's original sin.

Seventy-seven times—he's not simply raising the ceiling even higher on Peter; he's saying that there is no floor to God's grace.

Seventy-seven times.

God's forgiveness for you in Christ is bottomless.

Make no mistake—

This is the radicality and the scandal of the Gospel.

This is the beating heart of Christianity.

I know I've said this before, but I also know that not everyone who shows up on a Sunday morning is a believer so I'm going to say it again.

What makes Christianity distinct among the world's religions is that, contrary to what you may have heard, Christianity is not a religion of *do*. Christianity is not even a religion, for that matter, it's an announcement—it's *news*—that *everything has been done.*

And Jesus gives you a hint of that here in his response. Jesus reframes Peter's question about the limits of the forgiveness we ought to do by alluding to the forgiveness God will do in him.

In other words, Jesus takes Peter's question about the Law (what we ought to do for God) and he answers in terms of Grace (what God has done for us).

Think about it—

When you make Christianity into a message of *do this* instead of *it has been done*, you ignore the trajectory of the parable Jesus tells where it's your failure to appreciate just how much you've been forgiven that produces in you unforgiveness for another.

The road to hell here in this story is paved not with ill intentions but with amnesia. What damns this slave is not his sin but his forgiven sin getting forgotten.

"Lord, how much do I have to forgive?" And Jesus responds: "For this reason the kingdom of heaven may be compared to a king..."

As if to say, the very question "How much forgiveness do I have to give out to those who owe me?" reveals you've forgotten how much mercy has been given to you.

Ten thousand talents worth.

The key to this entire text today is in the numbers.

Seventy-seven times of forgiveness.

Ten thousand talents of debt.

As soon as Peter and the disciples heard Jesus say that the Kingdom of God is like a slave—a slave—who owed his king ten thousand talents, they would've known instantly that Jesus is taking forgiveness out of the realm of *do* and recasting it in terms of *done*.

In case you gave up Lou Dobbs for Lent and are rusty on your biblical exchange rates:

1 Denarius = 1 Day's Wages
6,000 Denarii = 1 Talent

This slave owes the king 10,000 talents. When you do the math and carry the one—that comes out to roughly 170,000 years' worth of debt.

The Kingdom of God is like a slave who owed his king a zillion bitcoin, that's how Peter and the rest would've heard the setup.

What's more, ten thousand was the highest possible number expressible in Greek; it was a synonym for *infinity*.

"What's the limit to the forgiveness we ought to give, Jesus?"

"There was a king who had a slave," Jesus says, *"and that slave owed that king infinitely more than what Nick Cage owes the IRS."*

Ten thousand talents.

It's a ridiculous amount he owes his king, which makes the slave's promise to the king all the more pathetic: "Have patience with me, and I will pay you back everything."

I'll pay you back? To infinity and beyond?

This is what heaven sounds like to God: *I'll make it up to you, God. I'll do better. I'll get my act back in the black. Give me another chance, God. Be patient with me.*

This is what heaven sounds like—a cacophony of our pathetic pleas all of which drown out his promise that a debt we can neither fathom nor repay has been forgiven.

Look, it's great that God, as the Bible promises, is patient and slow to anger, but God giving you another chance is not what you need.

God's patience is not what you need.

You need pardon. Jesus' point right at the get-go here in his parable is that God's patience will not really remedy your ultimate situation.

This is why the Church doesn't charge you admission because of all the outlets in the world only the Church is bold enough to tell you the truth about yourself.

Your problem is infinitely bigger than your best self-improvement project.

No good deed you do can undo your unpayable debt.

Before God, you are like a slave so far in the red it would take a hundred thousand lives to get it AC/DC.

Or, it would take just one life.

Seventy-seven times, ten thousand talents—one life.

Remember the amount.

It's a kingdom's worth of cash the slave is in hock to the king. So when the king forgives the slave's debt, the king dies.

In forgiving his servant, the king forsakes his kingdom—he forsakes everything—because there's no way the king can dispose the servant's debt without the king also sacrificing his entire ledger.

The king's whole system of settling accounts, of keeping score, of red and black, of credits and debits, of giving and receiving exactly what is earned and deserved the king DIES to that life so that his servant can have new one.

But notice.

After the king gets rid of his ledger, who's still got one?

Who's still keeping score?

No sooner is the slave forgiven and freed than he encounters a fellow servant who owes him, about three months wages. Not chump change but small potatoes compared to his infinite IOU.

He grabs the servant, demands what's owed to him, and he sends the man to prison, turning a deaf ear—notice—to the very same plea he'd pled to the king: *"be patient with me and I will pay back everything..."*

How many times do we gotta forgive somebody, Jesus?

When the king finds out he has failed to extend the same mercy he had received, the king gives to the slave exactly what the slave wants.

You want to keep living your life keeping score? Even though I died to score-keeping? Fine, Have it your way. But that way of life—I gotta warn you—it's torture.

You see, even before the slave ends up in prison, that slave was already stuck inside a cage he couldn't see.

"Why can't I just wipe the slate clean and move on?" the woman at Starbucks asked me.

I sipped my coffee.

"Look," I said, "provided you're willing to be exploited for the purposes of a sermon illustration someday, I'll give you the goods, straight up, and you won't even have to pay for the refill on my coffee."

She smiled and nodded.

"It's not about wiping your ledger clean. It's about getting rid of the life of ledger-keeping altogether—it's about dying to it.

The ledger is the whole reason you've forgiven him but still don't feel free."

And I paused, wondering if I should tack on the truth:

"And my guess is as long as you're holding onto your ledger it doesn't matter how many times you've told your husband you forgive him—my guess is he doesn't feel very free either."

She bit her lip.

"When the Bible says, "Christ is the end of the Law," I said, "it's just a pious way of saying that Jesus is the end of all score-keeping. He's gotten rid of all it—the sins and the spreadsheets both."

And I could tell what she was about to counterpunch me with so, being an Enneagram 8, I interrupted her and talked over her:

"We say "forgive but don't forget," sure.

But Jesus says: *Don't forget—you've been forgiven with a forgiveness that has forgotten all your sins in the black hole of his death. Ditto for whomever has trespassed against you and whatever was that trespass against you. Remember that you've been forgiven with a forgiveness that has forgotten everything—remember that and, eventually, you can forgive and forget."*

She took off her glasses and wiped the corners of her eyes.

"I don't know," she said, shaking her head, "that doesn't sound fair."

"Of course, it's not fair," I said, "if God were fair we'd all be screwed."

And then her phone rang, and she had to leave as quickly as she'd came.

The woman at Starbucks and the slave in the story, they're not the only ones clinging to their ledger.

Admit it—

Some of you excel at *Excel*, carrying around a ledger filled with lists of names:

Names of people who've hurt you.

Names of people who've taken something from you.

Names of people who've wronged you.

People that no matter what they do, there's nothing they can do to change their name from the red to the black in your book.

Some of you cling to ledgers filled with balance sheets, keeping score of exactly how much you've done for the people in your life compared to how little they've done for you.

Jesus says with his story that in order for you to enjoy your forgiveness his death makes possible you've got to die too—to that whole way of living that produces questions like *"How many times do I have to ...?"*

No—just as there is no empty grave without a cross, there is no salvation for you without your death.

You've got to die to your life of book-keeping.

Limitless forgiveness—of course it sounds impossible.

I get it.

Forgiveness without limits comes so unnaturally to us it first had to come to us as Jesus.

And—no less than then—Jesus comes to us still today.

Jesus comes to us in his word. He comes to us in wine and bread

And Jesus comes to us preaching the promise of this parable:

The promise that those who know how much they have been forgiven—ten thousand talents—in the fullness of time, through word and wine and bread, much will they be able to forgive.

So, come to the table where Christ comes to you.

Taste and see that God is not fair; God is gracious.

Come to the table where Christ comes to you.

Taste and see and enjoy *your* forgiveness, for the promise that everything has been done for you—that promise alone has the power to enable you to do for another.

THE POWER TO DO IS NOT IN YOU!

THE POWER TO DO IS IN THIS PROMISE OF *DONE*.

So, come to the table; so that, you might become what you eat.

Blinded by The Light
Luke 17.20-37
Taylor Mertins

Jesus was doing his Jesus thing when, yet another group of Pharisees showed up and started badgering him with questions. They were mystified by all the mysteries, nonplussed with all the parables, and they just couldn't take it anymore.

"Enough is enough, Jesus. When is all of this actually going to happen? And, for once, could you just give us a straight answer?"

"You and your friends all want one thing: a sign. You want some big demonstration that what I've been talking about is getting set into motion. You flock to Twitter and assume that with every new major scandal or devastation that it's a sign of something greater happening. Yeah, I see what you all do on the Internet, I know your inner monologues of conspiracy theories—I've even eavesdropped on some of those mid-afternoon gossip sessions you've been having.

"But if you've been listening to anything I've been saying, the more you go looking for the kingdom somewhere else, the more you will miss it. Because the kingdom, my kingdom, as I've been trying to knock it into your brains, is already here. Seriously. It is among you, hell it's even within you. Perhaps it's best if I put it like this: It's lost in you and only when you admit that you are lost as well will you actually start to see it."

"C'mon Jesus, what in the world are you talking about? We don't want some sort of mystical kingdom. We want you to overthrow the powerful and the wealthy. We thought you were going to take the throne and let us reign over the earth. How can your kingdom be among us when the world still feels like garbage—better yet, how can the kingdom be in me when I feel like garbage?"

"I know I know. You all can't stand the stuff I'm bringing, but I'm bringing it anyway. I know all of you well enough to know that even my talking about it as clearly as I am right now won't leave you feeling like it's all settled."

"You think you're being clear right now? For God's sake, Jesus, just tell us something true!"

"All of you will point to things as if I have some master trick up my sleeve, as if I'm working behind the curtains and pulling all of the strings. You will pick and choose the signs that match most with your own sensibilities, you'll probably even lord them over other people and tell them that this was my work or that I have something to do with the craziness that's going on in the world. And all of that squabbling and pontificating and gesturing will be for nothing because it will be a denial of everything, I've already done for you."

"I believe you Lord. I know you're telling the truth."

"Peter, such a good boy. Maybe you're good with everything I'm saying, though when push comes to shove, you'll deny it, but I'm getting ahead of myself. No matter how all of you feel about this stuff, there will be others who point at the craziness. They'll say that mass shootings are my way of getting you back to prayer. They'll say that locking up immigrants is a sign of holy justice. They'll point and point and point and say my name. For God's sake, literally, don't go running after all that nonsense and don't you dare follow their examples. Those people haven't a clue in the world.

"When I come in glory it won't be in a particular place or through a particular people. When I show up in glory it's going to be like lightning—all over the place and all at once showing the truth to everyone and everything.

"But before being blinded by my light, the Son of man will have to endure suffering and be rejected by those in power."

"Of course, you will, Jesus. No one is going to buy anything you're selling."

"But don't you see? I'm not selling anything—I'm giving it all away. It will be just like during the days of Noah. Remember him? He was in on the whole mystery of death and resurrection before just about anyone else, but even he didn't really know it at the time. He was a sign that the whole world was going to hell in a handbasket and that God had plans to use death to save the world. But everyone during the time of Noah ignored it; they wouldn't think about anything except their precious little lives. They had dinner parties to go to, vacations to plan, tennis matches to watch. And they went right on doing all those things until the very end when Noah packed up his ark while the rest of the world drowned.

"Are you starting to get it now? The message I'm giving you to share with the world is that even in death you will be fine because death is my cup of tea. The problem isn't death—its' with all the people who are so committed to their version of whatever they think living is that they can't let go. When I come in glory it's the people obsessed with holding onto their lives that aren't going to be very happy.

"Imagine your neighbor being up on his roof replacing a wonky gutter and he sees me risen from the dead. What good would it do him to go into the house to grab his wallet and check his hair before joining me in glory?

"Picture someone mowing the lawn. Do you think they should go inside to finish filing their tax return before joining me in the blinding light?

"Do you remember the story of Lots' wife? When everything was finally out in the open, God had done a strange and new thing, and it was time for her to go with God's flow, she decided to have a nostalgia binge and look back to her old life in Sodom. And you know what happened to her? She turned into a pillar of salt!

"Plenty of you are going to try to save your lives like that, and you're going to lose it all. You're so obsessed with what you've done, and what you've earned, and what you've accomplished that you can't see the truth even when its standing right in front of you. And, I can't blame you, we've all been conditioned to hold onto our lives with every fiber of our being so losing that control will literally feel like losing our lives.

"I know this kingdom stuff isn't easy to digest because everything and everyone else will try to sell you a different story.

That's called idolatry. Whenever you feel compelled to worship something else, whether it's a person or an institution or heaven forbid a political party, those things can't give your life. In fact, they suck away the marrow of your life. They portend to tell you what to do, and what is important, and what is good and true and beautiful. And those things aren't necessarily bad, they might even be significant, they make differences in the ways we live and move, but they aren't the difference that makes the difference—that's me.

"And believe you me, things are going to get worse before they get better. You will pit yourselves against each other over the dumbest things, you will reject one another because of a wayward comment or a foolish story, and at some point, you're going to look back at your life and wonder where everyone went.

"But when it comes to my kingdom, remember the one that's already around you, it's going to be even more confusing. Some people are going to accept it and others won't. You'll see two friends out in a boat fishing and one of them will say yes to my death and resurrection and the other will say no. You'll see friends on a trip to the market and one will go for the deal and the other will say they need to think about it, forever."

"Enough Jesus! Where is this going to happen? Just cut the small talk about about the mystery and give us something real."

"Where the corpse is, that's where the vultures will gather... Oh, you don't like that? Are you feeling uncomfortable? It's all about death! Haven't you been listening to any of the stories I've been telling you? I know that death is the one thing you all choose to avoid more than anything else, not just your literal deaths but even talk about death, and yet death is the one thing you don't need to worry about. Because you can put the dead anywhere and the vultures will find the bodies—that's what they're good at.

"Don't you see it now? I'm in the death and resurrection business, that's what I'm good at. I will come and find you wherever you may be. So, forget all of your anxiety about the question of 'where?' And, while you're at it, get rid of you 'hows' and 'whens' as well. The only thing that matters is you trust me to do what I say I'm going to do, and then get out there and tell other people to trust me too—because in the end that's all you can really do—I'm going to take care of everything else.

"Stop worrying about where you are or who you're with— I'm with you." Amen.

God in the Hands of Angry Sinners
Matthew 21.35-45
Jason Micheli

"What do you think he'll do when he comes back?" Jesus asks on the eve of his own destruction.

"When he comes back, what do you think he'll do?"

And they said to him: "When he comes back (when he comes back to judge the quick and the dead) he will put those wretches to a miserable death."

"What do you think the owner of the vineyard will do when he returns?"

Here's another question—

Since today is the fifth Sunday in Eastertide, here's a resurrection question for you.

Why is the very first reaction to the Easter news fear?

Across all four Gospels, the immediate response to the news *Christ is Risen* isn't *Christ is Risen indeed! Alleluia!* It's alarm and abject terror. Why?

Mark and Matthew, Luke and John—none of them tell the Easter story in the same way.

Except for the fear.

Fear is the feature Matthew, Mark, Luke, and John all agree upon.

The soldiers guarding the tomb faint from *fear*. The women, come to anoint the body, run away, *terrified*. The disciples lock the door of the upper room and <u>cower</u> in the corner.

When he comes back, everyone—they're white-knuckled terrified.

Just what do they think he'll do?

———————————————

Before you get to the New Testament, the only verse in the Old that explicitly anticipates resurrection is in the Book of Daniel, chapter twelve.

And the resurrection the prophet Daniel foresees is a *double* resurrection:

"Those who sleep in the dust of the earth shall be raised up, the righteous to everlasting life, and the unrighteous to everlasting shame and contempt."

It's a double resurrection the Bible anticipates.

A resurrection to reward, or a resurrection to punishment.

Those who have remained righteous and faithful in the face of suffering will be raised up by God to life with God in God's Kingdom.

But those who've committed suffering by their sins—they might be on top now in this life, but one day God will raise them up too, not to everlasting life but to its everlasting opposite.

The "good" news of resurrection in the Book of Daniel is predicated entirely upon your goodness.

Resurrection was not about yellow peeps and metaphors for springtime renewal; resurrection was God coming back with a list of who'd been naughty and who'd been nice in order to mete out to each according to what they deserved.

Resurrection wasn't about butterflies.

Resurrection was about the justice owed to the righteous and the judgment owed to sinners.

In the only Bible the disciples knew, the Old Testament, resurrection was good news.

If you were good.

If you weren't, if you were wicked, resurrection was the first day of a miserable and wretched fate.

They all respond to the Easter news with fear not because they fail to understand resurrection but exactly because they do understand.

They know their Bible—better than you.

They knew resurrection was good news or godawful news depending on where you fell according to the righteousness equation.

And they know that as God's elect People in the world God had called them, Israel, to be tenants of God's vineyard.

And they know all too well that when God set them apart as his peculiar, pilgrim People, when God gave to them the Law on Mt. Sinai, they promised God not just their effort or their obedience but perfection.

"All of this we will do and more," they swore at Sinai, "we will be perfect before the Law as our Father in heaven is perfect."

When they weren't—

When they failed to return God's love with love of their own, when they chose to be like the other nations instead of a light to the nations, God sent them his messengers to call Abraham's children back to the righteous life owed to God as God's chosen People.

First, God sent them prophets.

And what did the People who'd promised him perfection do the prophets?

Zechariah, who told them that God would redistribute their wealth for the sake of the poor, was killed by the King of Judah on the altar of the Temple.

Jeremiah criticized them for turning a deaf ear to lies and making an idol of their politics.

They shut him up by stoning him to death.

And Isaiah was sawn in two near the pool of Siloam for speaking truth to power. "Thus says the Lord," Isaiah said, "I dwell among a people of unclean lips."

They killed the prophets.

So next this God of second and third and sixth chances, he sends them still another.

A final prophet.

And this messenger makes a way in the wilderness. And he baptizes in the Jordan with a baptism of repentance, and he calls God's wicked tenants a brood of vipers.

Wearing camelhair, he hollers about God's axe lying near, but in the end he's the one on whom the blade falls. A king of the Jews serves his head on a platter as a party gag.

Yet this God is not a Lord of ledgers but a Father of compassion.

After he sends his People prophets, after he sends them John the Baptist (it makes no sense at all) God sends them his only-begotten Son. The Kingdom of God comes in the flesh and our response is *my will be done.*

God's People say, "We have no king but Caesar."

And then they scream, "Crucify him!"

His own disciples—

They'd denied ever knowing him. They'd turned tail. They'd let the wicked world sin all its sins into him.

And then they left him forsaken on a cross.

When the owner comes back—and the word Jesus uses there is *kyrios*, meaning *Lord*—when the Lord comes back, what do you think he'll do?

Everyone in the Easter story responds to the news that Jesus is longer dead with dread because they expect the Lord to put wretches like them to a miserable death.

For the Bible tells them so.

They lock the doors. They run and hide. They faint and cower because, according to scripture, resurrection for sinners means judgment.

They have every reason to expect the Lord who's come back to condemn them:

I was naked and you were not there to clothe me.

I was thirsty and you were too long gone to give me something to drink.

I was a prisoner and you stood in the crowd pretending me a stranger.

If Jesus was risen indeed, then there weren't any alleluias for them. Resurrection could only mean one awful thing for wicked tenants like them.

But no—

When he comes back, he doesn't pay them the wages their sins had earned. He doesn't put wretches like them to a miserable death. The Lord who'd sent messenger after messenger, prophet after prophet, slips past their locked doors and he doesn't give them payback. He gives them pardon.

"Peace," he says.

When he comes back, he doesn't give them what Daniel promised they have coming to them, everlasting punishment. No, he gives them his Holy Spirit that he had promised would come to them.

He gives them his Spirit.

He gives them his pardon.

And he gives to them the ministry of pardon. "Wherever you forgive the sins—any sins—of anyone, their sins are forgiven," Jesus commissions them.

Even Peter, who'd lied and denied the Lord thrice, when he comes back to wretched Peter, he doesn't indict Peter and condemn him. He invites Peter to confess his love for him.

Three times.

A do-over:

"Yes, Lord, you know that I love you."

"Yes, Lord, you know that I love you."

"Yes, Lord, you know everything. You know that I love you."

When he comes back to his wicked tenants...

Wait—

WHERE'S THE BRIMSTONE?

Resurrection is supposed to be a double-edged sword. Resurrection is about reward and punishment. Resurrection is about the justification of the righteous and the judgment of the unrighteous.

The Bible tells them so—that's why they're terrified.

But when the Lord returns to his vineyard, his tenants do not receive what they deserve.

They receive what only he deserves.

As though, resurrection isn't a double-edged sword so much as an exchange.

Eight years ago, exactly to the day, I was in Old Town Alexandria shopping for a black tie to wear for the funeral of a boy

I was burying. He'd been a little younger than my youngest boy is now. In a closet filled with Lego pieces and action figures, he'd done it himself with a fake leather belt bought at Target.

It was a couple of days before the day that Harold Camping, a huckster preacher and president of Family Christian Radio, had predicted the world would end, in judgment and fury, the twenty-first of May.

Standing on the corner of King Street, blocking my path, were four or five of Camping's disciples. A couple of the "evangelists" of were holding foam-board signs high above their heads. The signs were brightly illustrated with graphic images of God's wrath and damnation.

I remember one image—an image borrowed from the Book of Daniel—was of an awful-looking lion with scars on its paws. At the bottom of one of the signs was an illustration of people, men and women and *children*, looking terrified to be caught in their sins by Christ come back.

A young twenty-something man tried to hand me a tract. He didn't look very different from the models in the store window next to us. He gave me a syrupy smile, and said, "Did you know the *wicked* world is going to end on May 21? The Lord is coming back in just two days. What do you think he'll do when he returns? To sinners?"

Then he started talking about the end of the world. I flipped through his brochure.

"Martin Luther said Revelation was a dangerous book in the hands of idiots," I mumbled.

"What's that?" he asked.

"Oh nothing, just thinking out loud."

Now, I'm still new here at Annandale United Methodist Church. Maybe you don't yet know. Sometimes, I'm prone to sarcasm. Sometimes, my sarcasm is of the abrasive varietal. But that day, the day before I had to bury that boy who'd died by his own foolish hand, what I felt rising in me was more like anger.

Because *evangel* in scripture means literally *good freaking news.*

And these "evangelists" weren't dishing out anything of the sort.

"Lemme ask you something," I said, "since you seem to know your Bible."

The evangelist smiled and nodded. He looked electrified to be, all of a sudden, useful.

"Doesn't the Bible call Jesus the Lamb of God who takes away the sins of the whole world?" I asked, feigning naïveté.

He nodded a sanctimonious grin.

"Well then, which ones did he miss?"

He looked confused, as shoppers pushed past us to get to the bus stop.

"Sins," I pressed, "which sins did Jesus miss?"

I'd raised my voice now, my pretense falling away and my righteous anger welling up in the teardrops at the corner of my eyes. "Did Jesus take away *all* the sins of the world, or did he only get *some* of them?"

No sooner had he started to mouth the word "all" than I was back down his throat.

"Really?! Because from your signs and pamphlets, it sure as hell looks like Jesus missed a whole lot of sins, that he's none too pleased with folks who can't get their act together."

He started to give me a patronizing chuckle, so I pressed him.

"And, wait a minute, didn't Jesus say, whilst dying for the sins of the *whole* world, 'It is finished?' Isn't that, like, red-letter?"

He nodded and looked over my head to his supervisor behind me. I was shouting now.

"And doesn't it say, too, that in Jesus God has chosen all of us from *before* the foundation of the world?"

"I think so," he said. "I'm not sure."

"Well, damn straight it does," I hollered. "Ephesians, and, looking at you all with your bullhorns and pictures of lions and dragons and brimstone and judgment, I'm just wondering how, if God's chosen us all in Christ from before the beginning of *everything*, you think so many of us with our puny, pathetic, run-of-the-mill sins—which have all been taken away already—can gum up God's plan?"

"Riddle me that," I shouted.

Okay, so maybe I was feeling a little sarcastic.

"I'm not sure you understand how serious this is, sir," he said to me.

"Oh, I got it, all right."

He suddenly looked like he was trying to remember the safe word.

"I get how serious it is," I said, "I just think it's you who doesn't take it seriously, not enough apparently to take Jesus at his word that when he comes back he'll come back already bearing every sin we've ever sinned in his crucified and risen body. The Judge has been judged in our place. It's not about reward and punishment anymore. It's about promise. The Gospel promise that he has gotten what we all deserve and we're given *gratis* what he alone deserves."

You wonder why I repeat myself Sunday after Sunday—

It's because this "evangelist," this *preacher*, just stared at me like he'd never heard the Gospel before. He hadn't.

"The only basis on which God judges now is not our works—not our *behavior*, good or bad (thank God)—but our belief. Our faith. The only basis on which he judges now is on our simple trust that he's gotten out of the judgment game. It's in your Bible, man: "There is therefore now no *judgment* for those who are in Christ Jesus.""

"It's "There is therefore now no *condemnation,* not no judgment."" he tried to correct me.

"It's the same word," I said. "*Krima*. Judgment. Condemnation. *Krima*. Same word. And when St. Paul says *in Christ Jesus,* he's talking not about behavior but about baptism."

It was right about then I became aware that I was creating a scene.

But I didn't care.

Standing there, needing to buy a necktie I could wear beside a four-foot coffin for a boy I'd baptized, let's just say, it was not an academic debate.

"When the owner of the vineyard comes back, what do you think he'll do to those wicked tenants? And they said to Jesus: "He will put those wretches to a miserable death."

And Jesus doesn't respond: WRONG ANSWER.

Pay attention, this is important.

Jesus tells all of his parables of judgment in the space of four days before his crucifixion—that's the interpretative key to them.

We're supposed to read the parables of judgment as pointers to the cross.

You see, it's not that after three years of preaching about God's bargain free grace and bottomless forgiveness Jesus suddenly gave up and decided to preach instead like John the Baptist. The Gospel is not a bait and switch. Jesus doesn't take away with these parables of judgment the grace he already gave with his left-hand.

The judgment at the center of these dark parables is the cross.

When you read them in light of the cross, you discover that the parables of judgment, every bit as much as that one about the father and the fatted calf, are Gospel not Law.

The cross is our judgment—Jesus already told you that at the very beginning of the Gospel: "This is the judgment, that the light has come into the world, and people loved darkness."

He's talking about the cross.

It's likewise with Paul. "God made Jesus to be our wickedness," Paul writes, "... and through the cross God put to death—krima'd—the enmity between humanity and God."

The cross is our judgment.

"He will put those wretches to a miserable death," they tell Jesus.

And Jesus doesn't correct them or contradict them because they're right. We're all put to death in him. "Do you not know,"

71

the Bible promises, "that all of us who have been baptized into Christ Jesus were baptized into his death...we have been buried with him by baptism into his death for sins so that we might be raised up with him."

That promise is no different than the promise with which Jesus ends the parable today.

Our judgment on the cross is the cornerstone of God's new creation.

All that the world has to do now to escape judgment is to trust that in Jesus Christ you've already escaped it.

That's it.

And that's red-letter: "God the Father judges no one," Jesus says, "God has given over all judgment to the Son...and he who trusts in him is not judged."

Let me make it plain.

GOD'S NOT MAD AT YOU.

God's forgiven you for every single thing—and that thing too.

God's not mad at you.

It doesn't matter who you are.

It doesn't matter what you've done.

It doesn't matter what you've left undone.

On account of Jesus Christ—*propter Christum*, the first Protestants liked to say—God literally doesn't give a damn.

After Jesus Christ announces from his cross, "It is finished," there is now—for those who trust it—nothing but the "blessed silence of his uncondemnation."

No matter who you are or what you've done.

There is no case against you.

There is no indictment filed. There is no evidence locked away in storage. There's not even a courtroom for you to exhibit all your good works.

There is therefore now no judgment.

Because when the Judge came back to his vineyard, he came carrying not a gavel in his hands but nails. He returned wrapped not in a Judge's robe but naked.

Forsaken.

For you.

What Jesus says at the end of this parable is dead on—the indiscriminate acceptance of his uncondemnation, it crushes those of us who persist in our stubborn belief that God's judgment is about rewarding the rewardable.

God's free grace isn't just a stumbling block to those of us who insist on supposing that being well-behaved is more important to God than just trusting his forgiveness.

It breaks people like us to pieces.

It kills people like us who'd prefer to think of ourselves as good than loved.

In the end, that's what's so scary about this parable of judgment.

You and I—the quick and the dead—we're slow to believe that all he's ever wanted was for us to believe.

Death and Taxes
Matthew 17:24-27
Taylor Mertins

The church is weird.

It is weird for a lot of reasons, least of all being that people like you and me are part of it.

The church is weird, at least according to the world, because we worship a crucified God and boldly proclaim that death has been defeated in the person of Jesus Christ.

Add to that the fact that we dump water on babies telling them they've been baptized into Jesus' death and every month we proudly eat Jesus' body and drink his blood... I don't know if things could get much stranger.

Last Sunday was Easter which, or course, is one of the more bizarre Sundays in the church year. We looked around the sanctuary and saw people we've never seen before, we remembered the shadow of the cross from Good Friday, and we triumphantly sang "Christ Is Alive!"

And yet here we are, a week later, on the other side of the resurrection story. We, like the disciples before us, are experiencing the whiplash of discovering a strange new world that has been changed, for good, by Jesus Christ. The resurrection is the event that shatters all of our previous expectations and assumptions and it is the lens by which we read the entirety of the Bible.

As I said last week, if the Easter story were not included in the holy scriptures then we would've thrown out our Bibles a long time ago.

But now we jump back into the story, back into the ministry of Jesus. We have pressed the rewind button to re-enter the realm of the bizarre.

This act of worship through which we proclaim the Word of the Lord is often nothing more than entering the strange new world of the Bible and hoping that we can find our way through together.

Or, to put it another way, if you thought Jesus rising from the dead was crazy, just check this out...

A bunch of tax collectors went up to Peter as soon as the disciples reached Capernaum and asked, "Hey, does your guy pay the temple tax or not?" Peter said, "Yeah, of course he does."

But then when he got to the house where Jesus was staying, Jesus brought it up before Peter got a chance to open his mouth. "What do you think Pete... Who do the wealthy and powerful tax? Do they take money from their own children or from others?"

Peter replied, "From other people."

So, Jesus said to him, "Then the kids are free to do as they please. But we don't want to scandalize the collectors of the temple tax, so why don't you head on down to the sea and go fishing. When you hook your first fish, look inside its mouth, you will find enough money to pay for you and me."

What?!

This feels incomprehensible. And, upon reading the story, it's no wonder that the disciples were such a group of bumbling fools. How can we blame them when Jesus tells the chief disciple that he can find his tax payment inside of a fish's mouth?

Over and over again in the gospel narratives, the disciples struggle to make sense of what they see and hear from Jesus. Sure, they witness miracles, and experience profound truths, but they are also bombarded with a strange new reality straight from the lips and actions of their Lord.

He was weird.

The weirdness is as its fullest when Jesus comes to the realization, or perhaps he has it the whole time, that the kingdom of God is inextricably tied up with his own exodus, his death and resurrection.

The parables, therefore, are seen in their fullest light on this side of the resurrection. I have made the case before that for as much as we want the parables to be about us, they are about Jesus. That's one of the reasons that Jesus sternly ordered the disciples not to tell anyone what they saw or heard until he had been raised from the dead.

Of course, upon first glance, the money in the mouth of the fish might not sound like a parable. For whenever we hear the word *parable,* we are quick to jump to the good Samaritan or the prodigal son—we conjure up in our minds the stories Jesus *told.*

But this is a parable that Jesus *lives out.*

What makes it parabolic is that it points to something greater than its parts and it leaves us with more questions than answers.

The tax collectors were out to find the temple tax, the didrachma. It was a two-drachma tax expected of all Jews and it amounted to about two day's pay. But they weren't simply looking to collect—they are asking a question to discern what kind of person this Jesus really was.

"Does he pay the temple tax?" is but another version of "Does he follow the Law?"

Peter, ever eager to jump in without thinking much about what he was saying, assures the collectors that Jesus in fact pays his taxes and then he returns to the house.

And Jesus, who was not privy to the conversation, questions Peter upon his arrival, "Who do the powerful take their taxes from? Their own families, or from others?"

And Peter responds accordingly, "From others."

And that was good enough for Jesus who says, "Then the children are free."

Before we even get to the miraculous and monetized fish, Jesus is establishing something remarkably new through the spoken truth of this parabolic encounter. Jesus and his followers in whatever the new kingdom will be are under no obligations to the old order represented by those in power.

The former things are passing away and Jesus is doing a new thing.

The children are free from taxes; they don't have to do anything. Which, to our Americans ears starts to sound a little disconcerting. Some of us will immediately perk up in our pews when we hear the news that Jesus is apparently against paying taxes, while others of us begin to squirm when we think about what would happen if we all stopped paying our taxes.

But that's not what's going on here.

Jesus and his disciples do not have to do anything because they are God's children, and only God has the right to tax God's creatures. This wasn't money for public school education, or for infrastructure repairs, or national defense. This was for the Temple, the religious establishment, the same Temple that Jesus eventually says he has come to destroy!

But then he moves on from words alone to the action of the parable, the part that, if we're honest, leaves us even more troubled than with questions about our taxes.

Jesus says, "But you know what Pete, we shouldn't scandalize the tax collectors so go catch a fish, and inside you will find a coin that will be enough."

Interestingly, the coin in Greek is a STATER which was worth exactly four drachmas, which would perfectly cover Peter and Jesus' contribution.

And how to the temple tax collectors respond to the aquatic audit?

The Bible doesn't tell us.

What about Peter's response to actually catching a fish with a coin in its mouth?

The Bible doesn't tell us.

All we're given is the parable.

Jesus knows that his own death will be at the heart of the new order, the kingdom of God. And in this strange and quixotic moment, he shows how free he and his disciples are from the old political and religious and messianic expectations and decides to make a joke about the whole thing.

And for the living Lord this is nothing new. He was known for breaking the rules, and eating with sinners, and questioning the authorities. But now, in this story, Jesus lives and speaks into the truth of his location being outside all the programs created by those with power to maintain their power.

He is free among the dead.

He is bound to the last, least, and lost.

The coin in the fish's mouth is the great practical joke of God's own creation against the powers and principalities.

It's but another version of saying, "You think all of this religious stuff is going to save you? You think your morality and your ethics, and your economics are enough? Even the fish in the sea have a better chance than all of you!"

The children are free.

Free from what? The children are free from the religious forms of oppression and expectation. Whatever religion was trying to do during the time of Jesus, and sadly during our time as well, cannot be accomplished by our own religious acts but can be and are accomplished in the mystery of Jesus' death and resurrection.

The children are free.

The parable of the coin in the fish's mouth is far greater than an episode by the sea or even a treatment on the levying of taxes. It is a profound declaration of freedom.

But herein lies one of the greatest challenges for us.

Because when we hear the word *freedom,* we bring all sorts of our own definitions to that word. We hear "freedom" and we see red, white, and blue. We talk about freedom in terms of getting to do, and say, and believe whatever we want without repercussions.

But Jesus brings a radically different version of freedom— freedom from religion; freedom from the Law.

Religion, in the many ways it manifests itself, often only has one thing to say: people like you and me need to do something in order to get God to do something. We need only be good enough, or faithful enough, or merciful enough, until we tip the scales back in our favor. But this kind of religious observance, which is most religious observance, traps us in a game that we will always and forever lose.

It's bad news.

But Jesus comes to bring Good News.

I have come not to abolish the law but to fulfill the law.

Again, and again in the gospels Jesus stands against what the established religious order was doing and trying to do.

The Devil offers him power over the Temple during the temptations and Jesus refuses.

Jesus rebukes the hard and fast rules of not eating with sinners, and of not helping others on the sabbath.

After he enters Jerusalem, with the cross ever present on the horizon, he marches straight into the temple and flips over all the tables of the moneychangers.

And even in his death, as he hangs on the cross, the veil of the Temple is torn into two pieces.

The old has fallen away and something new has arrived in its place.

Jesus says he doesn't want to scandalize those trapped in the Law and by religious observance but his cross and resurrection are fundamentally scandalous. We are no longer responsible for our salvation. We do not have to be the arbiters of our own deliverance.

We are free!

Truly and deeply free!

Jesus has erased the record that stood against us and chose to nail it to his cross!

Jesus has taken the "Gone Fishin'" sign and hung it over the doorpost of the ridiculous religious requirements that we have used against one another and ourselves.

Jesus has come to bring Good News.

The children are free. Amen.

(un)Like A Virgin
Matthew 25:1-13
David King

The parables are stories Jesus tells about himself. That is, the parables make no sense apart from who Jesus is and what God does through Jesus on the cross. So, you can imagine my surprise when Jason told me last week that I was preaching on the parable of the 10 virgins.

I mean, talk about a first impression.

In all seriousness though, if the parables are stories that both are made sense of through the cross and shed light on the mystery of the cross, then the story we have in today's scripture presents a difficult passage to make sense of.

Like last week's scripture, this parable is categorized as a parable of judgment. And, on the face of it, the parable reeks of an inhospitable bridegroom shutting the door in the face of the virgins. In fact, the story tells of all doors being shut to the foolish virgins. And before we start associating ourselves with the wise virgins, remember to whom and for what purpose Jesus tells this parable. Jesus tells it to the disciples, knowing full well that they will fall asleep when he asks them to stay awake in the Garden of Gethsemane, just a chapter later in Matthew's narrative.

The parable of judgment – this parable of the kingdom – it presupposes the disciples unfaithfulness to Christ.

Why, then, do we so often read the parables of judgment as parables of condemnation, as verses and stories declaring the sorting out of the faithful from the unbelievers that we think will happen at the end of days, that great and glorious time when we can whet our tongues with the wine of heaven while all the non-Christians weep and gnash their teeth?

Stories, parables like these, we so often read them to satiate our need for validation of our faith in a world that often feels hostile to it. We so often do it to feel better than "those people." However, the image of the ten virgins, undivided with respect to their purity indicates to us that the people being judged are members of the church. Their virginity is symbolic: it indicates their preparedness to be married to the bridegroom who is Christ. As St. Paul writes in 2 Corinthians 11:2, "I promised you to one husband, to Christ, so that I might present you as a pure virgin to him."

Already, then, the popular interpretation of this as a judgment levied against non-believers is moot. The virgins are united in a community called "Church," their virginity imputed to them as a symbol of grace.

Further, what this shows to us is that this parable of judgment, it needs to be read through a frame, a lens, that presupposes the gift of grace. We read the parables of judgment not with condemnation in mind, but with, as the theologian Robert Capon insists, an interpretive lens of inclusion-before-exclusion.

This is all the more important since the parable begins with the ever-important word, "then." Earlier in Matthew's Gospel, Jesus describes the Kingdom using the phrase, "The Kingdom will be like" x, y, z. But here, Jesus begins by using the word "then," indicating to the disciples that this is not a parable of judgment preceding the cross. Jesus is speaking of what the kingdom in the wake of the cross is like.

The wedding has happened – the grace has been offered. The virgins are preparing to celebrate their marriage.

What, then, is all the fuss about the oil? Fleming Rutledge, who I will only mention once since she's really Jason's gal, asks the pertinent question: what really is in those lamps?

Before I answer that question, I must admit that one of my guilty pleasures is listening to bad Christian talk radio. You know, the all love but no Jesus kind of Christian talk radio. You know, the kind that prides itself in its acceptance of saints but rejects the sinner. The kind of Christian talk radio that will couch an hour long sermon on judgment in between two hours of financial planning "from a biblical perspective." I love that stuff.

So, as I was driving in to work here this week, listening to Christian talk radio, learning about how I can plan my retirement in accordance with biblical standards of stewardship and bookkeeping, the oil and the lamps finally made sense to me.

St. Augustine, in his sermon on Matthew 25, notes that the foolish virgins wish to please people with their abstinence and good works, but in doing so, they forget to carry what he calls "the necessary oil," which is faith in the Gospel.

That is, the parable, the oil stored up by the wise virgins, it can't be good works because, as Augustine sees, that would make their entrance to the wedding celebration a matter of payment, a payment that no sum of works can make. It is for this reason that the foolish virgins fear for their selves. They ask the wise virgins for the oil, saying, "give us some of your oil; our lamps are going out." They fear, that is, that their works will be insufficient, and rightly so! For they think that the oil the wise carry is something that can be transferred, something that can be given or earned.

You see, the foolish virgins misunderstand the purpose of the oil. They misunderstand its nature, and in so doing, represent for us the fundamental misconception we so often make when it comes to the Gospel: that anything besides the grace of God could possibly give us entrance on the final day of judgment. They misunderstand what the wise get right: that the oil is their sin, transformed by the grace of the cross and not by their works. Truly, then, the oil is non-transferable; it is non-refundable. The oil is their sin, an oil that which can be taken up by only one person: Christ the bridegroom.

Notice, too, what the text says: "but while they went to buy the oil, the bridegroom came, and those who were ready went with him to the wedding banquet, and the door was shut." Matthew does not say that the wise virgins go in with the bridegroom because they had extra oil, nor does he say they go in because their lamps are lit. Matthew does not accredit their entrance to any act that they participated in to distinguish them from the foolish virgins.

Matthew tells us that the wise virgins enter in strictly because they were ready. The readiness of the wise virgins is qualified not by their own glorification or righteousness, but by their readiness to lay their sin, their oil, before the bridegroom who is Christ. Their readiness is the posture of the Church in light of the cross.

The foolish virgins feared, for they misunderstood the nature of the oil. They did not bring extra oil precisely because they thought they could gain entrance on their own accord. But at the approach of the bridegroom, they doubt their own righteousness. For this, they panicked. The wise, however, brought extra oil, oil of a different kind, because they knew the only thing they could possibly do is bring their sin to the feet of the bridegroom. they knew that the preparedness for the wedding celebration, the celebration of the already-given grace of the cross, required but one thing: their sin, laid at the foot of the cross, given to the bridegroom who bears it on their accord.

The foolish, however, bring what they think is enough oil to get to the door, the gate of judgment. But they despair and fear for when the bridegroom arrives, and indeed they flee to seek extra things, to earn their way in. And in doing so, they miss his arrival. They leave the place already prepared for them. In this, they personify and exemplify the mistake so many of us make: the mistake of trying to find somewhere else, of trying to earn through our own actions, our ticket to Christ's wedding celebration.

The oil we anoint babies within their baptism, the oil we used to anoint Maddox this morning – it is an oil not of our works, but of the work of God in Christ. The oil represents not what we can do, but the forgiveness of sins which can never be merited. The oil is the blood of Christ that has cleansed our sins. The oil the virgins bring is the oil with which we are baptized: the oil that is the blood of the lamb, the ointment for the disease we are born into and cannot escape.

You see, the bad Christian talk radio made the parable clear: it matters not if you state the name of Christ at the beginning of your designated radio hour if what follows is not a message proceeding from the grace given in the cross. To declare one's belief in Christ, and to immediately scramble around, hunting for a means of self-sanctification, is to miss the good news embedded in His name altogether.

This is what makes sense of the judgment cast on the foolish virgins. The foolish virgins, returning in the dark to the door of the party, having found no works to pay their entrance, encounter a Lord who claims not to know them. They call his name, "Lord, Lord!" and he responds with "truly I tell you, I do not know you."

The word for knowledge used in the Greek is "οἶδα." It is a word that comes from the root of the verb that means, "to see." The bridegroom, we ought to note, literally says he cannot see them. They, the foolish virgins, have sought the light of grace where it could not be found, and in so doing, miss the very point of the message.

Notice, again, that the text never tells us that the extra oil is used. The wise bring the extra oil, but we are never told if it is used. The bridegroom comes, not when the extra oil has been used, but when the ones who think that entrance can be bought have left.

That is, the judgment levied, the door closed, is against those who obscure the judgment of the cross, the judgment of God on God's self, for the sake of all humanity.

Punished by Rewards
Matthew 25:31-45
Jason Micheli

I celebrated a wedding last weekend for a family from my former parish.

I hate weddings.

Wedding planners are the bane of my existence—they're almost always like those women Sandra Bullock brunches within *The Blind Side.*

No matter who gets married, every single time they stick me at the grandma table for the wedding reception.

And when it comes time to get my party on and do the white-man overbite on the dance floor, almost always all the guests hide their drinks and keep their distance from me because we all know *Pastor* must be an ancient Greek word meaning *Fun Sponge.*

I hate weddings.

As a pastor, I'm not even a fan of parties.

I avoid parties. I go to parties only begrudgingly, and whenever I'm at a party, I'm tempted, like George Costanza from *Seinfeld*, to pretend I'm anything other than a pastor—a marine biologist, say, or an architect.

Nothing stops party conversations in their tracks—or starts unwanted conversations—like saying you're a pastor.

The problem with wedding parties, though, is that you can't pull a Costanza. You can't lie and pretend to be an ornithologist because everyone has already seen you in robe and collar.

At wedding parties, I'm stuck being me.

So, there I was at this wedding party. The DJ had already played like his fourth Harry Connick Jr. song.

I was nursing a beer and gnawing on nibblers like a beaver when this salt-and-peppered guy wearing white pants, a seersucker jacket, a bow tie, and suede shoes ambled up to me.

"You must be a lawyer," I said.

"How'd you know?"

"Well, the guy who wrote the *Bonfire of the Vanities* is dead so you're not him," I said, "so you must be a lawyer."

"That was an interesting sermon," he said, "if that's your thing."

Here we go, I thought.

"I'm actually a marine biologist," I said, "that's my day job."

"Really?"

"No. No, I'm a pastor. Believe it or not, people really pay me to do this."

He nodded.

"I'm not a Christian," he said, putting up his hands like a suspect getting nabbed red-handed, "but I do try to live a good life and to be good and to help people when I can. When you scrape off all the other stuff, isn't that what Christianity's really all about—the golden rule?"

And I thought: "Wow, that's really deep. Did you come up with that all on your own or is that the fruit of years of philosophical searching? Damn, I should write that down: *It's really all about doing good for others.* I don't want to forget it. I might be able to use that in a sermon someday."

Instead I said: "Yep, that's Church—everything you learned in Kindergarten repeated Sunday after Sunday after Sunday after Sunday after Sunday and then you die."

And he looked at me like he felt sad for me, giving my life to something so boring. So I raised my beer to him and said: "But sometimes we get to argue about sex."

If you want proof that deep-down we want the comfort of merits and demerits rather than the indiscriminate acceptance of Easter, if you want evidence that in the end we prefer the Golden Rule instead of the Gospel, you need look no further than the fact that Matthew 25 is every Methodist's favorite parable.

The parable of the sheep and the goats is Jesus' final parable.

And, sure, this final parable sounds like it's *finally* the end of Jesus' preaching on bottomless, unconditional, no-matter-what-you-do-I-do-for-you grace.

The closer he gets to his passion; it sounds like the prodigal father has run out of fatted calves and now is going to reward the rewardable.

It sounds like Jesus has pivoted from gift to grades, from mercy for sinners to merit pay, from free undeserved pardon to punishment.

Grace is God's unmerited favor.

Grace is God's one-way love.

Grace is the melody the New Testament returns to over and over again: "By grace you have been saved through faith, and this is not your own doing; it is the gift of God—not the result of good deeds you do—so that no one may boast about what they've earned."

But—

There seems to be a lot of earning and deserving going on here with the sheep and the goats. As a Shepherd, this King doles out punishments and rewards based not on our faith but on our deeds alone.

(We think.)

The sheep fed the hungry. The sheep gave water to the thirsty. The sheep welcomed the stranger. The sheep clothed the naked. The sheep cared for the sick. The sheep visited the prisoner.

The sheep did all the things you need not believe in the Good Shepherd to believe are good things; nevertheless, the Good Shepherd rewards them for the doings they did.

And the goats did not do those deeds.

And they are punished precisely for not doing them—we think.

Salvation is based not on what Christ accomplished for us (so it seems here)

Salvation is based on what we accomplish for Christ.

The Gospel (it sounds like here) is not Christ the Lamb of God became a goat so that goats like us might be reckoned among the Father's faithful flock.

The Gospel (it sounds like here) is that you must get over your goatness and become a better sheep by doing what the Good Shepherd tells you to do.

The promise (it sure sounds like here) is not that everything has already been done for you in Christ and him crucified

The promise (it sure sounds like here) is that Christ is for you *if you do everything for him.*

Even though Jesus thus far has studiously avoided making badness an obstacle for admittance into his Kingdom and spent all of his time eating and drinking not with sheep but with goats, it sure sounds like Jesus here has scrapped the prior three years of his preaching, taken off the velvet glove of grace and now put on the brass knuckles of the Law.

Your sins of omission—what you've left undone—they're sins against me, Jesus says.

We think.

Based on the conventional, cliched reading of this parable, even a busy flock like you all better buckle down and pump up the volume on your good deed doing.

No matter how much you're doing, do more.

Do more; so that, when you meet the Lord for your final exam, your performance review, your everlasting audit, you can say to Christ your Savior: *You gave us the course curriculum in Matthew 25—you gave us your marching orders.*

And we did what you said to do.

And with our report cards and resumes in hand, with our discipleship diplomas and extracurricular accomplishments—with all our good deeds done for another—we will be able to give our valediction to Christ our Savior:

Graduate us, Lord, to what we've earned.

Pay us what we're owed.

Give us what we deserve.

Except—

If we said such to Christ, we wouldn't be speaking to our Savior because he told us what to do and we did it so, really, we saved ourselves.

Let me say it again:

If Christianity boils down to doing what Christ said to do, then Christ is not a Savior, for by doing what he said to do we've effectively saved ourselves, which is sort of unfortunate because Jesus promptly goes from here to Jerusalem where he's bound and determined to save us from our sins by dying for them.

As the angel at the gates of heaven says to the do-gooding dead guy in C.S Lewis' *The Great Divorce*: "Nothing here can be bought or earned. Everything here is bleeding charity, grace, and its yours only by the asking."

It's yours by the asking.

The Bible says the Law is written not just on tablets of stone, but on every human heart too. Every single one us—we're all hard-wired to be score-keepers and debt collectors, hellbent on turning the Golden Rule into a yard stick by which we can measure our enoughness over and against our neighbors.

And because I'm just like you, I can bet what some of you are thinking right about now.

Does this mean our good deed doing doesn't matter?!

Of course, what we do matters.

The Paul who says that you are saved by grace through faith not good deed doing is the same Paul who tells the Philippians that "God is at work in you and through you to will and to work for his pleasure."

So, don't misunderstand me.

Yes, good works are important.

Yet—

We're so stubborn about shaping Jesus in our scorekeeping image, we're so determined to turn Jesus into the Almighty

Auditor from the Department of Afterlife Affairs, that we miss the embarrassingly obvious epiphany in this parable.

The big reveal behind this parable *of judgment* is that good godly works cannot be tallied up on a scorecard.

The good works that count for the Kingdom cannot be counted because—notice now—when the Shepherd hands out report cards neither the sheep nor the goats have any idea, they've done what the King says they've done or left undone.

When the King of the Nations separates them as a Shepherd one from the other, the sheep are not standing there waiting to be handed their magna cum laude for a lifetime of charitable giving and community service hours.

No.

For the sheep and the goats alike, there's just *surprise:* "When was it that we saw you hungry and gave you food?"

The sheep are *surprised* by the grade the Good Shepherd gives them.

They're stunned.

To use this parable to exhort members of the flock to go and do good deeds for the Shepherd is to ignore the point that the sheep are blissfully ignorant that they've done good deeds for the Shepherd.

Wait, wait, wait—when did we do that?

They're surprised.

They're surprised because they weren't thinking at all about doing the good deeds they did.

All their good works—the sheep did them not because they were told that's what sheep ought to do.

The sheep just did them as they were caught up in the joy of their Shepherd.

The good works that count were not done to be counted; the good works that count were unpremeditated, done out of love—organically, such that the sheep weren't even aware they'd done them.

Listen again to who was counting.

"Then those on the King's left will answer, saying, "Lord, when did we see you hungry or thirsty or a stranger or naked or sick or in prison, and did not minister to *you?* "'

It's amazing how we mishear this parable.

It's not that the goats didn't do any good deeds.

It's that they felt justified in having done enough.

We fed the hungry. We clothed the naked. We did all those things—when did we not take care of you too?

It's not that the goats didn't do any good deeds.

It's that the goats come to Jesus dependent upon their good deeds.

The goats think they're good enough; meanwhile, the sheep were so in love with their Shepherd they're stunned to hear they've got any good grades on their report card at all.

The danger in taking the Bible for granted is that we're all natural-born Pharisees and so we turn the Gospel into Law without even realizing we've done it.

We're as stubborn as goats when it comes to this parable.

We insist on hearing it in terms of reward and punishment, earning and deserving, but that contradicts the clear conclusion Christ contributes to it: "Come, you that are blessed by my Father, *inherit* the kingdom prepared for you *from the foundation of the world...*"

Notice, Jesus does not say to the sheep *Here's your wage. Here's your reward.*

No, Jesus says to the sheep *Inherit the Kingdom.*

The Kingdom is not their compensation. The Kingdom is not their accomplishment.

The Kingdom is their *inheritance.*

You can't earn an inheritance.

Not only is this parable about inheriting instead of earning, Jesus says as plain as the nose on your face that this inheritance has been prepared for the sheep *from before the foundation of the world.*

Before God put the stars in the sky, God made this promise to you.

Think about it—

This parable isn't about our works, good or bad, because before any of our works, good or bad, had been done, what work was God doing?

Preparing a place in the Kingdom for you.

For all of you.

For every last one of you.

How do I know?

Notice—

In the parable, the King doesn't say to the goats what he says to the sheep.

He doesn't say to those on his left "Depart from me, you cursed ones, into the eternal fire prepared *for you from the foundation of the world.*"

No, he says "Depart from me, you cursed ones, into the eternal fire prepared *for the Devil and his angels.*"

Sure, we can get our sphincters all in a pinch over that image of eternal annihilating fire.

But if this parable is about our inheritance, then the point is that the place of punishment wasn't prepared for them.

Don't you see—the place where the goats are going is not a place they were ever meant to go.

The place the goats go is not a place that was prepared for them.

Where the goats are going, they don't have to go.

Don't you see—

No one is out who wasn't already in.

Nobody is excluded from the Kingdom who wasn't already included in the Kingdom from before the foundation of the world.

The goats get themselves where they're going by stubbornly insisting, they're earned what can only be inherited.

The goats are like the elder brother in that other parable, pouting with his arms crossed and gnashing his teeth in the outer darkness beyond the prodigal's party. *Father, I've worked for you all these years. I deserve that party.*

In Heaven, there is nothing but forgiven sinners.

In Hell, there is nothing but forgiven sinners.

The only difference between the two is that those in Hell don't think they deserve to be there, and those in Heaven know they don't deserve to be there.

The DJ at the wedding party had stepped onto the parquet to lead some of the guests in dancing to the song *Uptown Funk,* which isn't exactly eternal conscious torment but it's close.

I was sitting at the grandma table, watching and picking at the leftovers on my dinner plate, when a woman in a mauve dress pushed some of the plates to the middle of the table, and sat down next to me.

She sort of laughed to herself and shook her head and looked straight down at her lap, and when she looked back up at me, I could see she was crying.

I held up my hands.

"Don't look at me. I'm a marine biologist."

She smiled and sniffed her runny nose. She looked to be about sixty.

"Seeing you do the wedding," she said, "I couldn't help but think of my daughter."

"Did she get married recently?"

She winced at the question and wiped her eyes. Then she took a deep breath like she was coaching herself up, and she told me her daughter was gay.

She told me how her daughter had MS and how she'd found a partner, someone who would be there to care for her one day.

"Watching these two get married today, it just reminded me of all the things I've heard people in my family and in my church say about my own daughter."

"Like what things?" I was dumb enough to ask.

"They say she's abomination. One of my good friends told me, matter-of-fact, that my daughter wouldn't be with me or Jesus when she died, that she'd go to Hell like she deserved, but that I shouldn't worry because in the Kingdom I won't even remember her anymore."

That and the rest she told me—it honestly took my breath away.

"What do you think?" she wiped her nose and asked.

"What do I think? It's not what I think; it's what the Church and the Bible teach—and that's that not a one of us gets in by the uprightness of our lives nor are even our awful sins an obstacle for admittance. We're justified by grace through faith, *alone*. When it comes to the Kingdom, the only relationship of your daughter's that matters is the relationship she has with Christ. Saying "I do" to that Bridegroom is all any of us gotta do to gain entry into the party."

"But my friends say that she and her partner will go to Hell..."

I cut her off.

"They might go to Hell—sure—but if they do it won't be because Jesus sent them there and it won't be for the reasons you fear. In fact, those Pharisees you call family and friends—they might be surprised how things shake out for themselves too. Jesus is annoyingly consistent on the matter—the only ones not in the Kingdom are the ones who insist they ought to be there."

I didn't think of it until this week as I studied this scripture text.

That mother at the wedding, worried sick over whether her daughter was a sheep or a goat, I could've pointed out to her that according to Jesus here there is one fool-proof way of knowing for certain that he is with you.

This parable of judgment—there's a third category of people here.

Not just sheep. Not just goats.

There's a third flock of people in this parable.

Those in need.

Jesus says it bluntly: the place where his presence is promised—where there should be no surprise or speculation—is not with the good but with those in need.

And so, if you're worried about whether you're a sheep or a goat, then your refuge should not be the work you've done for Christ but the work you need from him.

The assurance that Jesus Christ abides with you lies not in your merits out measuring your demerits.

The assurance that Jesus Christ abides with you—is for you—lies in your lack.

The guarantee that you are not alone—the guarantee of God's blessing upon you—is not your awesome list of accomplishments but your inadequacy.

I should've told that mother that the very fact of her tears and grief, the very fact of her daughter's illness, the very fact of their rejection by and estrangement from others, the very fact that a lot of self-identified sheep treat them like goats and presume to do the King's work of sorting and sending for him—those very facts are red-letter proof-positive that Jesus Christ—if he's with anyone, he's with them.

Because Jesus puts it plain to both the sheep and the goats alike—he makes his office is at the end of your rope.

I didn't think to tell her.

But I can tell you.

Has the treadmill of good works alone left you exhausted and starving?

Do you thirst for the kind of faith and joy you see in others?

Are you sick of all your best efforts to be a good sheep?

Or are you just sick?

Is there something in your past that leaves you feeling naked and ashamed?

Are you in a relationship locked in resentment?

Are you captive to abuse? Or addiction?

Do you feel out place, wondering what the hell you're even doing here?

If so, hear the good news.

In the same way you come up here with the gesture of a beggar to receive him in bread and wine, Jesus Christ is present to you in your poverty.

The ticket to this Table is the only ticket you need for his Kingdom.

Your need. You need only know your need.

The Kingdom is yours only by the asking.

Give Me Liberty and Give Me Death
Luke 14:15-24
Taylor Mertins

I wrote three versions of this sermon.

In the first version I, the preacher, encouraged you, the listener, to imagine yourself as a party host. You worked diligently to prepare a feast, ordered the perfect set of invitations, and you even hired a wine sommelier just to make sure everything was in harmony. For months you laid awake at night not worrying about the extravaganza itself but imagining all the profoundly kind compliments you were about to receive.

And then, as the day of the shindig got closer and closer, the RSVPs started to arrive and with every "No" your heart started to sink deeper and deeper until you realized that no one, not a single invitee, would be coming.

You fretted over what to do next. After all, you had spent a small fortune to set the whole thing up and you couldn't just return everything. You began calling all your family members, and knocking on the doors of all your neighbors, but it still wasn't enough. It got to the point that, like a crazy person, you started yelling at people on the street demanding that they come to your party.

But it wasn't a very good sermon. It wasn't a very good sermon because it made all of you, the listeners, out to be like God. You became the divine party host and when no one showed up, it just left you with a bit of rage.

And where's the Good News in that?

In the second version I, the preacher, encouraged you, the listener, to imagine yourself as one of the invited guests. You received an invitation in the mail to a very posh party and though you were initially excited about the prospect of attending, you quickly realized that the celebration would be an impossibility.

You knew that it would not be responsible to accept such a grand invitation and you thought about how it was all really such a waste. You pictured in your mind all of the hungry children across

97

the globe and you just shuddered with the thought of such delicious food in the midst of a broken world like ours.

So, you came up with a list of reasons why you would not be attending. For some of you it was because of your spouse. For others you had responsibilities in the home that could not be overlooked. And still yet a few more of you simply lied because you had better things to do.

But that one wasn't a very good sermon either. It wasn't a good sermon because when all of you found out about the lengths the host went to make sure the party was full in your absence; you weren't really jealous. I mean, he invited all of the delinquents and riffraff from the community; who would want to go to a party with those people? You became satisfied by your excuses and patted yourselves on the back for a job well done.

And where's the Good News in that?

The third version was my favorite. In it I, the preacher, encouraged you, the listener, to imagine that you had no business attending the party in the first place. You were down on your luck, worrying about how to pay your bills, fretting over your child's grades, overwhelmed by domestic trivialities. And all the while you saw the host preparing for the party. You witnessed truck after truck bringing in the wine and beer, you saw the caterers lugging in all of their equipment, and when the day of the party arrived you could hear the live band playing all of your favorite songs and yet, you weren't invited.

And then, miracle of miracles, the host came and knocked on your front door, grabbed you by the collar, and started dragging you to the party. And, because you were full of humility, you pleaded with the host to realize the mistake he was making. You didn't deserve to be at the party, you would never be able to return the favor, and you really didn't even have anything nice to wear.

To which the host simply waved his hand and told you to raid the closets at his house and take whatever clothes you wanted. The party simply must be full, and he didn't give a flip about who you were, he just wanted you to be there.

And so, you went, and you had the time of your life. You ate, and drank, and danced. You fraternized with people who never would have given you the time of day. And the longer you partied, the more people started showing up. And they, like you, had sparkles in their eyes because something like this was beyond all of your wildest imaginations.

And that sermon, that sermon was a good one. It was good because it spoke truly about the ridiculousness of grace, how unmerited it is, how we, even up to the moment we receive it, make excuses for why we shouldn't be the ones to get it. And I almost preached that sermon—one long story about being dragged to a party that you didn't deserve to attend—it was going to end with the host bringing out another case of wine as the sun rose in the east and everyone trotting back out onto the dance floor to do it all over again.

But I'm not preaching that sermon.

Nope.

I'm not preaching it because the Good News sounds too good.

Jesus is still at the dinner table when our scripture for today begins. He has already healed a man much to the chagrin of everyone else at the party, he has called everyone out for wanting to sit in the best places, and he just commanded them to invite the wrong people to their own parties when someone inexplicably stands up to shout, "Blessed is anyone who will eat bread in the kingdom of God."

The comment sounds like the man is mocking Jesus. As in, "No one is going to buy whatever you're selling. Blessed would be anyone, and apparently everyone in your kingdom Jesus, but that ain't the way it works."

And Jesus won't stand for it.

What the interrupting man doesn't know, what he can't know, is that the very kingdom of God he referenced was sitting right there at the table with him, and none of them want it. They don't want to eat bread in the kingdom if it means what Jesus was describing. They had all worked too hard to get where they were, and it doesn't sound like good news when the first are told that they are going to be last.

So Jesus jumps into another story.

A man had invited many to his awesome party. Everyone had already responded to the card in the mail, but when the day of arrived, they were no-shows. Each of the guests, in their own way, said, "Hey Lord, I'll spend time with you later. But right now, I've got other things to take care of."

And all of the people at the table hearing Jesus' story, are like the people in the parable with their excuses—they had pursed the sensible paths, they were what we could call successful, and Jesus tells them, to their faces, that it is precisely all their pursuing that keeps them from the party.

For this crazy Lord of ours, the one we worship and adore, he has no use for winners, people only concerned with their own definitions of what it means to do and to win in this life. So instead of bringing all of the right people to the party, the host, Jesus, goes out looking for all the wrong people.

One way or another, the host will fill the tables—the food will be eaten—the drinks will be consumed—the band will be enjoyed.

It sounds too good to be true, but this is the gospel: the losers of life are the winners at God's table. On a day when they wake up expecting nothing, or worse, they rise to a new way of being that surpasses even the people who first received their invitation.

The last, least, lost, little, and dead never get invited to parties because they run counter to everything the world tells us to do.

But in the kingdom of God, lastness, leastness, lostness, littleness, and deadness are all Jesus is looking for.

As Jesus has been saying again and again and again throughout all of these parables in different ways, shapes, and forms, you and I don't get to earn our spot at the party. There's no to-do list to get in.

In this particular parable none of the people who had a right to be at the party came, and all of the people who came had no right to be there. Nothing in the kingdom has anything to do with rights; God is going to deal with us in spite of our deservings, not according to them.

And that just gets under our skin or we completely ignore it. We're so accustomed to a way of being about earning and rewarding that free grace sounds irresponsible or too good to be true.

But hear this, hear it in all of its craziness and bizarreness: Grace works by raising the dead—not by rewarding the living.

This story from the lips of Jesus is about liberty. Not liberty from monarchy like so many of us celebrated this week with our food and fun and fireworks. But a liberty from all of the labeling that comes about in this life. Liberty from the truest tyranny that the world has ever known - sin and death.

This party of Jesus', the parable of the host dragging in people from the street, it shows us how God in Christ gives us liberty in death. It even shows us how free we really are right now for we have been baptized into Jesus' death.

Or, at least, it shows us how free we should be.

Because most of us aren't, me included. I too am shackled to the expectations of the world, of the need and the desire to appear first even when I am really last. The need and desire to appear wealthy even when I'm in debt. The need and desire to seem as if I've got it all figured out even when I really have no idea what I'm doing.

I want to be a winner, but Jesus saves losers.

I want to be first, but Jesus is for the last.

I want to be in control of my life, but Jesus wants me to die.

Jesus wants me and you and all of us to die to all of these overwhelming expectations we place on ourselves and on others. Jesus tells these stories to break down all of the labels we throw around and to show how salvation, our salvation, has already been figured out.

Jesus turns things upside down. The whole gospel is one topsy-turvy tumbling narrative. The chosen people of this world, the privileged, the powerful, the righteous, the religious, the pious, they will not be the ones filling up the dance floor because they often ignore the invitation.

But at God's party, it's those of us who've been crippled by our sin, blinded by our shame, and made lame by our guilt who eat, and drink, and dance. We do so precisely because we were a bunch of outsiders and nobodies who never thought we had a chance in the world.

God desires a full house—God wants the party to be bumpin'—and we're all invited. Amen.

Everything You Need to Know You Did Not Learn in Kindergarten
Luke 10:25-37
Jason Micheli

I've had it sitting in my sermon file for years, a review of the book *In the Land of Magic Soldiers: A Story of White and Black in West Africa,* by the journalist Daniel Bergner, whose book documents the gruesome aftermath of the civil war in Sierra Leone.

The title of Bergner's book refers to the popular—desperate—belief in the region that certain rituals, going even to the extreme of cannibalism, will guarantee immunity to bullets. Hence, the term "magic soldiers."

What caught my attention in the review is the section that begins with this line: "What is of value in this book is less what it says about Sierra Leone than about the human condition."

Specifically, the reviewer is referring to one human, Neall Ellis, whose story in the book says something offensive about the lot of us.

Neall Ellis is a white aviator from South Africa. After a brief stint in the Rhodesian Army, he joined the South African Air Force, where he was awarded the Honoris Crux in 1983, and later attained field rank.

After retiring from the SAAF, Ellis used his savings and retirement funds to pay the tuition costs for local schoolchildren in war-torn Sierra Leone.

He sent one young woman all the way to England, set her up with lodging, and paid her way through nursing school and, after nursing school, midwifery school.

He covered all the expenses of another young man's medical school education in Johannesburg, as well as the extensive plastic surgeries required by a young woman who had been badly burned during the conflict in Sierra Leone.

And not just her—Ellis raised the funds to construct an entire burn hospital.

I've got a note that says it's named after the Good Samaritan.

Ellis told the journalist that he was building the hospital, "because right now there isn't a place like that in the whole of Sierra Leone, nowhere a victim can go to get that type of treatment. Seeing such a need, I can't just pass on by."

Admit it—you expect a sermon on this parable to segue into an illustration just like this of some real-life *Good* Samaritan making good on the lessons we all learned in Kindergarten.

Whenever you hear the Parable of the Good Samaritan, you expect to hear a story about someone like Neal Ellis.

Well, here's the rest of Neal Ellis's story.

After he retired from the South African Air Force in the 1980's, Neal Ellis took a job as a mercenary for the government of Sierra Leone, piloting the sole combat helicopter the nation owned.

He took the job not for the pay, he admitted to the journalist, but for the work. He loved the thrill of rocketing and machine-gunning from the air, confessing to Bergner: "It's better than sex. . . . There's a lot of adrenaline going. You're all keyed up, and when you realize you're on target, that you've taken out the enemy, it's a great feeling."

According to Human Rights Watch, they've documented dozens of dead and wounded civilians, women and children, in scores of towns that Neal Ellis attacked. The burn victims whose medical bills Neal Ellis covers—Neal Ellis is responsible for their condition.

They're in the hospital, because he put them there.

Even after *In the Land of Magic Soldiers* went to print, Ellis emailed the author mentioning another civil war that had broken out on the continent and how he was "hoping for a possible contract."

Writing about Neal Ellis, journalist Daniel Bergner doesn't call him a Good Samaritan.

Instead, Ellis makes Bergner question if there's any such thing as a *Good* Samaritan.

Until the complexity of casting someone like Neal Ellis as Jesus' protagonist in today's parable has stuck in your craw, you've not really comprehended Christ's answer to the lawyer.

We've all heard about the Good Samaritan so many times the offense of the parable passes us by.

It's so obvious we never notice it: Jesus told this story to Jews.

The lawyer who tries to trap Jesus, the twelve disciples who've just returned from the mission field, and the crowd that's gathered round to hear about their Kingdom, work.

Every last listener is a Jew.

And so, when Jesus tells a story about a priest who comes across a man lying naked, maybe dead, in a ditch, and says that priest passed him by, none of Jesus' listeners would've batted an eye.

When Jesus says, "So there's this priest who came across a naked, maybe dead, maybe not even Jewish body on the roadside and he passed by on the other side," NO ONE in Jesus' audience would've reacted with anything like, "That's outrageous!"

When Jesus says, "There's this priest and he came across what looked like a naked, dead body in the ditch, so he crossed to other side and passed on by," EVERYONE in Jesus' audience would've been thinking, "What's your point? Of course, he passed by on the other side. That's what a priest must do."

Ditto, the Levite.

No one hearing Jesus tell this story would've been offended by their passing on by.

No one would've been outraged.

As soon as they saw the priest enter the story, they would've expected him to keep on walking.

The priest had no choice—for the greater good.

According to the Law, to touch the man in the ditch would ritually defile the priest.

Under the Law, such defilement would require at least a week of purification rituals during which time the priest would be forbidden from collecting tithes, which means that for a week or more the distribution of alms to the poor would cease.

And, if the priest ritually defiled himself and did not perform the purification obligation, if he ignored the Law and tried to get away with it and got caught (according to the *Mishna),* the priest would be taken out to the Temple Court and beaten in the head with clubs.

Now, of course, that strikes us as god-awful.

But, the point of Jesus' parable passes us by when we forget the fact that none of Jesus' listeners would've felt that way.

As soon as they see a priest and a Levite step onto the stage, they would not have expected either to do anything but, exactly, what Jesus says they did.

So—

If Jesus' listeners wouldn't expect the priest or the Levite to do anything, then what the Samaritan *does* isn't the point of the parable.

If there's no shock or outrage at what appears to us a lack of compassion, then—no matter how many hospitals we name after this story—the act of compassion isn't the lesson of the story.

If no one would've taken offense that the priest did not help someone in need, then helping someone in need is not this teaching's takeaway.

The takeaway is the *who,* who is doing the helping.

The point of the parable doesn't start with the *what,* but the *who.*

Just like Neal Ellis, this Samaritan has a more complicated backstory.

In Jesus' own day a mob of Samaritans had traveled to Jerusalem, which they didn't recognize as the holy city of David, and at night they broke into the Temple, which they didn't believe held the presence of Yahweh, and they ransacked it.

Looted it.

And then they littered it with the remains of human corpses, bodies they dug up and bodies killed.

Whereas, the priest and the Levite would not touch a dead body in the ditch out of deference to the Law and its ritual obligations, the Samaritans made a mockery of God's Law by vandalizing the Temple with bodies they'd robbed from the grave.

In Jesus' day there was no such thing as a *Good* Samaritan.

That's why, when the parable's finished and Jesus asks his final question, the lawyer can't even stomach to say the word "Samaritan." "The one who showed mercy" is all the lawyer can spit out through clenched teeth.

You see, the shock of Jesus' story isn't that the priest and the Levite fail to do anything positive for the man in the ditch.

The shock is that Jesus does anything positive with the Samaritan in the story.

The offense of the parable is that Jesus casts someone like a Samaritan as the protagonist.

We get it all backwards.

Jesus isn't inviting us to see ourselves as the bringer of aid to the person in need.

I wish.

How flattering is that?

It says a lot about our privilege that we automatically identify with the rescuer in the story.

We get it backwards.

Jesus isn't saying that loving our neighbor means caring for someone in need.

Of course, loving your neighbor means caring for someone in need.

But that's not what Jesus is doing here.

Not only do we forget that every last listener in Luke 10 is a Jew, seldom do we notice what prompts Jesus' story in the first place.

What does Luke tell you?

Luke reports, "The lawyer, *wanting to justify himself,* asked Jesus: 'Who is my neighbor?'"

107

This lawyer is attempting to establish that he is enough before God all on his own.

This is what Jesus is picking apart with his parable.

Jesus shows you what St. Paul tells you in Galatians—that, if justification could come through our keeping of the commandments (if it was as easy as this lawyer supposes), then Christ died for absolutely nothing.

So, what does Jesus do to this lawyer and his self-justification project?

To this expert in the Law, Jesus tells a story where the hero is the personification of *unrighteousness* under the Law.

Jesus skewers the lawyer's good, godly self-image by spinning a story starring an ungodly sort like Neal Ellis.

And then, like Jesus does in the sermon on the mount, Jesus amps up the expectations to an impossible degree. Jesus overwhelms the lawyer by crediting to the Samaritan a whopping fourteen verbs worth of compassion and care, count them up.

And finally, in order to blow the lawyer's self-righteousness to smithereens, Jesus lowers the boom and says, "Go and do likewise."

Pay attention.

This is where our reading of this passage tends to run off the rails. What Jesus is driving at here with his "Go and do" is heavy, and the demand is the same for me, and it's the same for you too.

Go and do like that Samaritan, Jesus is saying, *help every single person in need who comes your way, regardless of how busy you are.*

No matter the circumstances, no matter the cost, no matter the safety. Book them a room. Give the front desk your Amex Gold Card and put no restrictions on room service.

And do it, Jesus is saying, *like that Samaritan. Do it with the purest of intentions, with no thought about yourself, without any expectation of reciprocation or promise of reward. Do it spontaneously, provoked solely by the love of God alone, and do not be disappointed when they recidivate.*

Do it just like that—spend fourteen verbs on every single person. Do it no matter if they're wearing a "MAGA" hat or a "Black Lives Matter" tee.

Do all of that, perfectly, from the heart, and on your own, all by your lonesome, you will be justified.

How's that working for you?

This parable is not about helping people in need.

This parable is about helping you recognize your need.

For a savior.

YOU'RE THE ONE IN THE DITCH!

And while we were yet enemies, when there was "no health in us" and we were as good as dead in our trespasses, the Son of God condescended to us—he took flesh—and he got down into the ditch with us and he loved you, his neighbor, more than himself, carrying you in his body, lavishing upon you his every last verb, sparing no expense, until his love for you drove him to fall among thieves, bloodied and beaten and ditched by a world too busy to do anything, but pass him by.

In his book, *In the Land of Magic Soldiers*, journalist Daniel Bergner doesn't call Neal Ellis a Good Samaritan.

He calls him "a haunting figure ... haunting, because the strange blend of compassion and cruelty in his life is a reminder of what we all carry within us. He's a reminder of how fragile our human predicament is and of how we are all in need not only of rescue, but also repair."

Or, as the Apostle Paul puts in Romans, *rectification.*

We're in need not only of rescue, but also rectification.

We're the ones in the ditch.

But before Jesus Christ departed us by Death and Resurrection, he left us not his Discover Card, but his Holy Spirit.

He left us his Holy Spirit to nurse us back into health.

He left us his Holy Spirit to rehabilitate us.

To rectify—to make right—the image in which God, the Father Almighty made you.

Before he left, he left you his Holy Spirit.

And his Holy Spirit, the Apostle Paul writes to the Ephesians, is the *deposit* that *guarantees* the *inheritance* this lawyer was inquiring about with Jesus.

Eternal life.

The Holy Spirit is the deposit of eternity in time.

The Holy Spirit is the present tense down payment on the future life this lawyer seeks.

That's this lawyer's other error; he thinks eternal life can only *begin* somewhere down the line, past the present.

As Karl Barth liked to joke—what sort of eternal life would it be if it begins *after* something else? If eternal life is eternal, it cannot come after anything.

Because it's eternal, it's always already and always ongoing, and though it is always also still not yet, the Holy Spirit is the deposit of it in the here and now.

The Holy Spirit is the deposit of the not yet in the now.

The practices of the faith, therefore, are the work we engage in the Spirit:

The sandwiches you make at the mission center;
The tutoring you contribute to at-risk kids;
The service you offer to our neighbors;
The shelter you provide for the homeless, and
The support you send to churches along the border.

They are not ways we in Christ's stead help the poor.

They are the ways that Christ's Spirit uses the poor to heal us.

They are not ways we rescue the needy stranger.

They are ways the Spirit rectifies the stranger in need that you call "you."

They are not ways we go and do likewise—there's only one way for us to be justified.

The practices of the faith—they are not ways we go and do.

They are ways we are done to.

Done to by the Holy Spirit.

Until the Holy Spirit has rendered us likewise.

We're all born lawyers.

We need to be made Christians.

So hear the Good News:

While we were yet enemies, Christ died for your sins and was raised for your justification to be given to you not as your wage for what you go and do, but as an unconditional gift, no matter where you go or what you do.

By grace through faith, you already possess irrevocably what that lawyer pursued.

Your justification.

But your rectification?

For that, our Rescuer has left his Spirit.

So all you lawyers, lay all your doings down.

They can't cure what ails you still.

Lay all your doings down.

And come to the table.

Come and be done to.

Come and be done to by the Spirit of our Good Samaritan.

Come, and with bread and wine, be done to by the Spirit of the Samaritan, who is determined not only to rescue you from the ditch of Sin and Death, but to bind up all your wounds, heal your every affliction, and strengthen you in your weakness until you are what you eat.

Repent with All Your Heart
Luke 13:1-9
Teer Hardy

For the past few weeks, we have been spending time outside of the gospels but that does not mean we have spent time away from the Gospel. The beauty of the Gospel of Jesus Christ is it is spread throughout the entirety of the Bible. The Hebrew Bible points to the coming of God's kingdom, to be revealed fully by Christ (the gospels), and the Epistles look the fullness of Christ's ministry and how the ancient church was shaped by this Good News. So while the gospels may be a familiar space to spend our Sunday mornings, the Gospel is proclaimed throughout the entire Bible.

Last week Abram and the week before that Paul. This morning we find ourselves in the midst of the parables, stories used by Jesus, utilizing familiar objects and people, to explain what God's reign looked like and will look like. The following four chapters of the Gospel of Luke are littered with these stories.

As Jesus was making his way to Jerusalem he continued to minister and point to the coming fulling of God's glory. All of Jesus' teachings and healings pointed to one thing: the Kingdom of God.

As Jesus faced towards Jerusalem, we will arrive there with him in four weeks to shout Hosanna, he was told of the mixing of blood in the Temple along with the death of 18 people who died in the collapse of the tower of Siloam. Prior to this scene, Jesus had been teaching about settling disputes with an opponent:

> "when you go with your accuser before a magistrate, on the way make an effort to settle the case, or you may be dragged before the judge, and the judge hand you over to the officer, and the officer throw you in prison. I tell you; you will never get out until you have paid the very last penny."

Jesus was talking about the wrongs done by those who were listening to his teachings and not a hypothetical group of people not present. After he finished his teaching on the matter, the question of blood and falling towers were presented. It is almost as though, after hearing that perhaps those listening to Jesus' teachings were not blameless, to deflect attention away from themselves, two groups who had died in tragic manners were dragged into the conversation as though to ask, "didn't they get what they deserved?"

Jesus, is it obvious they died in these ways because of their sin?

If you have kids or have ever cared for more than one kid at a time you may have experienced a similar situation. You catch one child in the act of breaking a rule or doing wrong to someone else and instead of accepting responsibility for the act, the child defects attention toward a friend or sibling who has also broken a rule or done a wrong.

This behavior continues into adulthood. Politicians are really good at this but Christians, we are the best.

We will see a group of people and declare their sins, or what we perceive to be sin, as greater than the sins we have committed, and they, not us, need to correct their lives.

How many of you have ever been told, "You ain't livin' right" by someone you know to be a sinner as well?

I would be willing to imagine some of us have thrown that phrase—You ain't livin' right"—at someone, meanwhile our own sin continues unchecked, unacknowledged by ourselves.

So back to the original question Jesus is about to dodge—did those groups of people perish because of their sin?

Can we make sense of the complicated and unclear matters by examining the actions of those who have died?

The real question: "Did God kill those people? Did God deal out punishment for their sin?"

It is a tough and complicated question.

We can look to the Hebrew Bible and see God striking down the unjust, those who perhaps stood in opposition to Israel.

But we can also see in the ministry of Jesus healing and mercy where there had once been suffering and exclusion.

So, to the question Jesus would dodge, I am inclined to agree with Archbishop Michael Curry. If God dealt out punishment—judgment, and curse—in relation to sin, there would not be anyone left on the planet. All sin is against the will of God. All sin is incompatible with God's command to love God and love one another.

Yes, in Jesus dodged the question in his response but he had been teaching and exhibiting healing and mercy—grace— since he picked up the scroll in his hometown synagogue and declared the scriptures fulfilled. Since the manger, Jesus' life has been pointing to the healing and mercy of his kingdom. Where we expect, and at times demand, judgment curse, the Kingdom of God offers something quite different.

God's kingdom is different from Pilates. God's kingdom is different from Rome, and friends we live in Rome.

Pilate and Caesar ruled by muscle and fear while God rules with grace. Those listening to Jesus' wanted to talk about the sins of others and instead Jesus offered them the opportunity to repent of their own sins and to reorient themselves toward the kingdom he had come to make known and fully realized.

At its most basic level, repentance changes the way we behave in and view the world. Instead of our own perception, we begin to see the world as Christ does. When we want to focus on sin and judgment, Jesus invites us to look at the world differently.

Jesus had/has a Kingdom view of the world and in his invitation to repent, he is extending citizenship in his kingdom to us, the citizens of Rome.

When I was in St. Louis a few weeks ago the Westboro Baptist Church was there to greet us as we entered and exited the Dome at America's Center. Their least offensive sign extended an invitation to repentance. The problem with their invitation is the invitation is not theirs to make. The Kingdom of God belongs to Christ and it is his grace inviting us to change our orientation, even if it takes more time than others think it should. An invitation to enter into this grace and be completely transformed.

For Jesus—his life, death, and resurrection—the Kingdom of God is always at the forefront. The Kingdom of God is priority number one for Christ.

When we accept Christ's invitation to repent, we are intentionally turning towards his kingdom. In this turn, we begin to see, experience, and become a part of the healing, liberation, and compassion extended to all of creation by God through Jesus Christ.

The Good News is that in five weeks, through the emptiness of his grave, we see the healing, liberation, and compassion of God in its fullest. In the empty tomb we find the extravagant grace of the Gardener—God Almighty—as the healing grace of Christ is extended to us regardless of our ability, and willingness, to repent with all our heart.

God Hates Figs
Luke 13:6-9
Taylor Mertins

It was brutally cold in the middle of February as we lugged our recording equipment up to the arena in St. Louis, Missouri. We had somehow hoodwinked the powers-that-be at the General Conference that we were a reputable media organization, and they happily provided us with press passes. So my buddies and I parked as close as we could, but we had to get all of our podcast equipment to the designated Media Area.

We were all shivering, having not packed enough winter clothing, while waiting for the light to change in the sparsely populated downtown streets. Over chattering teeth, we opined about what and who we might encounter at the General Conference, and we even wondered whether they'd actually let us in or not.

However, by the time the arena came into view none of us were talking. Instead we were gobsmacked by the presence of representatives from Westboro Baptist Church picketing in response to our called General Conference.

Our denomination was meeting to discern the future for LGBTQIA inclusion or exclusion, and mere feet away from the main entrance were a handful of demonstrators who, by the signs and shouting, let everyone know how they felt about the whole thing.

NO WOMEN PREACHERS!

I thought, "They're going to be really disappointed when they realize that women preachers were the first to tell the disciples about the resurrection."

DIVORCE, REMARRIAGE, AND GAY MARRIAGE ARE ALL SIN!

I thought, "They're not necessarily wrong, but so is eating shellfish and working on the Sabbath so…"

BELIEVE IN JESUS THE DESTROYER OF SODOM!

I thought, "Wait a minute, Jesus was born centuries after Sodom was destroyed."

YOUR PASTORS ARE LIARS!

I thought, "Yep. Just like everyone else."

AMERICA IS DOOMED!

I thought, "Huh, maybe they're on to something…"

And the last sign—GOD HATES FIGS

Honestly, even with what felt like subzero temperatures, I started laughing right there in the middle of the street. God hates figs! These people really do read their bibles. Jesus rebukes a fig tree and curses it to never grow fruit ever again, and he tells a parable about a fig tree in which the owner of the fig tree can't stand its inability to do what he wants it to do.

And so I entertained the thought of crossing the line to the dark side to congratulate the protestors for their astute reading of God's Holy Word. I mean, I had problems with some of their claims, I could have pulled out the Bible from my bag and showed chapter and verse to contradict their signs. But GOD HATES FIGS? How can you argue with that?

It was only as we got closer, and the yelling through the megaphone grew greater in decibels did I realize how I misread the sign. It didn't say God Hates Figs.

It said God Hates Fags.

A man had a vineyard and, in the vineyard, he planted a fig tree. For three years he would wander out to his field of grapes to check on the prayed for figs, only to return to the chateau empty handed. So, one day he says to the gardener, "I just can't take it anymore. This fig tree has been wasting my soil for three years. I want you to cut it down."

But the gardener looks at his employer and says, "Lord, let it be. Give it another year. I'll spread some manure on it later today. If it bears fruit next year, all the better. But if not, then you can do whatever you want with it."

Short and sweet as far as parables are concerned. Unlike my parable of walking to the entrance at General Conference there are no superfluous details, nothing to distract the listener from what the story is saying, and the main thing stays the main thing.

And yet, even for its simplicity and brevity, there are a lot of weird and notable details in the parable. So many, in fact, that I preached on this exact passage a mere three months ago and there's still more to say about it. Honestly, I had to look up my sermon because I couldn't even remember what I said about it three months ago.

That's the enduring and endearing beauty of God's Word— it is a never-ending mine of glory from which we can glean again and again and again.

Ah, but back to the matter at hand: Why does the vineyard owner plant a fig tree among all his grapes? Don't you think he would be worried about an outside plant vying for the nutrients in the ground? Or was he just a sucker for a dry fig every once in a while? Or what if he was planning to start the first Fig Newton distribution service in Jerusalem?

We don't know. All we know is that the owner of the vineyard delighted in planting a fig tree among his grapes. Maybe it's a sign to us that God, as the vineyard owner, rejoices in us, his fig tree, but that we are also not his chief concern. We are not his bread and butter as it were. If that's true, it's all good and well, but it has the rotten luck of showing all of us how we are not nearly as important as we think we are.

But there are still more details—enter the gardener.

In terms of storytelling, it is notable that the gardener, not the vineyard owner, is the one who ultimately displays and offers grace to the fig tree.

Jesus could've told another quick and easy story in which the vineyard owner himself offers grace to the inexplicable fig tree among the grape vines. But that's not the story Jesus tells. Instead it is the owner himself who can no longer wait idly by with patience hoping for the blasted tree to grow some fruit. He wants to tear the thing down.

It is the gardener who speaks in defense of the speechless tree.

And what does the gardener say? "Sir, let it alone for one more year, until I dig around it and put manure on it." At least, that what it says in our pew Bibles.

But in Greek, the gardener says, "KYRIE, APHES AUTEN"

Literally, "Lord, forgive it."

Sound familiar?

Lord, forgive them, for they do not know what they are doing.

These might be some of the most striking words from the Bible both because they proclaim the apparent forgiveness of the Lord for no reason at all, and because they help us to *see* how little we can.

Three years ago, this week, a gay night club in Orlando, Florida was hosting a "Latin Night." There were about 300 people dancing in the club when the announcement went out for last call around 2am. And shortly after the crowds made their way to the bar for their final drink of the evening, a man walked into the club and started shooting indiscriminately.

There was the initial barrage of gun fire, a hostage situation in one of the bathrooms, and eventually a SWAT team entered the building to eliminate the shooter. By the end 50 were dead, including the shooter, and another 53 were in the hospital.

At the time it was the deadliest mass shooting by a single shooter in US history, only to be eclipsed by the Las Vegas shooter a year later. But it still remains the deadliest incidence of violence against LGBTQ people in the history of our country.

And, tragically, this is nothing new to an entire community of people. Nearly a quarter of all hate crimes in the US are committed against LGBTQ people and the number of incidents has increased every year since 2005. Many of those perpetrating the violence regularly cite religious convictions to defend their actions.

And just this week, a Sheriff's Deputy in Tennessee implored the members in his church to call upon the federal government to round up and execute members of the LGBTQ community.

Sometimes it takes decades of hearing a preacher belittle and ridicule people for their sexual orientation, and sometimes all it takes is seeing a protestor with a sign with three terrible words, and then someone can assault two men walking down the street hand in hand, or walk into a night club and shoot into the darkness simply because women were dancing with women and men were dancing with men.

Sometimes it takes a sentence in a book about incompatibility that becomes a shackle around the ankle of a church, a shackle that it is forced to carry ad infinitum.

In Jesus' parable, there are only two characters and Jesus paints them vividly for us—the vineyard owner, God the Father, and the gardener, God the Son.

The gardener, as Christ, invites the owner of the vineyard to forgive the fig tree and to live according to the light of grace. His words here, as we're already noted, are the very same words from the cross. Words that, if we're honest, haunt us.

Lord, forgive them, for they do not know what they're doing.

All of us, whether we like it or not, live under the decisive reign of forgiveness. And yet, the world usually thinks and is hellbent on acting otherwise.

The world thinks it lives and spins by merit and reward. The world produces people who can wave signs and sing slogans that, at times, result in people being buried simply because of who they love. The world likes to imagine that salvation comes from a God who rewards individuals for their righteousness, whether its biblical or not.

But the foolishness of God, the one who mounts the hard wood of the cross for us, is smarter than that.

The cross with which we adorn the sanctuary, in all of its ugliness, is a sign and testament to Jesus becoming sin for us— how Jesus goes outside the boundaries of respectability for us, how he is damned to the dump for us, and how he ultimately becomes the manure of grace for us.

Is there anything more striking in the story than the fact that the gardener offers to dump manure all over the fig tree, all over us? Only in the foolishness of God could something so nasty, so dirty, so grossly inappropriate, become the means by which we become precisely who we are meant to be.

It is the horrific nature of the cross, Jesus' profound death for all eyes to see, from which Jesus returns to us. And he returns marked by the grave and the journey to it—he comes with holes in his hands and feet, bringing along all of the nutrients our roots could possibly need, and he brings them for free.

Jesus does not wait around for our fruit before offering the manure we so desperately need; he doesn't wait until we master the art of morality. He returns, and he dumps the dung right on top of us.

Jesus doesn't give a flip whether we've got a fig on the tree or not. He only cares about forgiveness, a forgiveness we so desperately need because we have no idea what we are doing.

For if we knew what we were doing, we would've solved all of the world's problems by now. We wouldn't have to worry about a young girl being ostracized in middle school for dressing like a boy. We wouldn't have to worry about the safety of people dancing in a nightclub simply because of who they might be dancing with. We wouldn't have to worry about a person contemplating ending their life because of what a preacher said in a sermon about who they are and their incompatibility.

But we do have to worry about these things. Because this is the world, we live in. We turn on the news reluctantly, knowing that we are about to be bombarded not by the joys in the community but by devastation. We see images of violence so often that we become numb to how broken this world is. We hear people shouting from the streets of life about what they believe, and we walk idly by not thinking about the repercussions of what they are saying.

We are a fruitless fig tree standing alone in the middle of God's garden.

We are doing nothing, and we deserve nothing.

And yet, and yet (!), Jesus looks at our barren limbs and is moved to say the three words we deserve the least, "Lord, forgive them."

Which is why we come to the table, again and again, knowing that this simple meal is anything but simple—it is, believe it or not, the manure for our soil—it is, believe it or not, our forgiveness. So be it. Amen.

Go and Sin Some More
Luke 18:9-14
Jason Micheli

At the first unsuspecting church on which a bishop foisted me—we staged a Christmas pageant during the season of Advent.

During dress rehearsal that final Sunday morning before the performance, stomach flu had started to sweep through the heavenly host.

When it came time for the angelic chorus to deliver their lines in unison: "Glory to God in the highest" you could hear Katie, a first-grade angel, vomiting her breakfast into the trash can over by the grand piano.

The sound of Katie's wretching was loud enough that when the other angels should've been proclaiming "and on earth peace to all the people" they were instead gagging and covering their noses.

Meanwhile, apparently bored by the angels' news of a Messiah, two of the shepherds—both third-grade boys and both sons of wise men—started brawling on the altar floor next to the manger.

Their free-for-all prompted one of the wise men to leave his entourage and stride angrily up the sanctuary aisle, smack his shepherd son upside the ear and threaten: "Boy, Santa won't be bringing Nascar tickets this year if you can't hold it together."

Truth be told, the little church had neither the numbers nor the talent to man a lemonade stand much less mount a production of the Christmas story; nonetheless, a brusque, take-charge mother, who was a new member in the congregation, had approached me about staging a pageant.

And because I was a rookie pastor and didn't know any better—and honestly, because I was terrified of this woman—I said yes.

The set constructed in the church sanctuary was made to look like the small town where we lived. So the Bethlehem skyline was dotted with Burger King, the local VFW, the municipal building, the funeral home and, instead of an inn, the Super 8 Motel.

At every stop in Bethlehem someone sat behind a cardboard door. Joseph would knock and the person behind the door would declare: "Sorry, ain't no room here."

The old man behind the door of the cardboard VFW was named Fred. He was the oldest member of the congregation. He sat on a stool behind the set, wearing his VFW beret and chewing on an unlit cigarillo.

Fred was almost completely deaf and not a little senile so when Mary and Joseph came to him, they didn't bother knocking on the door.

They just opened it up and asked the surprised-looking old man if he had any room for them to which he would respond by looking around at his surroundings as though he were wondering where he was and how he'd gotten there.

Because, of course, he was wondering where he was and how he'd gotten there.

For some reason, be it haste, laziness, or a dare involving some sum of cash, the mother-in-charge of the pageant had made the magi responsible for their own costumes.

Thus, one wise man wore a white lab coat and carried a telescope.

Another wise man was dressed like the former WWF wrestler the Iron Sheik.

And the third wise man wore a gray and green Philadelphia Eagles bathrobe and for some inexplicable reason had aluminum foil wrapped around his head.

King Herod was played by the head usher, Jimmy.

At 6'6 and wearing a crown and a white fur-collared purple robe and carrying a gold cane, King Herod looked more like Kramer as an uptown gigilo than he did a biblical character.

When it came time for the performance, I took a seat on the bench in the back of the sanctuary where the ushers normally sat and, gazing at the cast and the production design from afar, I briefly wondered to myself a question you all cause me to ask from time to time too.

Why didn't I go to law school?

I sat down and King Herod handed me a program.

On the cover was the title: "The Gift of Christmas."

On the inside was a list of cast members' names and their roles.

As the pageant began with a song lip-synced by the angels, the other usher for the day sat next to me.

His name was Mike. He was an insurance adjustor with salt-and-pepper hair and dark eyes. He led a Bible Study on Wednesday mornings that met at the diner. He delivered Meals on Wheels. He chaired the church council. He supervised the coat closet. He mentored kids caught in the juvenile justice system. He was the little church's most generous donor.

And he was more than little officious in his righteousness.

Mike never liked me all that much.

Mike sat down, fixed his reading glasses at the end of his nose, opened his program and began mumbling names under his breath: *Mary played by...Elizabeth played by...Magi #1 played by...*

His voice was barely above a whisper, but it was thick with contempt.

Of all the nerve.

I knew immediately what he was implying or, rather, I knew what had gotten under his skin.

There were no teenage girls in the congregation to be cast. So, Mary was played by a grown woman—a grown woman who was married to a man more than twice her age.

She'd married him only after splitting up his previous marriage.

The Holy Mother of God was being portrayed by a homewrecker.

Of the three magi, one of them had scandalized the church by ruining his father's business to fund his gambling habit.

Another wise man was separated from his wife, but not legally so, and was living with another woman.

The innkeeper at the Super 8 Motel—he was a lifelong alcoholic, alienated from his grown children and several ex-wives.

Reluctantly shepherding the elementary-aged shepherds was a high school junior. He'd gotten busted earlier that fall for drug possession.

His mother was dressed as an angel that day, helping to direct the heavenly host. Her husband, her boy's father, had walked out on them a year earlier.

Elizabeth, the mother of John the Baptist, was played by a woman who was new to the church, a woman who often wore sunglasses to worship or heavy make-up or who sometimes didn't bother at all and just wore the bruises given to her by a boyfriend none of us had ever met.

The man playing the role of Zechariah, the husband of Elizabeth and father of Jesus' cousin John, owned a construction company and had been accused of and charged with fraud by several customers in town, including a couple in the congregation.

He'd bilked them out of thousands and thousands of dollars.

Zechariah—his name was Bill—every first Sunday of the month, Bill began to cry, tears streaming down his sunburnt carpenter's cheeks, whenever I placed a piece of bread in his rough, calloused hands and promised him, "This is the Body of Christ, broken for you."

Maybe more than anyone in that little church, he depended on the promise that when Christ says "This is my Body broken for you" *you* mean *me*, too.

"There's no conditions," I'd told him once after the you-know-what with his business hit the fan.

"It doesn't matter what you've done. For all of us, that *you* mean me. The forgiveness—it's for you. You've got to take Christ at his absolving word or you're calling God a liar, which is alot worse of a sin than any you've committed. The truth about you is never what you see in the mirror—good or bad—the truth about you is always found in the broken piece of bread placed in your hand. You're no different than anyone else here."

Mike, the insurance adjuster, held the program in his hands and read the cast members' names under his breath.

Then he rolled up his program and he poked me with it and, just when the angel Gabriel was delivering his news to Mary, Mike whispered into my ear:

"Who picked the cast for this? Who chose them?'

And because I'm not a brave man (and because I didn't much like her) I pointed at the mother-in-charge.

"She did. She cast them all. Blame her."

He shook his head in disgust and then he gestured towards Zechariah, pretending now to be struck mute, and he said: "It's one thing for him to even show his face here Sunday after Sunday without mending his ways but...this?! Do you really think he's the sort of person who should be sharing this story with our church and our community? What in the hell have you been preaching to him, pastor? *Go and sin some more*?!"

———————————

The narrator for the Christmas pageant that year was a woman whose name, ironically, was Mary.

She hadn't had the energy for any of the rehearsals. She just showed up at the worship service when it was time to perform the pageant pushing a walker, from which hung a black and green oxygen tank.

Mary was old and incredibly tiny, no bigger than the children that morning wearing gold pipe cleaner halos around their heads. Emphysema was killing Mary a breath at a time.

She had to be helped up to the pulpit once the performance began. I'd spent a lot of hours in Mary's kitchen over the time I was her pastor, sipping bad Folger's coffee and listening to her tell me about her family.

About the dozen miscarriages she'd had in her life and about how the pain of all those losses was outweighed only by the joy of the child she'd grafted into her family tree. About the husband who died suddenly, before the dreams they'd had together could be checked-off the list. About her daughter's broken marriage. And about her two grandsons who, in the complicated way of families, were now living with her.

As the children finished their lip-synced opening song, and as the shepherds and angels and wise men took their places, and as Billy climbed into his makeshift throne, looking more like a Harvey Keitel pimp than a King Herod, Mary struggled up to the pulpit.

With the walker resting next to the pulpit, the tube to her oxygen was pulled almost taut. Her fierce eyes were just barely visible above the microphone.

With her hands bruised from blood thinner, she spread out her script and in a soft, raspy voice she began to tell the story, beginning not with Luke or with John but with Matthew, the Gospel of Matthew.

I wouldn't have chosen Matthew for a Christmas pageant, but again I was terrified of the mother-in-charge.

The cadence of Mary's delivery was dictated by the mask she had to put over her face every few seconds to fill her lungs with air: "She shall bear a son ... (breath) ... and you are to name him Jesus ... (breath) ... f or he will save people from their sins...(breath)..."

Except—

That morning Mary didn't start by narrating the Christmas story.

She went off script.

I don't know if she went off script because she hadn't been at the rehearsals or if in her old age she was confused and rambling, or maybe she was just filling time while she tried to locate her spot in the script.

I like to think she'd heard the scuttlebutt about Mike and his righteous indignation over the likes of the people who populated the parish's pageant.

She began by introducing the passage.

128

"The Bible tells us about God being born as Jesus," Mary said, "only after a long list of begats." And she took a breath from her oxygen mask. "Emmanuel ... God-with-us ... (breath) comes from a family tree every bit as knotted as ours (breath) a family of scoundrels and unbelievers (breath), rapists and hookers (breath), cheats and those consumed by their resentment over being cheated upon (breath) all the way back to Abraham (breath) who wasn't righteous (breath) but was reckoned so on the only basis any of us are so counted, faith, alone (breath). Christ comes from a family just like us," she said and took a breath.

"He comes from sinners for sinners."

And I looked over at Mike, who'd been standing in the narthex passing out programs. In addition to everything else, Mike was the head usher too.

When the pageant began, Mike's ears had been beat red and the vein in his forehead throbbing so outraged and incredulous was he that we were "telling the story of our savior with those kinds of people," but, hearing that tiny little women with her Gospel promise, he suddenly hung his head.

He looked embarrassed—as though, God the Holy Spirit had just smacked him upside the head.

Humility is only ever something we discover because humility is something done to us.

Katie in the heavenly host nearly made it through the Christmas pageant in the clear, but when the wise men showed up delivering their gift-wrapped boxes, she ran to the trash can in the choir loft to deliver into it the last of her breakfast.

Mary never made it to the next Christmas. She died that spring clutching the same promise she'd preached to us that Sunday in Advent.

Zechariah left the church shortly after I did, and he became a preacher in a storefront start-up church, preaching the promise that whether we mend our ways or not, when it comes us, God never mends his ways. No matter what, God will deal with you tomorrow exactly as God dealt with you yesterday, by grace.

Turns out, he was a good preacher too—only those who know they're not good realize that the promise is too good not to believe.

After the worship service that Sunday in Advent finished, I stood outside near the front door to the sanctuary, shaking hands as the bell rang and the organ groaned out the last notes of the postlude. Mike was one of the last to leave. In addition to everything else, he always cleaned up the pews after worship and vacuumed up the communion crumbs from the floor.

His hand felt hot and sweaty in the December air, like he'd been wringing his hands in consternation.

"We've all fallen short of the glory of God, but I guess that doesn't stop us from measuring distances does it?"

But I didn't catch his meaning because as he started to walk home down the sidewalk, I thought to myself (and remember, this is a long time ago in a county far far away, back in my pre-sanctified days):
"Thank God, I'm not a self-righteous, holier-than-thou, bookkeeping hypocrite like him."

Two men went up to the temple to pray one Advent Sunday morning, the first a Methodist preacher—a professional Christian—the second a modern-day Pharisee named Mike.

The latter, not the former, went back down to his house justified.

But on some other Sunday?

You know as well as I do.

Under a different set of circumstances, it could just as easily be the former not the latter. Come next Sunday it could just as easily be the tax collector Ubering home whilst congratulating himself that he really gets how God's grace works unlike that holy-rolling bookkeeper who makes himself the subject of all his prayers and gets caught red-handed in his self-righteousness.

All of us—we're always, if not simultaneously then from one Sunday to the next, at once, sinners and saints. We leave church tax collectors enjoying our forgiveness, yet as soon as we get into the fellowship hall or login to Facebook, we're back to being Pharisees.

They're two different characters in the parable, but they're both in us.

No matter how hard you try, you *will* go and sin some more.

That's why (this might sound obvious to some of you, but I promise you it's not self-evident to many) the Gospel is for Christians.

The Gospel is *even* for Christians.

The Gospel is *especially* for Christians.

We tend to think of the Gospel (the promise that while you were yet hostile to God, Christ died for your sins and was raised for your justification)—as though it's for non-Christians.

Street-corner evangelists stand on street-corners not in church parking lots.

We tend to think of the Gospel of grace as a doorway through which we pass to get into the household of God; so that, we can then get on with the real business of living like Christ and doing as Christ for our neighbors.

But thinking of the Gospel as prologue to your Christian life, nothing could be more unbiblical.

The Bible teaches that Christ comes to dwell in our hearts by what exactly?

By faith.

And the Bible teaches that the faith by which Christ gives himself to us comes to us how?

Not by doing.

By hearing.

Christ gives himself to us by faith that comes to us by hearing the word.

And not just any word, the Bible teaches, a specific word.

The promise of grace.

The Gospel word.

The Gospel gives Christ himself to us the way a wedding vow gives a bride her groom.

The Gospel, therefore, is for Christians too not just potential converts.

The Gospel is for Christians especially because the Gospel that *gives* you Christ, the Bible teaches, is the same Gospel that *grows* Christ in you.

The way to grow in grace is to cling to the promise of it, to return to it over and again.

Living a grace-filled life is like learning a song by heart—this song.

Because we don't ever stop being a tax collector one Sunday and a Pharisee the next, we don't ever stop, we don't ever advance past, we don't ever level up beyond needing to the hear the Gospel.

This good word, the Gospel of Christ—just as Jesus said—is the Living Water without which first we get thirsty and then we get exhausted before finally our faith dries up, and we die in our sins.

The Gospel word that gives Christ to you is the Bread of Life that keeps on feeding Christ to you—that's what he means by calling himself Manna.

The Gospel is the Bread of Life, and we're always one meal away from starving.

And, without that meal, without the Gospel, we have nothing to offer our neighbor, we have nothing to offer the poor and the oppressed, we have nothing to offer them other than what the world already offers them and how the world offers it.

Which is to say, thank God.

God has not made us like other people.

God has made us Christians.

We *are* different from other people.

We are the particular people God has put into the world who've been set free by the Gospel to admit that we're just like other people. We're publicans and Pharisees all. We're worse than our worst enemy thinks of us, yet we're loved to the grave and back.

Thank God, we're not like other people.

We're different in that we have this Gospel that frees to confess that we're no different.

And that difference—A people set free to know and own that we're no different than other people ... That difference is the difference Christ makes in a world of Us vs. Them.

Possessed
Luke 12:13-23
Teer Hardy

Having turned and now facing Jerusalem and his coming death, Jesus had been teaching the disciples and the growing crowds that they needed to devote their lives to God. It sounds simple and obvious enough but the Bible we know is, at times, anything but simple and obvious. Before the incarnation, God taking on human flesh and dwelling among us in Jesus Christ, devotion to God was best accomplished by adhering to the Law God gave to Moses on Mt. Sinai.

The problem with seeking God's holiness through human means is that time and time again humans had proven our inability to fulfill the Law given by God. There was always room for improvement and thus there was always a barrier, it seemed, between humanity and God. Through the incarnation, Jesus revealed that the separation we, humanity, felt was one-sided as God had not abandoned that which God had breathed life into.

Jesus, through direct and indirect means, called the people back to living in the confidence of God's good purposes for not only them individually but to include all of creation, welcoming those through to be beyond the covenant established by God with Abraham.

God's good purposes are not to leave creation on its own, us to our own devices and imagination.

God's good purposes may not match the desires we have conjured up but God's good purposes do provide for our daily need—thus the line Jesus gave the disciples in last week's reading, "give us this day our daily bread."

Through parables, even when speaking of matters that are cut and dry, Jesus used earthly examples to reveal heavenly truths. Jesus was not telling fables with quirky and ironic endings. Rather through parables, Jesus revealed the nature of the Kingdom of God, his kingdom.

Jesus was approached by a man seeking Jesus' input and judgment on a family squabble. The dividing of assets after the death of one's parent caused then and causes today feelings to be hurt, especially when the cultural norm was to give more to the oldest son. This was a practical matter, done to ensure the family name and wealth lived on well-beyond the death of the father.

This younger brother received what was due to him by the cultural norms of the day but he wanted more. The younger brother approached Jesus with a question of greed cloaked in a dispute over fairness. Jesus chose to not intervene on the young brother's behalf as Jesus is not a celestial genie or judge. Jesus is the savior of the world—all of creation—revealing God's good purposes for us.

Jesus was not focused on patching up family disputes or incidental injustices. The Robert Capon put it this way, "(Jesus' ministry) is the bearing of the final injustice—death—and the raising up from it of an entirely new and reconciled creation."

After being unwilling to settle the family squabble, Jesus moved to tell a parable.

A rich man hit the agricultural jackpot. His farm had been producing enough to provide for him but then he hit a bumper crop. The abundance he had was nothing in comparison to the yields from his field during the latest harvest. The rich man tore down the existing barns to store all of the grain and goods his fields had given him. The man had an abundance on top of abundance.

His store of grain and goods was so great that not only did he tear down what he already had for the sake of storing more but he also made plans to take a hiatus from the farm to relax—eat, drink, and be merry.

The word fool seems to be a throwaway line used by Jesus. The word "fool" though is only used four times in the Gospels— two times in Matthew's Gospel and two times in Luke's Gospel. Each time "fool" is used Jesus uses the word to describe behavior contrary to God's good purposes for creation

Foolishness, according to Jesus, is not merely a flippant attitude but instead is an obsession/need for more—greed.

A need for more wealth for the sake of having more.

Jesus is not saying that wealth is wrong and that is where the parable trips us up. This is not a parable about selling off all of your possessions and then giving the proceeds to the poor. Jesus is warning the young brother caught up in a family squabble that the possessions he has and the desire for more will one day possess him. Jesus is telling us that the possessions we have and the desire for more will one day possess us.

The wealth accumulated by the rich fool blinded him of his foolishness in destroying the barns he already had so that he could accumulate more. The rich fool's use of the first-person language, along with his plans for a sabbatical without an end date, signal his true intentions. He was not storing up grain so that he would be prepared for famine or to be able to help a neighbor knocking on his door in the middle of the night seeking three loaves of bread.

Simply put… The rich fool was a rich blind fool, unable to see that what he had gained from the ground had now possessed him.

Back to Robert Capon for a moment—the now deceased Episcopal priest writes that in the eyes of Christ all of us—rich and poor—are "nothing but unreconstructed rich people." What Capon is getting at that is at some level all of us are rich fools because we live in a world where greed, extreme greed—Capon uses the word "avarice"—is the driving force behind the systems that created IRAs, the desire for second homes, and over-indulgent retirement plans. We clutch to our lives and our purposes for them rather than living into the new life in Christ we were clothed in when we exited our baptismal waters.

St. Paul wrote, "(you) have clothed yourselves with the new self, which is being renewed in knowledge according to the image of its creator." Once we clothe ourselves in Christ, we are no longer fools because we live in the knowledge of God's good purposes for the new creation inaugurated by Christ's death and resurrection.

The fool remained consumed, until his death, with wealth to the point that he lost his soul to that which had demanded so much of him—the possessions he clung to stored up in shiny new barns.

The "they" Jesus spoke of refers to the possessions that possessed the fool—claiming his soul—and demanding his life. The fool was rich in this life only to find the cruel reversal, the reversal his wealth would not warn him of that in death, apart from God we die in poverty. It is a cruel reversal to the story that will rearrange your mental furniture.

In Christ, we discover that the poverty we enter into at death—you cannot take it with you—and the sad comprehension of the cruel reversal turns into Good News. Just as Jesus fully revealed God's good purposes for creation in his earthy life, so too is it for us who have clothed ourselves in Christ at the time of our death. There is nothing left to do, no barns to take down or to build up, and instead, through the grace of Jesus Christ, we are invited to lean into God's good purposes revealed to us by Christ. Now we await the day when the fullness of God's new creation, made possible through the faithfulness of Christ, is finally revealed.

I Pity the Fool
Luke 12:13-21
Taylor Mertins

Weddings are important, and because they are important, I want the couple to grasp how crazy of a thing it is to get married in the first place.

I get asked to do a fair number of weddings and I will agree to participate so long as I can engage in at least a handful of premarital counseling sessions. Part of this is born out of a desire to know the couple well enough to actually stand before them, their friends, and their families to peach about the bizarreness of marriage, but it also my attempt to help prevent the hoped-for marriage from falling apart in the future.

On more than one occasion I have shared that the first question I ask any couple wanting to get married is, "Can you tell me about your last fight?"

It's a great icebreaker and within a few minutes I have a pretty good idea what the rest of our conversations will be like.

And yet, I know, that answering that particular question is uncomfortable. I've watched countless couples squirm in the chairs wondering who was going to bring up the proper location for dishes in the dishwasher, or who was going to raise the complaints about the over-bearing mother-in-law, or who would mention the frivolous spending from the bank account.

And sure enough, someone always caves, and we can begin the good and difficult work of approaching marriage from a theological perspective.

But that's not the only question that makes couples uncomfortable—no we quickly move to the subjects of sex and children, are you having it and are you wanting any, respectively. And the individuals slink deeper into their chairs and their cheeks get redder and redder.

But of all the questions I ask, and all the things we discuss, there is one subject that rules them all: money.

And, as should be expected, money is usually the most discussed topic during pre-marital counseling because it is at the heart of the majority of divorces in our country. I gently encourage couples to share with me how they currently handle their finances and how they hope to handle them on the other side of "I do." We then discuss habits and practices that can prevent the kind of deception that tends to rip couples apart around bank accounts and credit cards.

And then I get to ask a question that stops everyone dead in their tracks (Pun intended).

"How much money is enough money?"

Eyeballs always stare back at me with confusion or disbelief. So, I have to elaborate: "Is there an amount of money that, should you be able to achieve it one day, you won't want more?" Or "Have you considered a top salary that once you earn more than it, you'll give the rest away?"

"How much money is enough money?"

Someone in the crowd interrupted Jesus one day, "Lord, tell my brother to divide up the family inheritance with me."

The man probably has just cause even though the conventions of the day dictated that the oldest son would receive the inheritance. Who wouldn't want the Lord to decree that things must be divided evenly particular when it comes to money?

And Jesus snaps right back, "Hey, who made me a judge or a divider over all you people?"

Apparently, Jesus' work is bigger than the incidental patching up of family problems and financial squabbles.

But then Jesus does what Jesus does best; he tells a story.

There was a man who was doing well with his career. At first, he used the excess cash to fill his house with all sorts of trinkets and wares designed to show other people how wealthy he was. First it started with some original paintings, but then he ran out of wall space. Next he redid his entire wardrobe, but then his closet was full. And lastly, he decided to buy an extra car, but there was no room in the garage.

What was the man to do?

And he had a vision.... Why not tear it all down and build a bigger house to fit all of his stuff inside?

And that's what he did.

In the midst of the plans for reconstruction, while laying out ideas of what would go where, he said to himself, "You've done good, old boy. Time to eat, drink, and be merry."

When suddenly a booming voice shatters all the new windows, "You fool! This very night your life is being demanded of you. And the things you have prepared, whose will they be?"

Much to our chagrin, the line between evil and foolishness is frighteningly thin. Up to this point in the gospel story Jesus has been using those qualifiers interchangeably when denouncing the scribes and Pharisees, he has used both word for the powers and the principalities. But now they get turned against us.

Be on your guard against all kinds of greed, because our lives are about more than what we have.

But Jesus, what about my 401k?

But Jesus, what about my nest egg?

But Jesus, what about all that stuff I've accumulated to show people who I really am?

All of that stuff, all of that money, they are the hopes of the well-off and the envy of the poor who will never have them—nothing more, nothing less, and nothing else.

Our world, all of this, even in the church (sadly), it's all run on avarice. Extreme greed for wealth or material goods. It's the lie we were fed as children, and it's the lie that we feed to our children. It is reinforced on every magazine cover, on every Instagram post, and with every commercial on TV.

Happiness is yours if you acquire this thing.

And it's all a lie.

Because contrary to that false narrative, something hammered home relentlessly, we are not defined by our bank accounts or by what we hang on our walls or by what kind of car we drive. Poverty, not wealth; Death, not life—these are the ways by which God saves us.

Regardless of whether we're wealthy, poor, or somewhere in-between, all of us in Jesus' eyes are people who are sin-sick with our insatiable desire for more.

And not just more, but more more more!

We clutch at all that is around us rather than opening our palms to ever be open to anything else.

We'd rather receive than give.

Earn all you can, and save all you can, because it's an eat or be eaten world out there, right?

I don't know about you but this parable stings. It just won't leave me alone. It confronts and convicts me.

Jesus tells a story in which a man does what all of us do with our avarice, with our greed: We congratulate ourselves on all we have accomplished.

You graduated with that GPA? Wow, you definitely deserve to do whatever you want this summer.

Your grandchildren really are adorable, and their parents are paying for your next vacation? Sounds like it's time to relax and start enjoying your well-deserved retirement.

You just got that promotion you've been gunning for? Wonderful, you definitely have this whole adulting thing figured out!

And I have this job, it's a great job. My marriage is beautiful, I have a son who brings smiles to the faces of all with eyes to see. Good job Taylor! Relax, eat, drink, be merry!

But here's the really interesting thing about all of that stuff—from the GPA to the kids to the promotion to the bank accounts—we think we earn them or at the least we deserve them, when in fact each and every one of those things is a gift. They are good only because someone, or something, was good to us.

Jesus sets up the man as a paradigm of everything we think to be good, and right, and true. He's fiscally responsible after all. He's earned it. And yet, the man is only a master of a life that is completely and radically out of his control—he is nothing but the captain of a ship that has been taking on water since it left the dock.

You see, Jesus builds up the man as the pinnacle on financial responsibility only to knock him straight down to the ground: "You fool! This night they are demanding your life, and then whose will they be?"

Up until the Lord's interruption in his life, the fool has been living a monologue. The whole parable is just him talking to himself, congratulating himself, rejoicing in and with himself. All the while forgetting that his good crops, or his stock portfolio, or whatever the thing is, was always first a gift.

And gifts require givers.

Or, to put it another way, isn't it such great and sweet irony that the man who had it all discovers that his things had him?

And they do have us, don't they? We lay awake at night thinking not upon all the good that we have, not giving thanks to the Lord above and to the people around us who make our lives possible, but with worry.

And not just worry for the sake or worrying—we worry about our stuff.

Was that the right investment?

Am I going to be able to afford that new cable plan?

Was I foolish to buy that extra TV?

And yet, we keep acquiring new things and we try to control them. Or, at the very least, we try to control our lives with the accumulation of things such that it makes us appear as if we have our lives together.

We want to be rich, or we want to appear rich.

However, unlike Jeff Bezos and Warren Buffet and Bill Gates, the only truly rich person in the world in Jesus.

You and me, we spend our whole lives in the pursuit of wealth (both material and immaterial) only to come in the end to the greatest poverty of all: death.

This is the frightening and final tone of the parable, the one that lingers long after even being called a fool: no matter how much we make and no matter how much we accumulate, we all die in the end.

I pity the fool, particularly because the fool is me.

The fool is all of us.

We all live in these self-satisfied, fat, and ignorant monologues about all that is good in our lives and we forget, mostly because we avoid it, that we all die in the end.

But in Jesus, the one who tells this story precisely because it frightens us to death, all is turned upside down. The Lord offers grace to both the wicked in their moral poverty and to the rich in the death of all their stuff. Jesus becomes a new way in which all of our pointless pursuing and all of our foolish incomprehension becomes something we can call good.

We can call it good because Jesus is there for us in our deaths.

Nothing can separate us from the love of God in Christ Jesus, not our money or lack of it, not our stuff or lack of it, not our lives and not even our deaths.

We might not see it, and we might not believe it, but there is greater wealth in the salvation of Christ than in every bank in the world.

And it is ours for free.

We can't earn it.

We don't deserve it.

It's not cheap.

It's not even expensive.

It's free.

It's free for you and me and every fool the world will ever see. Amen.

God Gone Wild
Matthew 22:1-14
Jason Micheli

Last week, some of your lay leaders and I were emailing each other back and forth regarding what we should do about a homeless, undocumented man who's been sleeping outside near the trash bins at our mission center on Heritage Drive.

"You should see how he's dressed—the custodians are creeped out by him."

And so, we exchanged emails, weighing the merits of shelters and county services against our concerns about safety and liability on the one hand and the police and ICE on the other hand.

At some point during the Reply All email thread, Eldon Hillenbrandt, who—if you don't know him—is a wonderful, earnest, sincere man without a sarcastic or cynical bone in his body (in other words, he's everything I'm not) replied with a wonderfully earnest and sincere question. He asked us: "What do you think Jesus would do?"

WWJD—what would Jesus do?

Totally sincere question, not cynical or sarcastic in any way.

And probably Eldon had in mind a parable like the sheep and the goats. *I was a stranger and you welcomed me.* What would Jesus do about the stranger sleeping against the dumpster in his stinking, shabby clothes?

And because I'm the way my Maker made me, when it came to Eldon's completely earnest and sincere question, I couldn't help myself.

Like those salmon who swim upstream in order to mate even though doing the deed will be the death of them, I couldn't help myself.

Just as some artists work in oil or watercolors, I work in sarcasm and middle-school boys' bathroom humor.

I couldn't resist typing in reply: "WWJD? Cuff him! Hand and foot! Torture him! Kill him! Throw him in Hell!"

144

Fortunately, as I gazed upon my computer screen, the cursor still blinking at the end of my adolescent quip, I suddenly had what alcoholics describe as a moment of clarity and thought better about sending it.

In case you haven't met her, I call that moment of clarity Ali.

So, I deleted the comment and instead sent out some prosaic pastor-speak.

But the problem is—

We can't backspace our way away from the Jesus who tells this parable today.

As liberal mainline Protestants, we've all been conditioned into believing that Christianity boils down to being nice and doing nice; therefore, if we have any religious convictions at all it's that God is nice too. And maybe at first you thought that's where Jesus' story was headed.

An evite goes out for a great extravagant party, but those in the VIP queue—the fat cats and country club set, the season ticket holders and the keto dieters, the cronies of the rich man—mark the invitation *read* and forget all about it.

So, the rich man says, "Hey, I've already paid the photographer. I've got a Costco's worth of beef tenderloin under the broiler, and the DJ's already started playing the Electric Slide. Go out beyond the suburbs and bring in the folks from the Halfway House—and don't forget those guys who loiter around the 7-Eleven too. Let them come into my party. The 1 percent don't deserve my generosity."

Probably as Jesus' story was being read at first you thought you liked it. You like the idea of God going out like Bernie Sanders to the marginalized and the poor and the dispossessed and inviting them to a fine china, cloth napkin, open bar party.

It's a nice thought.

And it would be nice if Jesus just left it alone right there, which is sort of the way Jesus tells it in Luke's Gospel.

But Matthew?

I mean—all this festival of death needs to be more terrifying are creepy twin girls, an elevator full of blood, and Jesus with a hatchet saying, "Here's Johnny."

And maybe a ginger kid too—a ginger would make it scarier.

What gets you about Jesus' story in Matthew is not the graciousness of the King esteeming the lowly onto his guest list, as in Luke.

What gets you is this King's totally inappropriate and excessive behavior.

"Oh, the A-Listers couldn't be bothered to open the Paperless Post? Some clicked 'Maybe?' Really? Well then, I'll tell you what, Alfred. I want you get some of the hired help and I want you to cross them off the guest list permanently, if you know what I mean. No, that's right, you heard me correctly, hand and foot. Send them to a place worse than Cleveland! They'll regret sending their regrets when I get through with them!"

Then, as if the body count wasn't already high enough, in a flourish only House Lanister could love, there's Jesus' finale. Among the good and bad gathered into the King's party, this panhandling vagrant off Braddock Road makes it past the maître d' only to get himself shipped off to one of Dick Cheney's black sites *all because of the way he's dressed.*

"You there—yeah you."

Actually, the word the King uses in Greek is *hetaire*, which means, basically, "*Buster.*"

"Hey how'd you get in here dressed like that? We've got beluga on ice and Chateau Branaire-Ducru uncorked. This party is black tie and tails only, buster."

"Well, sir, I was sleeping outside next to the Mission Center trash bins only an hour ago, and they don't stock formal wear in the church's coat closet."

And the "gracious" King responds: "Really? Well then...Bind him, hand and foot! Throw him into the outer darkness where there will be weeping and gnashing of teeth!"

I know you—

It really bothers you that the formerly sweet baby Jesus in golden fleece diapers would tell a story like this to nice, well-mannered people like you. It bothers you to hear the Lamb of God who takes away the sins of the world roaring like a lion at...

At what exactly?

Failure to RSVP?

A party foul?

What gives?

Admit it—

We all want a God who says of our flagged but unopened evites, "Oh, your kids have a soccer game? You were up late last night? You can catch it online? That's okay, I know you're busy. We'll miss you at the party but no biggie. Raincheck?"

We want a God who is as cool and dispassionate about us as we are about him.

We don't want this irrational, incongruous God.

We don't want this God gone wild.

We don't want this King who is ferociously determined to celebrate his *free* party.

No matter the costs.

I mean—that much is obvious, right?

As much as it tightens our sphincters and gives nice types like us acid reflux, for his macabre little drama Jesus rudely casts his Heavenly Father as this bezerk, damn-the-torpedoes, party-or-bust King.

Which puts us where in the story?

Who are we supposed to be at this party?

The A-list?

Does Jesus mean for you to identify with those at the top of the King's guest list? The ones who for whatever reason (or none at all) don't accept the King's invitation? Actually, the Greek in verse three isn't as neutral as it sounds. The word is *amelsantes*, and it means literally, "They didn't give a damn."

"The King sent his servants to call those who had been invited to the party, but *they didn't give a rip,"* Jesus says.

Maybe that is who Jesus means us to be in the story because he conjugates the VIPs' apathy in the imperfect tense.

It's: *"They were not giving a rip..."*

That is, these A-Listers' snubbing of the King's call is an ongoing rejection; as if to say, the world will always be full of idiots who refuse to trust and enjoy a good thing when they hear it.

Free grace, dying love, unqualified acceptance, and unconditional forgiveness *for you*—it might as well be a prostate exam given the way some of us respond to it.

Is that us?

Obviously, you all give a rip.

You wouldn't have dragged yourself out of bed, showered, and shown up this morning for a subpar sermon if you didn't care.

But maybe like that first group of invitees, you make your way in life assuming that God's good, gracious nature means you're free to ignore his call upon your life until after you're finished with all your better plans.

Maybe that's why Jesus repeats the word *call* every other verse, from the top of his story to the bottom.

As though the King's call is a countdown.

Going once.

Going twice...tick tock.

What about that second batch of evites?

The King sends out his servants a second time to those on the guest list. And they deliver the message: *Look this party is off the hook! The oxen and the fatted calves (plural!) have been in the smoker since last night. The keg is tapped. Come on already!*

Notice—

It's not that those guests can't be bothered.

It's that they're too busy.

Some, Jesus says, are too busy with their farms to celebrate the King's party.

Others, Jesus says, are too tied up at the office to join the King's party.

It's not that they don't give a rip.

It's that they give too many.

Farming, business—those are *vocations*, good works God gives to us for our neighbors.

These guests are so wrapped up in the good work God has given them to do for others that they ignore the King's individual invitation to them.

They're so focused on doing good works for their neighbor that they've neglected, and thus put at risk, their personal relationship with the King—the very relationship to which their good works were meant to be a sign not a substitute.

Their busyness lulled them into forgetting that their personal yes to the King's invitation is an urgent eternal matter of life and death. We can be so bent over busy in our religious, deed-doing lives that we lose them.

And maybe they don't answer the King's invite because they assume they can get past the bouncers at a date they name later, on the merits of all their hard work and not on the King's gratuity.

Perhaps that's who Jesus means us to be in the story.

Or what about that poor bastard who's caught without a cummerbund and patent leather shoes? Does Jesus mean for us to be the guy dragged off by the King's SWAT team because of a wardrobe malfunction? I mean, even Janet Jackson got a second chance.

Is that who we are in the story?

Are you supposed to hear this parable and worry?

Worry that, yes, all are invited to the party of salvation, gratis, but if you don't meet the dress code? It's outer darkness for you.

In other words: *yes, yes grace, <u>but</u>...*

Yes, salvation is by grace.

But, your faith better bring something to show for it when you get to the party.

Yes, all are invited, gratis.

But, only some get to stay. You better show up wearing your three-piece suit of obedience, your gem-covered gown of holiness, or your mink of compassion.

Yes, yes grace, but...

Never mind for a moment the not minor point that as soon as you attach a *but* to grace, it's no longer grace, such a worrisome takeaway ignores the fact that whatever fancy duds these riffraff at the party are wearing, they're clothes the King has given to them.

Free of charge.

Upon arrival not prior to departure.

So, their ability to remain at the party is not conditioned upon the presence or absence of anything they brought with them—not their closet full of loving works and not their suitcase holy living.

The King gave them their garments upon arrival. So, for whatever reason, this eyesore who's still in his street clothes and bound for darkness, he didn't put on the bow tie and tux given out to all the other guests who got there on the same free ticket as him.

This guy didn't change his clothes.

He refused to change.

Is that it?

If he's who Jesus means us to be, then is the takeaway for us that, yes, we're invited but once there we better change and get our act together?

That might be one way to interpret Jesus' story if Jesus' story were told by someone other than Jesus, and if Jesus told this story at some point other than three days before he died not to improve the improvable or reform the reformable but to raise the dead in their sins.

And the only thing the dead do is stink.

So, the takeaway today can't be that we need first to apply deodorant before we're allowed onto the dance floor.

The Cross is Exhibit A.

Jesus saves us *in* our failures not just in spite of them.

"The gifts and invitation of God," the Apostle Paul says, "are irrevocable."

And the word Paul uses there is repentance.

The gifts and invitation of God *are without repentance.*

Therefore, the moral of this parable is not that God invites us to the party called salvation, but we better shape up or we'll get shipped off.

No, the parable doesn't have a moral because it's a parable.

It's not about you.

It's about God—that's why the King and his staff get all the verbs in the story.

Notice—no one else in the story even speaks.

You can't ask of a parable, "WWJD?"

You can only ask, "Who is this God who does to us in Jesus Christ?"

But that still doesn't answer where are we in this parable?

Last week the *Atlantic Magazine* published an article entitled *Parents Gone Wild: Drama Inside D.C.'s Most Elite Private School.* The story's about Sidwell Friends School, the Harvard of DC private schools whose Quaker motto is "Let the light shine out from all."

Bright lights sometimes illuminate the worst in people. The article details the shocking and over-the-top behavior of some of the school's parents, which has led to 2/3 of the school's counselors leaving their jobs. Attempting to help their children get a leg up in the college admissions competition, parents at Sidwell Friends School have engaged in what the school's headmaster calls "offensive conduct."

Among the excessive behaviors, parents have verbally assaulted school employees, secretly recorded conversations with teachers, made badgering phone calls to counselors from blocked phone numbers. Some parents have even circulated damaging rumors about other parents' children in order to give their own children an advantage over their peers.

As one college dean of admissions explained it:

"When you're talking about the love a parent has for their son or daughter, the plan they have for their child and all the work they've done towards that plan—it can lead to some pretty wild and inappropriate behavior. You could choose to focus in on the crazy behavior, or you could choose to see the parent's love behind it all. Either way, if you get in the way of that kind of love, if you get in the way of what a parent has planned for the child they love without condition, watch out."

If you get in the way of what the Father has planned for the Son...

That's it.

You and I—the baptized—we're not in this parable.

We're not.

We're so hard-wired to turn the good news of grace into the grim pills of religion that we go to Jesus' parables asking what we must do, or we leave Jesus' parables worrying about we're not doing. In doing so, we turn the Gospel into the Law; such that we miss completely the fact that, according to Jesus himself, we're not in the parable.

Yet.

We're not in the parable—yet.

Jesus told us at the top of the story. In response to the chief priests and the Pharisees who begrudge his relationship with the Father—his *relationship* with the Father—Jesus says the Kingdom of God is like ... what?

The Kingdom of God is like a King who gave not just a party but a wedding banquet.

A wedding feast for his Son.

His Son to be married to whom?

We're not in the parable—yet.

You and I, and all baptized believers, we're still waiting in the wings, offstage.

We're not in the parable.

We're in the parlor.

A friend's putting a finishing gloss on our fingernails while the curling iron gets hot and the string quartet warms up and the photographer shoots some candids of everyone getting ready and the white dress hangs uncovered from the curtain rod.

This isn't a horror story about what God will do to you if you don't get your act together and get your ass to his party.

No, for you—this is an absurd romantic comedy about the wildly excessive, inappropriate lengths the Loving Father will go to have every last detail of the party perfect, every seat filled, and everyone dressed to the nines with the custom-tailored clothes he's given away to every undeserving guest to celebrate his Son's marriage.

To you.

All are invited, but not all will accept the invitation—the whole world is invited to celebrate at Chez Yahweh, celebrate the Father's Son's marriage.

To you.

No wonder he acts so bezerk.

This parent has planned this party for his Son since before the foundation of the world, the Bible says.

Watch out if you frustrate this Father's feast-going.

He's not going to let anything get in the way of a five-star celebration for his Son's marriage *to you*.

Jesus left it assumed and unsaid in this story because he's already said it.

I go to prepare a place for you, and I will come again and take you to myself so that where I am you will be also, Jesus already promised. That's wedding language.

In my Father's house there are many mansions, Jesus promises. That's wedding language.

I am the way, the truth, and the life; no one comes to the Father except by me—that's wedding language too.

Not to mention, the word Jesus uses today for wedding banquet, *gamos,* guess the other place in the New Testaments it gets used—the freaking climax of the Bible, at the very end of the Book of Revelation where the angel declares "the marriage supper of the Lamb has been made ready" and Christ comes back to his Church who is prepared for him as what?

As a bride for her bridegroom.

So, Eldon, I don't know if you're here today or not, but What Would Jesus Do?

Welcoming the stranger, clothing the naked, feeding the hungry—that doesn't even begin to scratch the surface.

Because Jesus the Bridegroom would take his hand and pick him up and carry him across the threshold and say "My Beloved, let's dance."

Hear the good news—

You're not the one who blows off the party.

You're not the do-gooder who's too busy to attend the party

You're not the eyesore who wears the wrong garment to the party.

Though at times you might resemble all of the above, you're not any of them.

Because the party's for you.

By your baptism—

A promise signed by the Father and sealed in the Son's blood and delivered to you by water through the Holy Spirit, you are the betrothed.

You are free to do the things that Jesus did, and you are free not to worry about how little you're doing or how much you're leaving undone.

Because what God has joined together no one—not even you in your pathetic every day run-of-the-mills sins—can tear asunder.

No, you are his.

And with all that he is and all that he has, for better, for worse, no matter if your faith feels rich or if it is poor, he will cherish you.

This is his solemn vow.

Performance Anxiety
Matthew 25:14-30
Jason Micheli

Hey—

Hey, you got a flashlight? Or, even a match?

Yeah, I figured as much.

You can call me #3. No, I was never a *Next Generation* fan, why?

What about ear plugs? I'd give a kidney and my last pair of clean undies for some ear plugs. I mean, that gnashing sound is one thing.

If you've ever been married, then it doesn't take too long to get used to that sound of gnashing teeth.

But, the weeping? The weeping can mess with your head after a while. And, because of the darkness, because you can't see anyone, after a while you start to think the weeping is in *your* head. That, it's you. That, you're the one weeping.

You know that Groucho joke about how I'd never want to belong to any club that would have someone like me as a member?

Yeah, that's this place.

With the weeping and gnashing, you'd expect it to be a lot louder than it is. Instead, it's just creepy quiet. And, even though it's dark, you can just feel it—there's a lot of people here.

A lot of people, though not the ones you'd expect. I haven't bumped into one atheist, adulterer, or a TMZ reporter.

I mean, sure, Vladimir Putin is here; he keeps trying to assure Charlie Rose that he can influence a Divine election.

But, other than them and Justin Bieber, nobody here are the sorts of people you'd expect to find here.

Mostly, they're all people just like me. Just as surprised to be here as I am.

I suppose that's the money question, isn't it?

Why am I here?

So—

Just before my Master went away, he tells us a story—my Master was always telling stories. To people who weren't his servants, he never spoke anything but stories.

He told one story about a kid who wished his old man dead, cashed in his inheritance, then left home, and blew all the money at the MGM.

And, when the kid comes crawling back home, what's the father do?

The father blows even more cash—that would've been for his well-behaved, older brother's inheritance—on a "welcome home" party.

I know, *right?*

My Master told another story about a shepherd who had one hundred sheep and goes off and abandons ninety-nine of them to search for the one sheep who wandered away from the flock.

It's like that Woody Allen joke. Those who can't do, teach. And those who can't teach, shepherd.

My Master was always telling stories like that. I mean, my Master was killed—like he was determined to get himself killed—because, of the stories he told.

And, just before my Master went away on a journey, he tells us a story about another master, who had three servants.

The master gives the first servant five talents, and the master gives his second servant two talents—and one talent is worth about twenty years' income, so we're talking a crazy, prodigal amount.

It's like this master is forsaking everything for them before he leaves.

It's like he's dying to his riches, pouring out everything that's his, for their sake.

Even the master's third servant, who gets a single talent, gets more cash than he'd ever seen in his life, more than he could possibly know what to do with.

And that's the thing.

That's what I'm thinking as the Master is telling this story about a master.

What kind of fool would risk wealth like that on "nobodies" like them? I mean, at least Lehman Brothers knew how to handle money.

And, what kind of bigger fools would take that master's treasure and jeopardize it? Gamble on it?

But, in the Master's story that's what the master's first two servants do, and lucky for them (or lucky the master came back when he did), because they both managed to double their investment.

Five talents become ten and two talents becomes a fourscore gross.

Just the two of them turned those gifts into the equivalent of three hundred years' worth of wages.

And, their master praises them for it, "Well done, good and faithful servant."

The third servant, though—the one with the single talent that was still worth a fortune—he does the prudent, responsible thing.

He buries his master's talent in the ground, which is what you did in those days.

Don't forget, usury, lending at interest, was against God's Law. It violated the Commandments. So, investing that single talent or saving it in a bank account would've been as Bible-bad as spending it on prostitutes or Bacon Bits.

By not investing his master's money, I'm thinking this third servant's doing the faithful, biblical thing, right?

Wrong.

In my Master's story, when the master returns, he calls this third servant "wicked."

And "lazy," which might surprise some of you who think my Master's so warm and fuzzy it had to have been a huge misunderstanding that got him crucified.

No, my Master says that master calls his servant "wicked and lazy."

Pretty harsh, right?

That's what I thought, too. Then, this master ships his servant off to the outer darkness where there is nothing but weeping and gnashing of teeth.

At the time, I thought "outer darkness" was just a rabbinic euphemism for Cleveland, but it turns out I was wrong.

So, just before my Master went away he tells this story, and, sure, it didn't make much sense to me, but that's how it was with most of his stories.

Still, because it was one of the last stories he told before he went away, I figured it was important, so I tried to live my life according to it.

I tried to produce with the financial blessings the Master gave me. I didn't try to hide my stinginess behind caution or prudence. I took some risks for a higher yield, and other than a few shares of Uber and Redskins season tickets, I never wasted the wealth God gave me.

I earned as much as I could, so that I could give as much as I could.

That's the point of the story, right? A rising tide lifts all boats? Trickle down blessings?

But then—

When I saw the Master again? When he came back again to judge the quick and the dead?

No gold watch.

No, "My servant is good and faithful," bumper sticker.

Not even a Starbucks gift card.

No, instead I end up here, which I assume is the outer darkness. If there's a sign, it's not like I can read it. But there's definitely weeping and if that sound's not teeth gnashing, then someone should call a plumber.

I guess this is better than being cut up into tiny, little pieces—that's what happened to the fall guys in one of the Master's other stories.

And, maybe, it's better than what I would've guessed it to be like, fire and brimstone. But, it's God-awful cold here in the darkness.

And, for as crowded as it is, it's terribly lonely.

What day is it anyway? Or, year even?

I don't know how long I've been here, but it's still hard to believe I ended up here.

Or, not hard to believe at all, I guess.

The truth is-

How I heard my Master's story reveals an awful lot.

About me.

It shows how captive I was to money that I just assumed my Master's story was about money. If it's possible to see anything clearly in the dark, it's obvious to me now.

I really believed the only real, realistic wealth in the world was cold, hard cash. Not only did I believe it made the world go around, made me "successful" and made my family secure; I believed you needed it to change the world.

I really believed that you can't change the world one person at a time from the inside out.

I really believed that the only real change in the world comes through political change and, ever since Citizens United, that sort of change takes more than your spare change.

Like I said, it shows how captive I was to money that I just assumed my Master's story was about money.

Now, in the darkness, I can see the light. Or, see how stupid I was.

Why would I think he was talking about money? As though my Master subscribed to the Wall Street Journal. He didn't even HAVE money!

This one time—right after he told this story, actually—some hypocritical clergy (which might be redundant) tried to trap my Master with a question about taxes. And, he tries to answer them with an illustration.

So, he asks them if any of them have any money on them, as a sort of visual aid.

He asks them if they have any money on them. Because, he doesn't. He doesn't carry it, he doesn't have it, and he doesn't think the odds are in the favor of those who do have it.

He doesn't have anything positive to say about money at all, for that matter.

So why—how could I be so dumb—would I ever think my Master's story was really about *money*?

What would a Master like mine be doing telling a story like that?

What does it say about greedy, unimaginative me that when I heard this story, I just assumed it was about money? And making more of it. And, being rewarded for making more money. And, being encouraged to go make still more money.

What would a Master like mine be doing telling a story that just reinforced all the other stories we tell ourselves?

How could I be so blinded by greed that I didn't see the obvious?

The master in this story is supposed to be my Master.

And money—talent—that's not the treasure he gave us before he went away.

I don't know how I missed it before. He wasn't vague or coy.

The gifts the Master left us before he went away weren't cash and coin, or CODs.

No, he gave us bread and wine.

He left us water, for baptism.

He taught us how to pray.

He spent *fifty* days after Easter teaching us how to interpret Scripture.

And, he passed on to us his promise of absolution, giving us the authority—which only God has the authority to do—to forgive people's sins.

Before he went away, my Master gave us wisdom and knowledge, faith and prophecy, healing and miracles, and love.

Which is just another way to say that the gift he gave us, to each of us his servants, is the Holy Spirit.

And, sure, that gift comes to each of us in different amounts, but for each of us, the gift is more than enough.

More than enough—

To shape communities of mercy.

More than enough—

To announce his grace in places of conflict and suffering.

More than enough—

To teach that he is not dead, that he's a Living Lord, and that he is at work in our world even now, setting captives free, lifting up the lowly, and bringing down the proud and the powerful.

What he gave to us before he left, it's more than enough.

More than enough—

To bear witness that he is the only good and faithful servant whose perfect obedience has been reckoned as our own and *therefore, by His Grace, we have been set free to imitate him without any sort of performance anxiety, whatsoever.*

The gift comes to each of us in different amounts, but for each of us, the gift is more than enough for us to proclaim that he has taken away the handwriting that was against us, and it's more than enough for us to apprentice people into living lives that make his grace intelligible.

Even the servant with one gift—a grandma with the ability to pray, say, or a mother too busy to do anything but receive the bread of life in her hands, or a spouse focused solely on forgiving their spouse—even that servant is sitting on a fortune large enough to change the world, one person at a time, from the inside out.

That's what my Master wanted us to know before he went away.

Shoulda, woulda, coulda.

It wasn't until I was shocked to wind up here, buried in the darkness, that the shock of my Master's story finally hit me.

Think about it.

After spending so much time with his master, one of the master's servants still doesn't really know his master. He thinks his master is a hard, harsh master, and misunderstanding who his master is determines what he does with what the master has given him.

He hides the gift.

And then when the master returns, he tries to give it back. "Here," he says to his master. "Have what belongs to you," as though he doesn't realize that, as a servant—a slave—he belongs to the master, too.

The single talent is the master's possession, sure, but he's the master's possession, too.

There's nothing in the story that's not possessed—that's the key to the story!

The servant in the story misunderstands his relationship with the master completely; he doesn't understand that he's the master's valuable possession.

Not understanding who his master is and who that makes him, he fails to understand that the gift the master has given him—it's not something he has to do in order to please his master.

It's something he gets to do, because he has been made a participant in his master's pleasure.

The servant's work is not a gift he must offer back to his master in order to please his master.

The servant's work is, itself, a gift from the master who is already pleased with his servant.

Not understanding who his master is and who that makes him, it ruins all the fun! It turns the adventure of servanthood into an obligation.

It turns the zero-risk opportunity of the master's gifts into a high-risk burden that feels better buried away underfoot.

Here's the punchline.

There's only one servant like that in the story, but there's not only one servant like that.

There's only one servant like that in the story, but there's more than one servant, who so misunderstands the Master, they think a servant's work is a gift we must give to the Master to please him, rather than a gift given to us from a Master who is pleased with us.

There's only one servant like that in the story, but there's more than one servant who so misunderstands the Master, so mistrusts that they're the Master's prized possession—that nothing can take that status away—they bury away the gifts the Master gives them or they bear those gifts like a burden.

There's more than one servant like that.

Or else, I wouldn't be here, gnashing my teeth, weeping. The joke's on me.

Turns out, all my "sin" boiled down to unbelief.

A lack of faith in my Belovedness.

In the story, the master says to his servant, "You wicked and lazy slave! You knew, did you, that I reap where I did not sow, and gather where I did not scatter? Then, you ought to have invested my money with the bankers, and on my return, I would have received what was my own, plus some."

But—take it from me—what the master says in real life sounds more like:

After all the time you spent following me? Worshiping me? Learning from me? Hearing my Gospel? Eating in bread and wine my promise that I'm FOR YOU?
Still, you don't know me? You refuse to take me at my Word—that you are my beloved?
After I've given you all the gifts you need to do everything, I've taught you to do, you don't?
You don't do anything with the gifts I've given you?
Because, you're afraid of failing?
Because, you're afraid of me?
You can't even mess it up—there's no one keeping score, you're baptized; you've been handed my own permanent perfect record—but, still you don't bother with the gifts I gave you? What were you thinking? Whose job did you think it was?
My Kingdom is by Grace, yes.
And my Grace is free, yes.
But Grace is just an idea, if it remains invisible.
Evangelism requires exemplification.

Without witnesses, it's just words.
This Word took flesh, and it never stops needing to be put in the flesh.
I gave you these gifts.
And then, I invited you into the crazy, good fun of making my Grace visible.
But you still don't take me at my word?
You think I'm such a hard, harsh Bookkeeper that you bury my gifts in a deep, dark hole?
If that's where you think my precious belongings belong, then fine—but they're incomplete with you joining them there—you're my precious belonging too.
Outer darkness, for you.
You're sure you don't have any ear plugs you could spare?
No?
Well, make sure you pack some for yourself.
I mean, obviously I'm not a gambling man, but if I had to make a bet, you might here, too, someday.

Inescapable
Luke 17:1-10
Taylor Mertins

I don't like that this is true, but people are more often drawn to church out of problems than out of successes. People don't usually wake up the morning after receiving a raise to think, "You know what, I'm gonna swing by the church today." No, people usually come by when they find out they're being fired.

Which, to be honest, is probably a good thing. After all, the church is not a museum for saints but a hospital for sinners. It is here at church that we can finally dispense with all of the pretending and can admit the condition of our condition.

And our condition is bad.

Here's just a sample of some of the headlines this week:

"One in Ten Older Adults Binge Drink Regularly"

"Father Forgets Twins in Hot Car for Eight Hours Resulting in Their Death."

"Two American Mass Shootings in 24 Hours and the Third in a Week."

And we need not even look in the newspapers or on our favorite channels at night to see how messed up this world is; how messed up we are. Just take a drive down Route 1 for a little while and take in what you can see. We are stumbling, and in our stumbling, we are causing others to stumble.

So, what should we do about it?

Well, I've been thinking, and it's by no means an easy-to-handle solution, but I think it will largely take care of our problems. I've lined the back of our sanctuary with dozens of metal buckets, and with each bucket you can find a bag of quick dry cement. After the benediction at the end of the service, we're each going to take a bucket with cement down to the river, and we are going to make sure that none of us cause anyone else to stumble ever again.

Amen?

Now, before you start throwing your tomatoes, I stole that idea from Jesus. "Occasions for stumbling are bound to come, but woe to anyone by whom they come! It would be better for you if a millstone were hung around your neck and you were thrown into the sea than for you to cause one of these little ones to stumble."

So, who's ready to head down to the water with me?

Jesus is right. It is inevitable that scandals will come.

I know that sounds different than "occasions for stumbling" because it is different. But in Greek the word is our word for scandal. And the words we use are important.

Throughout the New Testament "scandal" is used when referring to something that occasions sins or temptation. But it is also used in reference to the cross of Christ. As in, to the weakness and foolishness of the method of salvation at work in the death and resurrection of Jesus.

It is absolutely a scandal to cause someone else to sin in their life. But it also absolutely a scandal that God chose to come into the world and die in order that we might live.

Which leaves us with a difficult question—What kind of scandal are we really talking about?

I mean, if you want to take Jesus literally here, while recognizing that each of us in ways both small and large have caused others to sin, then we can all throw ourselves into the Occoquan, but that doesn't sound like good news. In fact, it sounds like the worst news.

Let us, then, at least entertain the thought that the scandal mentioned here by Jesus isn't as we've so often heard it. Instead, perhaps the scandal that causes us and other to stumble isn't our own sin, though it certainly can, but the greatest scandal of all is the scandal of the cross.

Our sins are absolutely inescapable in this life, at least that the way we act regarding our sin. We label people by their faults and failure and those labels follow those people until the end of their days. But, in the same way, the cross of Christ is inescapable as well.

We then could read the verse in question differently: It would be better for someone to meet a violent end than to make someone else believe in a grace that requires them to do something to earn grace.

The cross stands as an uncomfortable and unwavering reminder that you and I don't need to do a thing for it. And yet so much of what we do as a culture, and heaven forbid as a church, tells people there is always more for them to do in order to get God to do anything.

And that might be the greatest stumbling block of all.

Jesus, of course, doesn't leave it all right there and begins to teach the disciples about real and unending forgiveness.

The disciples, bless their little hearts, are just like us and when they hear the Lord tell them to practice this kind of forgiveness it cuts against everything they, and we, have ever heard. It is bad advice, according to the world, to continue to forgive people who keep wronging us. But in the kingdom, the truth is that only those willing to lose can ever really win.

If we insist on being right and being perfect and only surrounding ourselves with right and perfect people then, according to the Lord, we will be out of luck regarding salvation. Moreover, our lives will be downright boring if that all we hope and yearn for.

The disciples, in this circumstance, hear the word from their Lord and recognize they haven't got nearly the right amount of spiritual resources to keep forgiving people so they naturally ask for the thing they need most: Lord, increase our faith.

And the way we often treat their request is to assume that we need to ask for the very same thing. If we only had a little more faith then we could do the kind of forgiving work Jesus was talking about, if we only had a little more faith then we wouldn't cause other people to stumble. And when Jesus responds to their request with talk of mustard seeds, we hear that as an approval to start small.

But that feels like we're actually going backwards. Notice—they ask for more faith, and Jesus tell them if they had even less faith than they currently have, a mustard size faith isn't much faith at all, the preposterous and impossible would seem reasonable and true.

In other words, Jesus looks at his ragtag group of followers, looks at each and every one of us, and declares for the thousandth time, that even when it comes to faith, we don't have to be winners.

And that sounds like much better news than marching down to the water!

It can be downright exhausting to be told over and over again that we just need to have more faith. Lost your job? You need more faith! Can't get a date? You need more faith! Worried about the bills? You need more faith! Blah blah blah.

Faith is not faith if it needs to be stronger, purer, or greater.

Somewhere along the line we crossed our wires and we haven't really figured out how to put them back. We have these absurd notions, even in the church, that we've got these little faith meters attached to our brains, and that after a lifetime of accumulating more and more faith, that we get to go on to our heavenly reward.

But the truth of the gospel is that we cannot be saved by our faith any more than by our measurements of mortality or supplements of spirituality. All of our talk of self-improvement amounts to nothing more than salvation by works, which in the New Testament, is rejected over and over and over again.

It is a crying shame that we have fallen into the trap of thinking "more" means salvation.

Which makes the mustard seed actually crazier when we take it in light of Jesus' words and work. Maybe faith isn't even essential in terms of salvation at all.

I mean, what does a mustard seed have to do to do anything? Be buried in the ground and die. So, perhaps even if we have no faith, really, even if we say no to Jesus again and again, we still die and out of our death Jesus still raises us.

I know that sounds crazy, but Jesus is pretty crazy. Over and over Jesus speaks of the all of salvation, the all of the cross, and it's we who put numbers and figures on the all.

Now, of course we won't be able to enjoy the Supper of the Lamb and we won't throw ourselves into the music on the dance floor unless we say yes to it. But Jesus' party is inescapable. Even if we don't want it, as crazy as that sounds, Jesus' nagging invitation to the celebration will never ever stop. Not now. Not ever.

Which leads us to the final movement in the scripture, the last part of the parable—the returning servant. Friends, we can and have really messed this part up. We've read this as a call for there to be certain kinds of people with certain kinds of rolls in the world. In fact, slaveowners used to use these last lines to keep their slaves in their places, but Jesus is far craftier than that.

Do you thank your slaves for doing the work they were commanded? No, of course not. They are your slaves and they have a job to do.

Coming in the wake of the scandal of the cross, and unending forgiveness, and limited faith, the final movement here sounds like Jesus knocking the disciples over the head with the gospel truth one final time.

Remember the unthanked and the unrewarded slave the next time you expect God to delight in any of your little good deeds. We followers of Jesus have only got one real job to do that's worth anything at all and that's to die. Die to ways we think the world works, and in the end die to the life we so desperately cling to. Because in the end, that all God's needs from us. Everything else that needs doing will be, and have already been, done by God.

I know it stings, but I also know it stings far less than thinking about cementing our feet into buckets. I know we don't like to hear it, but I also know that if we were honest with ourselves all of us know, deep down, that we could never earn the salvation from God we so desire.

No matter how good any of us are, no matter what kind of list of good deeds we could present at the end of our days, it would never ever compare with what God's doing and done for us.

The greatest scandal over which we stumble is the cross, because it shines like a beacon for all of us to see that we don't deserve it, but that God did it all anyway.

My sin, oh, the bless of this glorious thought! My sin, not in part by the whole, is nailed to the cross, and I bear it no more, praise the Lord, praise the Lord, O my soul. Amen.

And All of God's People Say: "What the F@#%?"

Luke 16:1-8
Jason Micheli

I was sitting on a barstool in her kitchen when Diane exploded at me, "He'll get what he has coming to him!"

Diane was standing in her kitchen gesturing emphatically with one of those decorative plates you can order from television, the ones with Elvis, Princess Diana, or Frank Sinatra on them.

I was sitting on a barstool in her kitchen, because that was the only place to sit. Diane's new house was unfinished, a messy maze of boxes, sheet rock, and plastic drop cloths.

Her yard outside wasn't even "unfinished." It was "unbegun."

No driveway. No grass.

Just a swampy stretch of mud from the road to the front porch (which was, also, unfinished). A row of rain-drenched, useless bags of cement sat orphaned in the side yard.

Their mailbox leaned loosely in the mud like a pick-up stick.

The mailbox had a blue and green mountain retirement dreamscape painted on it. She'd calligraphed their names on the mailbox, "Tim and Diane."

Tim and Diane were members of a church I pastored.

Diane was one of the ones who, after my first Sunday there, told me how much better she preferred the previous pastor's preaching.

Already, I had mastered the subtle Southern art of passive-aggressive politeness, so I replied, "Bless your heart."

Which, of course, meant, "Watch it, lady, I just may throw you through the stained-glass Good Shepherd."

Nonetheless, Tim and Diane were good people and good church members. And, in the way of small towns and small churches, they were related to nearly one-third of the names in the church directory—a fact she later wielded like a weapon.

Many months before that afternoon in her kitchen, against all the laws of common sense and wisdom, Tim and Diane had contracted Bill to build their retirement home on a mountaintop overlook outside of town.

Bill, who every Sunday sat with his family in the Amen corner pulpit left of that same church.

Bill, who was friends with Tim and Diane.

Bill, whose family comprised yet another third of my tiny congregation.

Bill, whose wife, Jane, had also been one of the ones to tell me how much more she preferred my predecessor's preaching.

"Bless your heart," I said, grinning like the Joker in the pale moonlight.

"Oh, well. *Bless your heart, too*," she replied, pinching my cheek.

Diane had missed church for several Sundays, so one afternoon, I decided to drive out to their new, unfinished home.

In my pastoral naivete and religious idealism, I'd driven out there for some Law-laying, to talk high-handedly about forgiveness and reconciliation.

Because, her unfinished front yard was a sea of mud, I had to take off my shoes.

Sitting in Diane's kitchen, I quickly discovered how hard it is to strike an authoritative posture when you're wearing your Superman socks and when said Superman socks have holes in the pinkie toe.

As she unpacked her decorative plates, Diane told me what I'd read in the local paper. Bill had taken their money for their retirement home and used it to pay off debts 0n business endeavors.

Now, Tim and Diane's savings were drained, their retirement postponed, their nerves frayed, and their home unfinished.

I said something foolish about needing to hear Bill's side of the story. Diane swung around from the box she was unpacking and screamed at me,

"Look here, preacher. I've been conned, cheated, and swindled. There is no "other side" to this story."

When I was in high school, I made a little money helping a carpenter put up sheet rock, so I know. If it's true that contractors have a vocabulary all their own, then it's axiomatic that those who've been cheated by contractors have an even more vivid linguistic arsenal at their disposal.

Diane said a lot of things about Bill, mostly along the lines of what Bill resembled, where Bill could go, and what Bill could do when he got there.

By way of conclusion, she gestured with a Princess Diana plate and said to me: "All I know is, he'll get what he has coming to him. He's got to answer to the Lord someday for what he's done."

I said a lot of things about Bill too, mostly boring, predictable preacher-like things, as in Bill needed to make restitution, do penance, and seek forgiveness. But it never would've occurred to me to say something like: "Sure Diane, I know Bill's a two-faced, crooked liar, but just look at how clever he was at draining your nest egg from you! You could probably learn a thing or two from him."

But I never would've said something that offensive.

Of course, that's just what Jesus does.

In Luke's Gospel, Jesus gets accused of consorting with tax collectors, who were no better than extortionists, colluding with the Empire against their fellow Jews.

In Luke's Gospel, Jesus gets accused of spending a suspect amount of free time with prostitutes (maybe that's why Jesus never has any money on him).

In Luke's Gospel, Jesus gets accused of eating and drinking—partying hard—with sinners.

In Luke's Gospel, the well-behaved begrudgers of grace, accuse Jesus of condoning sin by the sinful company he keeps.

173

And proving that he would make a terrible Methodist pastor, who are all conditioned to be conflict avoidant, Jesus responds to the acrimony by *inflaming* it.

He tells all the good, Law-abiding, religious people that God cares more for one, single sheep that wandered from the shepherd than he cares about those dues-paying, do-gooders who never wandered far from their flock.

And then, Jesus watches his stock drop further when he praises lying, cheating and stealing.

Don't forget—

The chapter divisions weren't added to the New Testament until the sixteenth century, which means Jesus has just offended everybody by killing the fatted calf for the father's lost-then-found son and comparing all of them to his self-righteous older brother, standing outside.

"Father, I wish you were *dead,*" the son had said. "Give me my inheritance!"

And, Jesus says God is just like that prodigal Dad, who never so much as says "thank you" to the son who stayed and slaved for his Father, and kept the church—I mean, the farm—running.

Then, as if he's trying to get himself killed, Jesus doubles down on the insult. With the second-guessing Pharisees looking on and listening in, Jesus gathers the disciples together and tells a story, just for them.

This story—

This story is meant to press salt into the wound cut in them by *that* story.

"Son, you're always with me. But we had to celebrate and rejoice, because this brother of yours was dead and has come back to life. He was lost and now is found."

"An executive at Goldman Sachs," Jesus says, "gets a memo from his HR Department that one of his managers has been cheating the company.

The boss calls the manager into his office, confronts him, and tells him to clean out his desk by the end of the day.

174

As the manager is about to leave the office, the boss adds, "And, I'll be coming soon to take a look at your books."

Riding back down the elevator, the manager thinks to himself, "I'm too old to start over again. I don't have any other marketable skills, and unemployment won't cover the family budget."

And, before the elevator doors open, the manager has come up with his own "severance package."

He's still got the firm's credit card, so he invites some his best clients to a pricey dinner in the District, and over drinks and foie gras, he tells them that he's canceling the balance of what they owe his firm.

"Just write it off, and we'll call it even," he says.

He may not have a job but at least when the pink slip comes, he'll have a group of wealthy, grateful people to help him land on his feet, instead of on food stamps.

Jesus tells his huddled disciples this story, and he doesn't end it with any woes or words of warning.

No, Jesus spins this story starring a corrupt guy that would make Aunt Becky from *Full House* proud, and he doesn't drop one word of woe.

He doesn't even use the story to warn us, like Carlos Santana that "we've got to change our evil ways."

He doesn't tell this story, turn to the Pharisees eavesdropping in on him, and exhort them to give up their dishonest ways and follow him.

Instead, Jesus says, "And his master commended the dishonest manager, because he had acted shrewdly. For the children of this age are more shrewd in dealing with their own generation than are the children of light."

And all of God's People say, "What the f@#%?"

You know, I watched you all while the Gospel was read this morning.

You all stood there as if this parable made perfect Sunday School sense.

At least in the ancient Church, no one swallowed this parable as calmly as you did.

Even St. Augustine, whose pre-Christian life makes Mar-a-Lago Club seem like an Amish Community Center, drew the line at this parable.

Augustine said he refused "to believe this story came from the lips of the Lord."

Julian the Apostate, a fourth-century Roman Emperor, used this parable of Christ's to crusade against Christianity. Julian labeled Christians "atheists," and said the Gospel encouraged its followers to be "liars and thieves."

And, St. Luke evidently had trouble with this parable, because Luke tacks all these other unused sayings of Jesus to the end of the parable after verse nine.

Luke has Jesus say that we can't love God and money.

True, but it's beside the point when it comes to this parable.

Luke also warns us how the person who is not faithful in a little, will not be faithful in much.

Again, it's true, but it's not faithful to the scandal in Jesus' parable; it's like Luke's obfuscating to get Jesus off the hook for violating our moral sensibilities.

And, maybe, getting Jesus off the hook is what you're expecting from me.

Maybe you expect me to tell you not to worry—in the original Greek story, the dishonest manager is more like a Robin Hood who rips off the wicked rich to give the money back to the righteous poor.

Yeah, not so much.

If someone like St Augustine didn't figure out a way to short sell this parable, then there simply isn't one.

What the manager did was to lie, cheat, steal, and lie some more.

And, what does Jesus do—

Jesus points to him and says, "Gold star."

"All I know is, he'll get what he has coming to him. He's got to answer to the Lord someday for what he's done."

We all met the next week in the church parlor: Tim and Diane, Bill and Jane, and the church lay leader.

The *Book of Common Prayer* contains an ancient worship service in it called the *Reconciliation of a Penitent*, and if I'm honest with myself, that's what I envisioned would happen.

With my keen powers of spiritual persuasion, Bill would repent. As a group, we would draft steps towards penance.

I would urge Tim and Diane to begin the process of forgiveness. It would all end, I thought, without permanent animosity or legal fees.

Instead, one Sunday Bill would confess his sins before the congregation and commit himself to straightening up and flying right.

And then, I imagined, without a dry eye in the house, we'd end the service singing *"Amazing Grace,"* that saved a wretch like him.

And, of course, as the script played out in my imagination, my congregation would be considered a paragon of counter-cultural Christian virtues, the sort of church you read about in the religion section of the *Washington Post*.

And, I would be the hero, easily elected as the Church's youngest bishop ever—the *Doogie Howser* of the Episcopacy.

What went down, though, was more like *Kramer vs. Kramer* than *Doogie Howser*.

We gathered in the church parlor. Tim and Diane sat in front of a dusty chalk board with half-erased prayer requests written on it.

Bill sat in a rocking chair backed up against a wall. That criminally tacky painting of the Smiling (Kenny Loggins) Jesus hung in a frame right above his head.

I opened with what probably sounded to everyone like a condescending prayer. No one said, "Amen."

Instead, Tim and Diane exploded with unbridled anger and unleashed a torrent of expletives that could've peeled the varnish off the church parlor china cabinet.

And Bill, who'd always been an unimaginative, sedate, boring church member, when backed into a corner, became intense and passionate.

There was suddenly an urgency to him.

With surprising creativity, Bill had an answer, a story, a reason for every possible charge.

I sat there in the church parlor watching the inspired and genius way that Bill tried to save his own neck.

I couldn't help but to turn to Tim and Diane and say: "I know Bill bled you dry and lied to your face and robbed you blind, but there's just something wonderful about the way he did it."

No, instead, in the middle of Bill's self-serving squirming, Tim and Diane threw back their chairs and, jabbing her finger in his direction, Diane screamed at him, "You think you can just live your life banking on God's *forgiveness?*"

And then she turned to me.

To second her assertion.

To say "No."

"No, you can't."

"You can't just live your life banking on God's forgiveness."

But I couldn't.

So, Diane pointed her finger at me instead and with a thunderous whisper said: "After all the good we've done for this church, we shouldn't even need to be having this conversation!"

Then they stormed out of the church parlor.

And they caused even more commotion when they left the church for good.

Meanwhile, Bill just sat there with a blank, guiltless expression on his face and that offensively tacky picture of Jesus smiling right above him.

After an uncomfortable silence, I said to Bill, "Well, I guess you're probably wondering if we're going to make you leave the church?"

He squinted at me, like I'd just uttered a complete non sequitur. "No, why would I be wondering that?"

"Well, obviously, because of everything you've done. Lying and cheating and robbing your neighbors. It's immoral. We're supposed to be *the light to the world* not just *like the world*," I said, in my best *Doogie Howser* diagnosis.

And, Bill nodded.

"The way I see it," Bill said, "This church can't afford to lose someone like me."

"Can't afford to lose someone like you? You're bankrupt. You can't even pay your own bills, Bill, much less help us pay our bills. What do you mean we can't afford to lose someone like you?"

Bill nodded and leaned forward and started to gesture with his hands, like he was working out the details of another crooked business deal.

"You're seminary-educated right, preacher?" he asked.

I nodded.

"And, of course, you know your Bible a lot better than me."

And, I feigned humility and nodded.

"I could be wrong' he said, "but wouldn't you say that the people Jesus had the biggest problem with were the scribes and the Pharisees?"

"Yeah," I nodded, not liking where this was going.

"And, back then, weren't they the professional clergy and lay leaders?" Bill asked. "You know, like you and them two?"

"And, again you've been to seminary and all, but who would you say Jesus would be harsher on? Someone like me, who knows he's not good and thinks the Gospel is the shadiest, too-good-to-be-true real estate deal of all time? Or, someone like you? Or, them," he said, looking over at the parlor door where they'd left, "someone who's pretty good and thinks that makes them good enough for God?

Who would you say Jesus would be harsher on? Someone who thinks they're good or someone who knows they're not?"

"You slippery son of a...." I thought to myself.

"Sure, I know what I deserve," Bill said, rocking in the rocking chair. "But, that's why you all can't afford to lose me."

"I'm not sure I follow," I said.

"Well, without someone like me around church, good folks like you are liable to forget how it's lucky for all of us that we don't have to deal with a just God. Without someone like me around, good people like you might take it for granted how lucky it is that we all have a gracious God, who refuses to give us what we deserve."

I can't prove it, but I swear Jesus' smile had grown bigger in that offensively tacky picture hanging above Bill on the wall.

Maybe his smile had gotten bigger, because Bill was smiling.

And, I wasn't.

Look—

Stealing is a sin. It's the Seventh Commandment.

Lying is wrong. It's the next Commandment.

Greed is *not* good. It's the last of the Ten Commandments. It's all there in scripture. It's wrong.

The Bible says so. Sometimes, Jesus even says so.

But, why is it that when Jesus says he's come to seek and save *sinners,* why is it that we always imagine Jesus is talking about someone other than us?

Why is it—what does it say about us—that we get all caught up with the supposed "offense" of this story, rather than grabbing a hold of the Gospel in this story's silver lining?

The silver lining in this story is that the crooked manager's only hope is your only hope, too.

The crooked manager banked on the mercy of his master.

When he got found out, his master's compassion and generosity were his only hope for the future. His judge became his savior.

And, so it is with you.

When it comes to the stewardship given you by the heavenly Master—your body and soul, your money and property, your vocation and family—admit it, I see how you spend your time on Facebook—at best we're faithful, *a little.*

Go ahead and deny it—you're only deceiving yourself.

Sure, the story's offensive *if* you somehow think you're good enough.

I'm not saying you're all crooks and thieves.

I'm saying that even the best of us aren't good enough.

The Law accuses all of us.

Every single one of us—even the saints-in-the-making—fall short of the glory of God.

I've no doubt most of you are better than the corrupt guy in today's parable—probably because you (like me) lack his energy and imagination.

But the crooked guy's only hope is your only hope, too.

Your hope is not that you are better than others.

Your hope is not that God has been blind to your wrongdoing.

Your hope is not that your good deeds will somehow, in the end, outweigh your misdeeds.

Your hope is in the very One who will sit in judgment upon you.

For the One who will come again to judge the quick and the dead, is the very One who was willingly nailed to a tree to be judged for you.

Recall the Collect of Purity, as the prayer book calls it.

Almighty God is the Master "to whom all hearts are open, all desires known, and from whom no secrets are hid."

You're not going to pull a fast one on him.

But more importantly, he knows that you are His.

And as His own, beloved by your baptism, He will never deal with you justly.

Don't forget how these parables begin, "The Kingdom of God is like...." You see, it's not that God doesn't give a rip about what you do. It's that the God we call Jesus Christ will do anything—*anything*—to get what he wants, including calling a fraud like you.

More than Jesus?
Luke 16:19-31
David King

Would you all pray with me? Lord, you are the God of
surprises. Open us again to the surprise of your presence, for you
come first to those least deserving. And now may the words of my
mouth and the meditations of all of our hearts be acceptable in
your sight, our strength and our redeemer. Amen.

In the town of Bakersfield, there are two McDonalds, one
downtown and one just on the town's borders. Bakersfield is a
small, formerly industrial town that now sits on the backrow of
America. Sandwiched between the two McDonalds on the now
vacant streets are several churches, many in buildings never
initially designed for worship. Besides the McDonalds, the only
gathering place for the people left out of America's innovation are
the churches there. The churches sustain the memory of their
lives, a project very important when there is no one else to
remember them and give them the hope of a different life.

Jeanette is a native of Bakersfield, the child of immigrants
from Mexico. She runs a church by the name of Full Gospel
Lighthouse. On Sundays, they offer two services, one in English
and one in Spanish. On one particular Sunday, Jeanette had
invited a photographer by the name of Chris Arnade to come to
Full Gospel Lighthouse. He was working on a book called
"Dignity: Finding Respect in Back Row America," and he wanted
to interview Jeanette about her work with the church.

The English service was small and quick, but the Spanish
service gathered a larger crowd in the oppressively hot building.
After an hour, Chris leaves.
Once the service is over, Chris gets a text from Jeanette that asks to
meet at the McDonalds down the street from the church. It is there
that Chris asks her about her work in the church.
After hearing the story of Jeanette's former husband, who drank so
much that he left the family and became homeless, Chris asks the
question he came to ask: "What does your religion mean to you?"

Jeanette waits a moment, almost confused by what she considers a question with an obvious answer. She tells him without God, she would be lost. Without God, she wouldn't have peace. Without God, she tells Chris, she would be dead.

I think it is fair to say that the condition of Lazarus that Jesus starts the parable with is not one of peace. Like Jeanette, Lazarus has found himself on the back row of society, totally cast aside from the consideration of the high-powered tellers of Wall Street and Rome. There is no avoiding the fact that Lazarus, for all intents and purposes, is dead to the world.

The rich man, on the other hand, wears fine linen made of purple and feasts sumptuously every day. Not only that, but he is secure in his life. He goes to and from work, in and out of the gate, with the surety that he matters in the world, that the world needs him. He is, after all, wealthy. The rich man has learned to live his life from the safety of the world; he has learned to live as though God does not exist.

In Jesus' time, there was a strong association between wealth and the mark of God's blessings. The dominant theology of the time was one of prosperity, one in which the gaining of wealth was both an indicator of the presence of God and an entrance to the life of God.

You see, the rich man's wealth gives him access to the temple, to the priests, to God. The rich man was so wealthy that he could buy a goat for every sin he committed, and given the picture Jesus is painting, that's a lot of goats. The rich man is capable of making himself clean, of maintaining ritual purity in the eyes of the law.

Lazarus, on the other hand, couldn't even get up to walk to the temple. And in fact, if he had, he wouldn't have been allowed to enter. The Law would have precluded him from entering the presence of God because he had been made unclean by the dogs who licked his sores. Not only was Lazarus down and out, but he was quite literally precluded from the presence of God. Not only was he ritually unclean, but he could do nothing about his condition. In the rich man's eyes, Lazarus is hardly even recognizably human.

Enter death. Despite the rich man's best efforts at replicating the immortal banquet, death comes for both of them. The great equalizer comes onto the scene in a flurry of immediacy, and boom, we're in the afterlife. Lazarus is whisked away into the bosom of Abraham, and the rich man, having had what we can infer to be a funeral of opulence, finds himself in torment.

The rich man dies, and when he does so he is not one whit less dead than Lazarus. Neither of them makes it out of life alive.

That's it. That's all we are told. Lazarus and the Rich man simply end up where they are. When the rich man cries out in anguish to Abraham, Abraham reminds him that…well, he reminds the rich man that this is simply how it is. Abraham does not list off the times the rich man ignored Lazarus. Abraham notes Lazarus only as a foil for the rich man's experience. There is nothing of moralism in Abraham's description, because it is precisely that: a description, not a proscription. In the eyes of the rich man, there is no rhyme or reason for his anguish.

That's the rich man's rub. The distinction he made between him and Lazarus, it doesn't come through. Neither Lazarus nor he got what they deserved. Both are sinners. For all the rich man's gestures towards purity, he ends up in Hades. For all of Lazarus' impurity, ritual and not, he ends up in bliss with Abraham. The state of affairs after death is nothing but a reversal of their earthly existence.

That's the thing – the difference between the two figures is that Lazarus doesn't do anything. Did you notice? Lazarus doesn't speak a word, he doesn't make any motions. He, like the unjust steward from last week's scripture, banks on God's work, not his own. What we so often miss in this parable is the fact that its main character *isn't* the story's main character. The circumstances that make Lazarus' life a version of death also make it so that he is absolutely inadequate to the task of doing anything for himself, much less for God.

Lazarus' condition makes him entirely dependent on grace. And before anyone assumes that I am worshipping poverty, we ought to note that Lazarus' life is a living hell that I would not wish on anybody.

By the world's standards, Lazarus' life makes him so *un*deserving of God's grace. By the world's standards, Lazarus does not need to be saved – he is dispensable and expendable, a sinner caught in a net he has no hope of getting out of. And yet, Lazarus is raised into the bosom of Abraham. And yet, the world does not have the last word.

This is a parable about resurrection and undeserving grace. The rich man in the story has not understood that. Even in death, he cannot accept his position: to him, Lazarus is still a tool to be used. The grace offered and on display here is so offensive to the rich man – a grace that does not have favour that can be gained, but that is offered to even the most impure and destitute. In fact, it is a grace that is offered first to them.

The God who condescends in the flesh of Jesus Christ holds no regard for status. Or, if he does, it is the status of the poor. The morals of this story, the reversal of fortune for the poor and the rich, it stands true *only if* the poor man named Jesus is raised from the dead. The resurrection is not incidental to the ethics of the story. The resurrection is what makes the ethics intelligible, for it reveals the kind of God we worship.

That's why Abraham won't send Lazarus to the rich man's brothers. They are so set in living without God that even the resurrection will be explained away. The God who makes the dead live again with an unabashed grace simply does not make sense. But God abandons no one, not even the rich man in Hades. The word for "torment" used in verse 23 in the Greek means "the extraction of the truth." The rich man's torment is being confronted with the truth revealed by grace in the cross: the utter truth that we are dependent on God, not us, for our salvation. No one is outside the realm of such grace.

This is a parable that teaches us that such things as a resurrection, such things as underserving grace matter to our lives. If Jesus is not raised from the dead, and if he does not raise up the undeserving like Lazarus, then our faith is in vain.

When Jeanette told Chris in the McDonald's in Bakersfield that without God, she would be dead, Chris writes that he was cured of his atheism. He is not a Christian, but he no longer thought that faith was a thing used to explain away the world. Chris tells Jeanette that the kind of community he saw in the church and in the McDonalds is something that he has seen in much of America's back row. He asks her if she goes to the McDonald's often. She pauses and thinks.

"Our lives used to be centered around work and church," she says. "Now, it is centered around McDonald's and Church."

McDonald's is not where we expect to find God – but neither do we expect to find God in Lazarus. But the fact that we do should come as no surprise. We worship a God who has condescended to us in our own flesh, who rose from the death we proscribed, and who makes his presence known to us through bread and wine. When we gather around the altar to remember and celebrate the mystery of Good Friday, we are being gathered by a God who can make a church out of such bad Christians as ourselves. We are being gathered by a God whose grace can lift up someone like Lazarus. Our God is a God of surprises. May our lives celebrate such a truth.

Justice Is Blind
Luke 18:1-8
Taylor Mertins

The courtroom was eerily silent as everyone waited for the judge to enter.

The jury had been through the wringer answering particular questions that would determine whether or not they were fit to serve.

The lawyers sat at their respective tables with their clients looking over all their prepared statements and pieces of evidence.

The stenographer even sat in raptured silence with her fingers hovering over the keys.

When the bailiff ordered the room to rise they responded accordingly as the judge, dressed in black, made his way to the highly raised chair at the front of the courtroom.

"What's on the docket today?" He mumbled as everyone sat down again.

The clerk promptly carried over a stack of cases through which the judge began to scan, until he lifted his eyes above the rim of his glasses and looked at down at the plaintiff. She was sitting there in her Sunday best trying desperately to keep her smile as sincere as possible.

And then the judge blurted out, "Weren't you in here last week?"

She unfolded the hands in her lap and very calmly replied, "Indeed I was, and I'm still looking for justice."

And with that the judge ordered her out of the room so that he could get on with the real work of justice.

The next day each of the common characters went through their repetitive routines until the judge ascended to his perch and was bewildered again to see the same woman, in the same spot as she was the day before.

"Ma'am, how many times will I have to kick you out of my courtroom before you learn your lesson."

"As long as it takes to get my justice, your honor."

For weeks they went through this new pattern every morning, and eventually it started to wear on the judge. At first, he relished in his commands to the bailiff to remove the woman by any means necessary. But every day she came back, looking a little worse than the day before.

He had no pity for her, he was still familiar with her case and he knew there was nothing to be done. And yet every night he lay awake in bed troubled by her bringing her troubles into his courtroom. The black robe felt heavier and heavier each time he put it on, and he discovered that he was starting to develop an ulcer, which he attributed to the woman.

But then one night, the judge came to himself and realized that if he just gave her what she wanted, she would stop bothering him and he could be done with the whole thing. So he gave her the justice she was hoping for.

The end.

Jesus says that's what God is like. Not like the widow who persistently goes looking for justice. Not like the bailiff dutifully following orders. No even like the stenographer observing and recording every minute detail.

God is like the unjust judge.

So, I guess, it's good to be bad?

Jesus, here, breaks a lot of common conventions, particularly when it comes to storytelling or, dare I say, preaching. Jesus, unlike your esteemed pastor this morning, did not have the benefit of attending a highly regarded seminary in which he would've learned about the importance of using good examples of good people to show the goodness of God.

Instead, Jesus hands us this story in which God, as the unjust judge, is supposed to sound good.

I don't envy the judge in the story, particularly when considering the fact that the judge ultimately takes on two subjects the rest of us find diametrically opposed to one another. The business of grace and the business of judgment.

This is a tough dance for the church to do no matter the circumstances.

We want to be able to hold these things at the same time when they seem to be completely opposed to one another—we want to be gracious toward all people but we also don't want people getting away with everything under the sun—we want to tell people that God loves them no matter what but we also want to make sure they know there are certain behaviors that God, in fact, does not love.

And we know how the story is supposed to go. After all, the judge is in the business of the law and therefore should be just in his sentence. But in the end of Jesus' tale, the judge breaks all the rules of his vocation and actually seems to put himself out of the judging business altogether.

The judge is bothered not by any normal character under the law, but specifically a widow. To our contemporary ears we can still imagine the plight of the widow in this circumstance, but in the time of Jesus to be a widow was to have no hope in the world whatsoever. For a woman to lose her husband was to become a complete and total loser—no social standing, no economic prosperity, no property period. And yet, this widow refuses to accept her deadness in life—she shows up at the courthouse looking for justice and the hope of discovering some kind of wealth in the midst of her total poverty.

She really is dead, at least according to the values of the world, and she knows it. The widow knows, deep in her bones, that she has no hope in the world and knows that the judge will not give her the justice she wants, but she also has no other choice but to ask.

And, for reasons that appear suspect and strange to us, the judge decides to change his mind regarding the plight of the widow. We would hope that the judge would be moved by pity, or hope, or even faith, but Jesus plainly declares those things have nothing to do with it.

The judge changes his mind simply because it will make things more convenient for the judge. The judge is willing to be unjust just so he can have some peace of mind.

Jesus then continues by telling those with ears to hear to listen to the unjust judge!

Jesus is saying to us here, in ways both strange and captivating, that God is willing to be seen as bad, to let God's justice be blind, for no other reason that the fact that it will get all of us off of his back.

Jesus spins the tale and we are left with the bewildering knowledge that God is content to fix all of our mess even while we're stuck in our futile pursuits of moral, spiritual, financial, and all other forms of purity.

In other words: While we were still yet sinners, Christ died for the ungodly.

There are few sentences in scripture as unnerving and beautiful as that one. It's beautiful because its true and it includes all of us. But it's unnerving precisely because it includes all of us!

We might like to imagine that God is waiting around hoping to dispense a little bit of perfection like manna from heaven if we just offer the right prayer or rack up the right amount of good works.

But Jesus' story about the unjust judge screams the contrary. It's as if Jesus is saying, "Do you think it makes the least difference to God whether or not you are right, or if your case is just? Truly I tell you, God isn't looking for the right, or the good, or the true, or the beautiful. God is looking for the lost, and you are all lost whether you think you are lost or not."

This is Good News because, like the parable of the lost sheep, God's never going to give up on us. The problem that we don't like to encounter is admitting that we are, in fact, lost.

Jesus jumps from the story to some sort of moral with the declaration that God delights in being merciful, whether we deserve it or not. And more than that, God will be merciful on God's people *soon*.

This story is told as Golgotha and the cross get clearer and clearer on the horizon. This is God's mercy made most manifest. Just like the unjust judge, God hung up the ledger-keeping forever while Jesus was hung on the cross. The cross is God, as the judge, declaring a totally ridiculous verdict of forgiveness over a whole bunch of unrepentant losers like the widow, like me, and like you.

It is the stuff of wonder and awe that God chose to drop dead to give all of us a break. Like the widow's verdict, God was tired of the world turning to self-righteous competitions and judgments thinking it would lead to perfection. And while watching the world tear itself apart, God destroyed God's self rather than letting us destroy ourselves.

The cross is a sign to all of us and to the world that there is no angry judge waiting to dispense a guilty verdict on all who come into the courtroom—there is therefore no condemnation because there is no condemner.

God hung up the black robe and the gavel the day his son hung on the cross. No one but an unjust judge could have ruled in our favor when we don't deserve it. No one but a crazy God like ours could have been merciful to throw a party and invite the very people that we wouldn't.

And yet, the parable is not over. It ends with a lingering question from the lips of Jesus: When the Son of Man comes, will he find faith on the earth?

The implied answer, much to our disappointment and embarrassment, is no. This story prohibits us from believing that any of us is just enough for the judge. We struggle with faith. Not because we don't know whether to believe God exists or not, but because we can't believe that God would do for us what God did for us. Our faith trembles in the recognition that the us in that sentence is *us*.

We worship a crucified God, a God who wins by losing, and that's a hard thing for us to have faith in because we are part of a world that refuses to let go of our insatiable desire to win all the time.

And this really is the heart of Jesus' parable of the unjust judge.

The confounding nature of God's work has made this whole parable series difficult for me, as I imagine it has been difficult for many of you. The parables are challenging because

191

Jesus' stories run counter to just about everything we've been told over and over again.

We call the Good News good, but more often than not we preach it and receive it as bad news.

I can stand up here week after week and tell you that God is angry with our behavior. I can proclaim that God is so good that none of us will ever have a chance of getting close to God. I can spend all of my time convincing all of us to get our acts together in order to appease God.

I can even command you to fill the offering plates to the brim enough to get all of us into heaven.

But the one thing I can't do, the thing we almost never do, is tell the truth that God cares not one bit for our guilt, or our good deeds, or even our tithes. We can't rejoice in the ridiculous Good News that God has gotten rid of all the oppressive godly requirements we think are part of our ticket out of death. We can't talk about those things because it sounds too good or too crazy.

And here's the truth: God is indeed crazy, and so are we.

God stays on the cross instead of coming down and punishing us until we behave properly.

God has already given us more than we could ever possibly earn or deserve.

And those two things are really unjust when you think about it.

They are unjust because God, our God, chooses to be blind to who we are.

There's no better news than that. Amen.

There's Nothing You Can Do to Make God Love You Less

Luke 15:1-10

Jason Micheli

This week I did something I never do. I reread all the old sermons I've written on today's text. If the files on my floppy disks and USB drives are correct, then this is the fourth time I've had to preach on these parables from Luke 15.

The first time was in Charlottesville, at a small Methodist church behind the Downtown Mall: Hinton Ave. UMC. The church was only a few miles from my dorm, but it could not have been further away from the life I knew on campus. It was literally on the other side of the tracks, near the public housing complex and the Salvation Army kitchen.

It was the kind of church that was always an offering plate or two away from financial ruin, where the janitor's first duty every morning was to paint over a fresh coat of vandalism and where the sanctuary smelled of varnish and black mold.

The outside stairwell of the church smelled of booze and piss. Homeless men slept in the stairs at night, and dealers lingered by the stairs during the day. It was the kind of church where on Sunday mornings undocumented workers and welfare mothers and poor whites would sit alongside the few remaining blue-haired matriarchs who'd founded the church.

I was still a college student then, 19 or 20. I knew the pastor, Edward, from a summer camp where I had worked. He often guilted me into attending worship at Hinton.

One spring Edward asked me to fill in for him in the pulpit. Without really knowing what I was doing, I did.

Now, I was still a new Christian at that point; it had been only recently that faith had "found" me. It hadn't been that long ago that I'd been steeped in doubts and questions. I could remember what it was like to have life blow past me because I was trying so hard to run away from God. I knew what it felt like: to feel pain where others said they felt the presence of God. I knew what it felt like to be lost.

And so, did everyone in that congregation.

So back then, the first time I stepped into the pulpit armed with this scripture—with who I was and who they were—it was good news all the way.

When they heard the Pharisees grumble about how Jesus chose to spend all his time with sinners and outcasts, they smiled, and they nodded their heads and they said "amen" because that meant them.

When we heard the parable of the lost sheep, it was each one of us. I was the poor, tuckered out lamb, draped across my redeemer's shoulders.

I was the one so full of gratitude and relief that I'd been found that I vowed to never wander from him again. I was the silver coin lying in some dark corner of my life until the good woman who will not give up on me sweeps me into the light.

They were stories about me. They were stories about each one of us there than morning, and they were good news.

We sang "Amazing Grace" to close out the service, and we sang it with gusto. Some cried. Some men, normally too cool to sing along, sang it with the quiet plaintiveness of Ralph Stanley. Some women raised their arms to heaven and praised God in Spanish and others knelt over the altar rail as if they were falling safely into their own beds.

And as they left that morning one man even told me that if it wasn't for my earring and unruly beard I could be a preacher someday.

It was different the second time.

The second time I carried these parables into the pulpit it was at a small Methodist church in Jersey. I was older. I was no longer a new Christian, and my "lost" years were further behind me. Rather than a one-shot deal, I preached at this church every week. Instead of being a guest preacher, I was the one who wore the robe. They were the first people to call me "pastor" and they referred to themselves as my "flock."

They were good people. There were only about 40 of them, but they kept that tiny church going even though the odds were against them. The bills were always paid. Vacation Bible School was always offered to the community. Repairs were never put off.

And because they were my flock, I knew them.

I knew who read scripture to the shut-ins on Mondays. I knew who taught Bible study at the prison on Friday afternoons. I knew who took in foster kids, who cashed in a chunk of their retirement to replace the roof and who volunteered at the AIDS clinic in Trenton. I knew who responded faster than the EMTs when there was a death in the congregation.

They were good people. They were faithful and devoted and they cared about their church. And I cared about them. I think that's why I didn't much like these parables the second time around.

Of course, I could've just dusted it off, printed it out and preached that same sermon from Charlottesville. But there wasn't a lost sheep or a lost coin or a lost son in that congregation. They were the flock.

They were the ones who'd never wandered off and gotten themselves lost. They'd never strayed very far. They didn't need finding because they loved their Shepherd and they always had, and they had always worked to stay close to him.

The second time around I read this scripture in a whole new way, and I didn't like it. I mean ... this is no way to shepherd a flock, abandoning the 99 to fend for themselves while you chase after the one who keeps straying and pursuing their own whims and may not even want to be found.

What was I supposed to say?

Look, I know you all make sacrifices to be here every Sunday. You're faithful in your giving. You make sure the soup kitchen's never without volunteers, but the fact is all that rates less in heaven than one prodigal being dragged back to the flock. We call that grace. Isn't that wonderful?

Or: I know you all love God and you study your bible and your deliberate in your prayer life, but the fact is if Jesus were here today he'd rather be with somebody else.

In seminary we referred to that as "the scandal of the gospel" and in the comfortable confines of a classroom it sounded provocative. But within a congregation, to a flock, it just sounds insulting. It trivializes their devotion. Why should they bother? Why should they bother if what would make God really happy would be for them to run off and follow their own desires and then one day, eventually, come back to the fold?

That second go-round I hewed to the shock of Jesus' message instead of the sentiment.

We closed that service too by singing "Amazing Grace" but, I noticed, it was like the words got stuck in the congregation's throat, like we were all singing a song that didn't belong to us. And on the way out that morning, no one in my flock said so but I'm sure they all felt like I'd told them to get lost.

If the files on my USB are correct, then my third stab at these parables came about two years ago. In this pulpit.

Don't worry, if I were you I wouldn't remember it either.

It was fine, I suppose. No more than the usual people fell asleep.

That third time around with these parables, I was more interested in mobilizing you as a congregation, getting you out of the pews and beyond these walls. So instead of focusing on the coin or the sheep or the son, I pointed to the shepherd, to the woman. "That's who we are in the story," I preached.

"We're not called to forever rejoice in our found-ness. We're not meant to stay gathered here with the rest of the flock and do nothing until the Shepherd comes back. We're meant to do the searching, the finding, the looking for what is lost and precious to God."

Like I said, it was fine. Probably, we sang "Amazing Grace" that day too. And afterwards, on her way out, Charlotte Rexroad probably told me it was a wonderful sermon and he-who-will-not-be-named probably told me something quite different.

Reading through those old sermons this past week, here's what I noticed: they're all about me. About you. Us.

I'm the lost sheep.

We're the flock of 99.

You're the coin that causes much searching and rejoicing.

We're either the prodigal son or the resentful brother.

Our first impulse is to cast ourselves somewhere in the story.

By my count, this is my fourth attempt preaching these parables from Luke 15.

But it's my first time as a father.

This is the first time I've read about the woman who searches every corner of her house for that lost coin—it's the first time I've read that story, knowing what it feels like that when I lock the doors at night and turn off the lights what I treasure most in the world is tucked in bed beneath posters of Spiderman and Superman.

This is the first time I've read about the lost sheep knowing what that charge of panic feels like when Gabriel gets lost in the crowds and commotion at Tysons Corner.

This is the first time I've read about that father with two sons, knowing that no matter where my boys go in life, I will never let go of them.

This is the first time I've read these parables as a father. Here's what I noticed: these parables, they're about God.

Jesus isn't asking us to decide if we're the wayward sheep or an obedient member of the flock. He's inviting us to imagine what God is like.

I'm a father with two sons.

My son Alexander is seven years old. By most ways of counting that makes him our oldest son, yet, because he only came to live with us when was already nearly six, in an odd way he's both our oldest and our youngest son.

Alexander joined our family last fall. I haven't told you all much about that time. It's his story, and he should get to decide

197

how to tell it. But I want to share a bit of it because it's determined how I read and understand today's scripture.

When Alexander first came to us he'd already experienced more upheaval and loss and grief than any kid deserves. "Permanence" is not a word he would've used to describe family or home.

When he first came to us, he had no reason to trust that it would be forever.

In those first weeks and months, Ali and I had to work to reassure him of the unconditionality of our love.

Alexander had to know that we weren't auditioning him to see how good he was before we committed our love to him.

He had to know that there wasn't any rule that if he broke it all bets were off.

And I'm sure, in his way, in ways we didn't even notice at the time, he tried to reject us in those weeks, to push us away before we could tell him to get lost. Bedtimes were the hardest time. I even made up a song to reassure him. You don't get to hear that.

There was one bedtime last year when the emotions swelled up in him and the routine of reassurances wasn't working and my song failed to soothe.

And I remember holding him on my lap in his reading chair. The glow of his nightlight made his tears look orange and burnt onto his face. And I made him look at me, and I told him: 'There's nothing you can do to make me love you more. And there's nothing you can do to make me love you less.'

And I didn't think about it at the time, I didn't think about it until I read Jesus' parables again this week but I'd just taught him the Gospel.

Narrow Hearts. Narrow Minds. Narrow Doors.
Luke 13:18-30
Taylor Mertins

It must've been very frustrating to be the Messiah. Hey Lord! Can you fix my bum leg? Hey Lord! We're getting hungry, can you whip up some dinner? Hey Lord! What's the kingdom of God like?

Everywhere he went, through all the different towns among all the different people, questions just kept coming. And, bless his heart, Jesus responds. Sure, take up your mat and walk. Sure, we can eat—anybody got any bread or a few fish? You want to know about the kingdom? Hmmm...

You know what, the kingdom of God is like a mustard seed.

The kingdom of God is like yeast hidden in some flour.

Do either of those make sense to you?

Well, it seems like one of the disciples mulled over parabolic answers from the Lord for a few days before asking yet another question: "Jesus, will only a few be saved?"

Well, it's like a narrow door and, believe it or not, a lot are going to try to enter and they're not getting in. Imagine that the owner of a house has already shut the door for the night, and you go knocking loudly. He's not going to let you in, no matter how much you can claim to have done with the owner.

Today, we live in a world in which we are always walking on eggshells. We have to be careful about what we say, and to whom we say it, and even how we say it. And, especially in the realm of the church, we do this with an ever-greater degree of attention.

And can you blame us? We want everyone to know that God loves them. We want everyone to feel welcomed. We don't want to upset anyone.

But then what in the world are we supposed to do with Jesus' words about the narrow door? Because it sounds like whatever the kingdom of God is, it is inherently an exclusive endeavor.

One of my favorite theologians, Karl Barth, was once questioned about his theological position regarding universalism, an understanding of salvation such that all are saved.

And when pushed to respond his answer was this: "I don't know if I'm a universalist, but I do know this: I won't be disappointed if heaven is crowded."

I like that a lot—but how can heaven be crowded if, to use Jesus' words, many will try to enter and will not be able?

The kingdom of God is like a mustard seed. When mustard seeds get talked about in the church they are mostly known for their size. They are tiny. And it is from tiny things that great things come. That's all good and fine. But one of things we almost never talk about is that for a mustard seed to do anything, it has to die.

It has to be buried in the ground.

The kingdom of God is like yeast mixed with flour. When yeast gets mentioned in church it usually falls into the category of its hiddenness, or its reactivity in terms of making something new a la bread. But one of the things we almost never talk about is that for the yeast to do anything, it has to die.

It has to be buried in the flour before it is baked away.

Death has been stinking up all of these parables we've been encountering week after week. And the more Jesus confuses his disciples, the more he mentions death, the city of Jerusalem hangs brighter on the horizon and the view of the cross comes sharper into focus.

Death is, and will be, the mechanism by which God makes all things new.

And so, it is on the heels and very much among the theme of death that the question is asked, "Lord, will only a few be saved?"

Now notice Jesus doesn't answer the question. He just hears the question and starts in with another one of his bizarre and meandering stories.

Strive for the narrow door my friends—many will try to enter and will not be able.

It's as if Jesus looks out at the crowds with a twinkle in his eye only to say, "You bet there will only be a few that get saved. Many of you will go crazy studying for the final exam, an exam that you will fail."

Now, I know a lot of you well enough to know that this Jesus doesn't square up nicely with the Jesus in other parts of the Gospel story. We like to think of Jesus as the one standing with open arms, the one who reaches out to the last, least, lost, the one who even offers Judas a spot at the table.

And even our church, it can have all the open hearts/minds/doors it wants, but it doesn't make much of a difference if they only open narrowly.

Jesus goes on to add a little more flavor to the story with the aside about the one who refuses to open the door once it has been shut and the imagery of our exclusive Lord and Savior looks more like a divine bouncer standing outside of Club Heaven than the Good Shepherd who goes looking for the one lost sheep.

And yet the narrow door is precisely the image of the story, the one that stays with us long after our Bibles have been closed and put away.

The door is narrow friends, but not for the reasons we so often think. The door is narrow because the door is Jesus himself.

We've been saying this a lot over the last two months, so I apologize for banging on the doors of all of our brains with this repetitive declaration—the parables are primarily about Jesus, and only secondarily about us.

It is the Lord who makes the door what it is, with all of its narrowness, because we can't get through it on our own. For as much as it might make us cringe—the door that is Christ is inherently exclusive because it is not for us.

Jesus doesn't set up a long list of requirements meant to keep only the perfect inside of his grace. This is truly the only way to enter into the many mansions of the Father's house, and it's certainly not because we've earned a space or somehow gotten our name on the list with a smattering of good deeds.

We only get into the party because Jesus is the door.

For a long time, Christianity has been defined by its exclusivity—you have to do this, and you have to believe this, if you want a space at the table. It's an inherently narrow proposition. But the narrowness of the door in the parable actually comes not from being small or difficult. Its narrowness comes from the fact that it is so counter to everything we think and know that we are repulsed by it.

It has been my experience, and perhaps your own too, that people do not often hear what is said, but they hear what they are prepared to hear. Such that a parable about a narrow door immediately conjures up in our minds the innate difficulties of getting into the club rather than us actually listening to what God has to say.

It is so difficult to hear because it implies that this is impossible for us to do on our own, and we hate being told that something is impossible. We hate being told something is impossible because we are told throughout our lives that so long as we work hard enough nothing is outside of our grasp.

This is a particularly challenging parable because the narrow door that is Jesus lets in a whole heck of a lot of people who don't jibe with what we think the party is supposed to look like.

The whole last will be first and first will be last is actually frustrating because the lastness of the last is what makes them first in the kingdom—not because they did what was right, or because they earned all the right things. They are now first precisely because they were last.

And those of us who have done what was good, those of us who have earned all the right things by doing all the right things, we can't stand the idea that we've been put at the back of the line, in fact we wouldn't be caught dead at the back because we've worked so hard to be at the front.

And then here comes Jesus, who looks at all that we've done, or left undone, and says, "The door is narrow friends, and none of you are good enough."

This parable sets us up to be duped and radicalized. God doesn't want to let us into the house. No amount of banging on the door is going to do us any good. Even the desperate pleas of our self-vindication (But Lord I went to church every Sunday, I gave 10% in the offering plate, I fed the hungry, and clothed the naked, and befriended the lonely), none of it merits us anything.

But that's exactly where Jesus drops the bomb of the Good News. There will be weeping and gnashing of teeth when you all try to measure yourselves up to a standard of your own making and design. You will grieve all of your wasted energy, and all your accounts of self-righteousness. Because the door is too narrow for you.

AND THEN, the Gospel says, AND THEN, ONLY THEN, will people come from the north, south, east, and west to eat with God.

There are definitely two ways to read the parable, and there are two ways to preach the parable. In version one we all leave church feeling pretty crummy about our chances of getting in through the narrow door. We leave with our heads hanging low as we contemplate our sins, or our problems, or our lack of faith, and we wonder if we'll ever be good enough. There is a way to read and preach the story such that God has closed the door of grace and locked out those who do not measure up.

In version two, the door is still closed. But the closing of the door can also be read and preached in a way that the door God closes is the one that says we have to do this that and the other in order to gain eternal salvation.

While the world's firsts, the winners by all definitions, are out there knocking their knuckles bloody on the locked door of righteousness, Jesus is quietly knocking at the narrow door of our own deaths trying to get us to let him in.

Remember, this narrow door follows the mustard seed and the yeast. All those two things have to do in order to do anything is die. They have to give up being a seed and being yeast, they've got to let the old fall away in order to become the new.

And yet we live by and in and world that tells us we have to do everything on our own. There are systems and norms that are largely designed to show us how we will never be good enough. And then Jesus shows up to say perhaps the most radical truth any of us will ever hear: Don't worry about how good you are or what you've been able to achieve, I am the door, and I'm coming to find you.

This parable, much to the consternation of preachers and Christians who want to scare others into behaving better, is actually about the opposite; Jesus is not busily thinking up new and frightening ways to keep people out of the kingdom—instead Jesus is actively and forever committed to letting himself into our kingdoms in order to tear them down.

At the very end, Jesus says the we who are knocking at the doors of perfect living and measured morality are nothing but workers of iniquity. Our good deeds are no more capable of getting us into the kingdom than our bad deeds are of keeping us out.

Christ died for us *while* we were yet sinners. Not while we were perfect, and not even while we were repentant, but while we were sinners. There is nothing on this earth that can make God love us any more OR any less.

That's the scandal of the Good News, but it's also why we can call it good.

And lest any of us remain unconvinced of the narrow door becoming the obliteration of any door keeping us out of anything, let us end where Jesus does—the meal.

It is after the weeping and gnashing of teeth, or own refusal to live under the unfairness of grace for everyone whether we deserve it or not, its only after our lamenting of the old world, that Jesus speaks of the meal—the meal that draws people literally from all directions.

The feast is not a trickling in of guests who, after becoming the paragons of perfection get a special invitation to the party, but instead it is a flood of uncountable people who, for free—for nothing, will be drawn by the love of Christ to the ultimate party that has no end.

Or to put it all another way: I won't be disappointed if heaven is crowded. Amen.

He Refused to Come In
Luke 15:11-32
Jason Micheli

The feast was the father's idea, his decree. The feast was how he'd wished for everyone to mark the occasion. The patriarch of the family—he's the one who'd called them all to his home. As far as feasts go, no expense was spared.

The food laid out across the long table was lavish and decadent and appropriately precise: with bottles of reds and whites, trays of lasagna and scampi, platters of artichokes and eggplant and prosciutto and, for later, tiramisu.

This wasn't comfort food or a potluck.

It was a celebration.

And everyone had dressed for the day. Women wore fur and broaches and heels. Men wore pinstripes and silk scarves. From the size of the crowd gathered there, it looked like the whole town had been invited to share in the celebration.

Music was playing, but the smooth notes of Frank Sinatra and Tony Bennett could barely be made out beneath the din of all the 'good to see you's' and the 'do you remember the time?' couldn't be made out above the laughter and the clinking of glasses and the scraping of serving forks across chafing dishes and more than one person saying to another 'I never thought this day would come.'

This was last winter, and I'd made the long journey to return to my family's home in Cleveland for my grandfather's funeral. The feast was his idea. Everyone on that side of my family is nominally Catholic. Food is their true devotion. So, it was fitting that we should mark his wake not with sadness but with celebration.

We'd been driving all day—my sister and my son, Alexander, and I—and we still got there late. We pulled up and got out of the car, and as soon as my sister saw my dad she ran in her

206

heels to him and smothered him with a hug and a kiss, wrinkling his tie and making a scene before he could even get a word out of his mouth.

When she finally let go of him, he looked at me with indecision and then sheepishly motioned like he meant to hug me too. Almost reflexively, I shook his hand instead.

He looked at his watch. "You're late," he said, "I was afraid you'd gotten lost."

"I haven't been here in a long time," I said with trace amounts of reproach on my lips, "but I found it."

My son Alexander was standing in front of me, standing on top of my shoes actually, looking up. "Who's that?" Alexander asked with his trademark subtlety.

I stammered. "X, this is your Grandpa Mark."

"Aunt Lisa's Dad?' he asked me.

'Yes, Aunt Lisa's Dad."

Crowded inside were several limbs and branches of my family tree, most of whom I hadn't seen since I was a boy. In the years that had elapsed many of them looked as though they had swelled while others, in their faces and hair, looked thinner to me. They were like approximations of memories, like artist-renderings of the people I remembered.

I've shared with you all before how my father walked out on us when I was 11 or 12, and how for another dozen years or so we spoke not a word. For a long while, he was dead to me, entombed in bitterness.

I've shared with you all too how I reconciled with him, just before I got married. We talked, and we agreed to "wipe the slate clean." But we never wrote anything else on that slate. Our reconciliation was only that in the strictest sense; it hadn't led to a renewed relationship. I think maybe he still felt too guilty to pursue it, and I think I just wanted the peace of mind; I just wanted to be able to tell myself that I'd done my religious duty.

I hadn't gone there to be angry, not at the start. I'd even looked forward to it in a way I was only vaguely aware of. I'd even taken Alexander with me—to introduce him to them, to show them who I was now, to make them proud.

Or, to rub their noses in my own pride.

The first thing that set me off though was that hug my sister gave him. That she would reserve such extravagant gestures for him of all people, that she'd brought him a belated birthday gift that I knew she couldn't afford, that all it took for her to be filled with joy was for the three of us to be together—it ignited some dormant fuse in me.

It didn't help matters that as soon as I went inside what I heard from nearly every relative there was: "It's so good to see you. We're so proud of your Dad. It's such a shame we don't see more of you." Like it was my fault! Like I was the one who'd ran out. Like I was the one who'd drank away what might have been.

And then there were the pictures.

All around the party, set on easels, were elaborately arranged and framed collages of family photos. Each collage was arranged chronologically so that the first frame of pictures by the front door were all in black and white, set in Italy, when my grandpa was just a boy. Looking from frame to frame, from picture to picture, I started to grumble under my breath.

I grumbled because I noticed how somewhere between the third and fourth frame of pictures, I stopped being in them. It was like *Back to the Future* except this time no one had bothered to notice how I was disappearing from all the pictures, from family Christmases and vacations and just the ordinary moments. And an anger that had been simmering inside me rose to the surface.

If I'm honest, I resented seeing how my father evidently had his life together: how the bottle was behind him, how he'd learned to be a husband to someone, and how he was a good father to her children, how with my grandpa gone he'd inherited the family's mantle. And it's not that I'd never wish that for him. It's that I wanted contrition first. I 'wanted penance first. I wanted a list of "I'm sorries" written in his small, slanted cursive and I wanted them to fill up one his yellow legal pads.

"Let's go sit down and eat," my sister urged.

"Not right now," I said, "I'm not hungry."

It's the party that sets him off, if you read Luke's parable closely.

Whatever resentments the older brother was harboring, whatever anger lay buried inside him already—it's the singing and the dancing and the feasting and the rejoicing that send him over the edge. Why shouldn't it?

Ancient Judaism had clear guidelines for the return of a penitent.

Ancient Judaism was clear about how to handle a prodigal's homecoming.

There was nothing ambiguous in Ancient Judaism about how to treat someone who'd abandoned and disgraced his family. It was called a *kezazah* ritual, a cutting off ritual. Just as they would have done when the prodigal left for the far country, when he returned home members of his community and members of his family would have filled a barrel with parched corn and nuts. And then in front of everyone, including the children—to teach them an example—they would smash the barrel and declare, "This disgrace is cut-off from us."

Having returned home, thus would begin his shame and his penance.

So, you see, by all means, let the prodigal return, but to bread and water not to fatted calf.

By all means, let him come back, but dress him in sackcloth not in a new robe. Sure, let him come back, but make him wear ashes not a new ring. By all means let the prodigal return, but in tears not in merriment, with his head hung down not with his spirits lifted up. Bring him to his knees before you bring him home.

Celebration comes after contrition, not as soon as the sinner heads home. Repentance is more than saying "I'm sorry" and mercy is not without justice.

It's the party that sets him off.

Here's the thing: the elder brother, he's absolutely *right*.

The music was still barely audible above all the remembering that was going on. Most everyone had sat down along the long table, tucked napkins into their collars and started eating, chewing and reminiscing as though both were sacred acts.

Meanwhile I was seizing any excuse I could find NOT to sit down and join in the celebration: I fussed with Alexander at the children's table. I went to the bathroom—four times. "Oh, gosh, I forgot something in my car" and while out there judiciously eyed the pressure in each of my tires. I checked messages on my voicemail, and I looked at the photo collages, staring at each picture intensely, almost daring someone to disturb me.

With the crowd and the commotion, I'm not sure if anyone noticed.

But there was a chair near my Dad that was refusing to be anything but empty. I'm sure he noticed.

I don't know how long my abstention lasted, but after a while my sister crept up next to me. "What's your deal?" she asked me.

"I told you I'm not hungry."

"Well, just sit down then."

I didn't move, and I didn't look at her. I was staring at one of the photos. It was in frame five in the corner near the bathroom and the piano and the fake potted plant. It was a picture of my Dad on a golf course somewhere sunny with my stepbrothers.

"What's my deal?" I said and pointed my chin at the picture, "I don't have a picture like that. I don't have any pictures like that."

"I know," she said, "but he's here now, and he's right over there."

Preaching to The Preacher
Luke 12:35-48
Jason Micheli

Blessed are those slaves whom the master finds alert when he comes; truly I tell you, he will fasten his belt and have them sit down to eat, and he will come and serve them.
Prayer

The internet and social media have made us all hyper-aware of everything that is happening all the time. Because of these things we have in our pockets and purses we know what is happening, where it is happening, and before its over we can look through all of the comments about what happened and where.

Some of this is good. We are more connected with people all across the world than we have ever been. Because of the instantaneous nature of communication and information we have been able to help those in need, we've been able to prepare for things we never could've imagined, and there is an invisible thing uniting us in ways previously impossible.

But, of course, a lot of it is bad.

A teenager posts a picture and is bullied for the rest of her adolescence.

An adult is radicalized through forums to commit horrible acts of violence.

Older individuals are regularly belittled for not being up to date with everything that, by definition, is changing faster than we can keep up.

We create and consume so much information today that, regardless of our age, we can barely recite that which we have received.

And, in a strange way, we are made most aware of all that we are missing.

In some circles this is called the "instagramification" of all things. We flock to places of social media, more often than not, to show all that is right in our lives when so much is wrong.

We gather the family together for a picture while on vacation and post it for everyone to know and believe that we have it all together, when in fact the family was screaming and pulling one another hairs just to get the picture taken moments before.

And when we see these images of friends, or family, or even celebrities we can't but help to judge and measure our lives against what we see on the screen.

Jesus, in his strangely parabolic way, has us imagine that we are waiting for our best friend to come from a wedding. A wedding we weren't invited to.

Weddings are all over the place in the Bible and are particularly profound in the New Testament. Consider: Jesus' first miracle is turning water into wine at a wedding, and one of the last images in the Book of Revelation is the marriage of the Lamb to his bride the New Jerusalem.

Jesus, the master in the parable, the friend in ours, returns to us after a wedding. The story makes the claim that we are to be awake and welcome him in glory, and we will be blessed by his arrival because he brings the party with him.

Whether it's the master with his slaves, or the uninvited friends, it is particularly striking that the one who has no reason to do much of anything, desires first and foremost to sit down and hang out, with us.

Jesus is crazy. He, again and again, contrasts the ways we so foolishly live in this world by showing how the opposite, in fact our dying, is the only good news around. And to make matters even more confounding, according to the Lord the sooner we die the sooner we can celebrate.

Now, of course, the ways we speak about and even conceive of our own deaths is inherently problematized—and yet, as Christians, our deaths are particularly peculiar. For, we are already dead. At least, that what we claim in baptism—By Jesus' death in ours, and ours in his, we have conquered the whole rotten game of the universe.

The sooner we can accept that our lives have already been changed, irrevocably, for good, the sooner the party arrives through the door.

Therefore, we needn't even worry about being invited to the party, we don't have to lay awake festering over whether we've been good enough, or popular enough, or even faithful enough. Our salvation, the party itself, is never contingent on our ability to make it happen.

All we need to do is be like those who know the party is coming through the door.

It is the greatest thing in the world that our friend stumbles into us in the middle of the night, perhaps in the greatest of moods a few sheets to the wind from the wedding reception.

See it and believe it: He does not come with sober judgments about why we aren't good enough, or with grim requirements about what we have to do or how we have to behave to get a ticket in.

Instead he comes humming along to a song from the distant dance floor, perhaps with a nice bottle of red stashed under his arm that he clandestinely removed from the open bar, and before we can say much of anything he's popped the bottle and is dolling out a full assortment of finger foods to quench every bit of our hunger.

It's a strange story. One that we often ignore, overlook, or disregard.

But it is there, and it is very much here.

We are blessed by the risen Lord, for he knocks at the door, even in our deaths, and he comes bringing the party with him. And this party is not far off and distant in both place and time from us, the party is here with us, right now. It's just that most of us are too stubborn to notice.

To return to our own parable, we've got our noses so stuck in our phones judging our lives against the lives of others that we can't even here Jesus banging on the door.

And then Peter perks up: "Lord, is this story for us, or is it for everyone?" A worthy question, for we should want to know who exactly is supposed to be around waiting for the Lord's party to arrive.

Jesus answers the question with a question, "Who is the manager that the master will put in charge of his slaves, to give them their food at the proper time?

The previous parable is certainly for all, but now the Lord put some things into perspective; the disciples are given a job, and those who continue in that line of work, dare I say pastors, are supposed to know their job.

Now, before we continue, I must confess that we have arrived a strange precipice, one in which Jesus is telling the future clergy (in a way) what they are to do. And yet here I am, your appointed clergy, preaching about what God has told me to do.

So, bear with me for a moment.

Pastors, the disciples in charge of the slaves as it were, are commanded to trust. Nothing more, less, or else. Pastors are not called to know everything, or to be enigmatically clever all the time, or to be fully of energy, or even to be talented.

They are to trust that the truth is in fact the truth. The greatest truth of all being that salvation does not come from a particular way of living or being. Which is a good word to those of us living in a world while drowning in efforts toward whatever we think life is supposed to be.

Contrary to what the televangelists proclaim, and pastors of all shapes and sizes, and even this one in front of you at times, the church does not exist to tell people like you to engage in acts of superior morality with the expectation that salvation will be your reward.

The foolishness of God is wiser than that.

God, more often than not, chooses what the world considers nonsense in order to shame the wise.

God, more often than not, uses fallible pastors to remind all of us that its the nobodies of the world, the last, least, lost, little, and dead who bring about anything we might call holy.

And so, as the only pastor in the room, I feel what can only be described as a sense of relief. After countless years in which people like me have been made to feel that forceful preaching, and masterful obedience, and perfect extraversion with just the right dash of introversion, is the name of the game—it's nice to be reminded, here in this parable, that Jesus expects the preachers of the church to be nothing more than half decent cooks.

"Who then is the faithful and prudent manager whom his master will put in charge of his slaves, to give them their allowance of food at the proper time? Blessed is that slave whom his master will find at work when he arrives."

Food at the proper time. And, to be clear, we clergy are not gourmet chefs or even casino buffet coordinators, but just some Gospel minded cooks who can rummage through the pantry of the Word to turn out a half decent and nourishing meal once a week.

And we then could turn to look at the meal of preaching, the Word made flesh in a certain way, every week. But it's much better than that. Because the greatest meal of all offered by the church has almost nothing to do with the preaching. In communion we find the sustenance that goes beyond all imagining - clergy need only serve it to those who are hungry.

So long as all of us, we who come to the table, get enough death and resurrection in our diet, so long as we are reminded with regularity that there is nothing we can do to earn it or lose it, then we will be, as the Bible says, filled.

And I wish we could end it there, but Jesus has more to say to Peter and the preachers…

"But if," Jesus continues, "If the manager thinks the master is taking his sweet time in getting back, and therefore beats on the other slaves and get drunk, then the master will return and cut him into pieces."

This is the moment that you can can offer up a prayer of thanksgiving to the Lord that you're not pastors.

To put Jesus final words another way: If the preachers decide to take matters into their own hands, if they make promises they can't keep, if they abuse the weak in their midst, if they create systems in which people can earn anything for themselves in the realm of salvation, then they will be torn apart, from top to bottom, whether at the hand of God or by their own undoing.

Preachers, managers, cooks of the gospel, whatever we want to call them, are to do nothing more than sit at the foot of the cross with words of what God has already done. They are to share the meal waiting at the table, a meal prepared long before the preacher ever preached a sermon.

This whole parable, for the laity and clergy alike, comes down to trust.

Not a trust that God is going to come and sweep down and fill all the potholes in our lives, but a trust that God has already changed the game for good.

Trust.

And when we've learned to live a life of trust, whether we wear robes or not, then we are living the life of grace. And in the life of grace, one in which we know what has already been done—something that can never be taken away—no matter how many doubts we have, or waverings, or questions, no matter how happy or sad we may become, no matter how awfully we sin—we simply trust that someone else, namely Jesus, by his death and resurrection, has made it all right, we can say thank you Lord and that's enough.

Our whole lives, from beginning to end, the mess that we are, they're leading to our own inevitable death. And it's all okay, because we've already died. It is Jesus who is our life, he is the one who comes for us from the wedding feast, he is the one who comes to us with the celebration under his arm and wants nothing more than to party with us. Amen.

The Dirt on You
Mark 4:1-10, 13-20
Jason Micheli

Listen.

There was a man I knew in a church I once served. Andy. And if you had just one sentence to describe him, you would probably say that Andy was a hard man.

His eyes were as dark as pavement and his voice as rough as gravel.

He'd been a cop, and I've always wondered if his jaded personality came as a result of his career or if his career choice had been a perfect fit. He was a hard man.

One time I was in my office on the phone and I heard Andy's gravely voice in the foyer—not shouting but barking in his cop's voice: 'Get up. Get your stuff. Move on out of here. You don't belong here.'

I hung up the phone and I went to see what the barking was about. A hitchhiker—a homeless man—had stopped at the church earlier that morning, looking not for money but for a meal.

So, when Andy came into the church office that day, he found this hobo seated on a dirty, green army duffel. The man was eating ham and sweet potatoes leftover from a church dinner.

The door to the church office had a little electric bell that went off whenever someone entered the building. That morning, before the bell even stopped ringing, Andy had appraised this stranger and was ordering him away: 'Get up. Get your stuff.'

For Andy, the 'real' world was the world he'd retired from—a world where people will do anything to get ahead and where scores are settled not forgiven. For Andy, that was the real world not the world as it's described in stained glass places.

He'd grown up in the church…without every really becoming a Christian.

In his moments of need—when his dad had died, when he'd lost his job, when he'd struggled with alcoholism—God had not been the one he'd turned to. He had two daughters, a wife and a house. Andy was happy with his life but not grateful. And he'd be the first to admit he'd made mistakes in his life, but he'd never call those mistakes sins.

If you asked Andy if he was a Christian, without thinking, he'd say: 'Yes, of course.' But if you asked his friends or his neighbors, they wouldn't know.

Andy came to worship whenever his wife or one of his girls was singing. Every time he came, he looked like he was restless to get to the main event, which for him never came.

When I preached, Andy would squint at me, suspicious of the agenda hidden beneath my words. And whenever I saw Andy sitting in the pews, I would practically throw the Gospel at him every which way, like he was target practice, hoping that some Word would take root in him. Nothing ever did.

When I heard Andy barking 'Get up. You don't belong here.' I got up and walked out to the foyer and, in my pastoral tone of voice, I asked Andy: 'What are you doing?'

And Andy smiled at me like I was the most naïve child in the world and, with the man still sitting there on the duffel, he said: 'He doesn't need to be here. He'll only bother the old folks for a handout or scare the kids.'

And I said: 'This is a church. We can't treat him like that. Whether he bothers the old folks or not, whether he scares the kids or not, we've got to treat him like he's Jesus.'

My words just bounced off him like seeds on a sidewalk.

Listen.

There was a family I knew for a short time. I met them at the hospital in Charlottesville when I worked there as a chaplain. The husband and wife were maybe in their early forties. They had three boys. Their oldest boy, Chad, was 12 or 13.

Chad was in the hospital with leukemia. Except for occasional respites at home, Chad was in the hospital for almost a year. And during that time, I saw him and his family once or twice a week.

The afternoon I first met them they welcomed me warmly. We talked about what they did, where they lived, the friends Chad was anxious to get home to.

And when I asked to pray with them, they said yes, even though they were visibly uncomfortable about it.

When I'd told them, I was a Methodist pastor they told me that they were Methodists too. So, I asked if I should contact their pastor for them. They said: 'No, he probably doesn't know who we are.'

I asked if they had a small group or friends from church that I could call to support them and again they said 'No.'

They blushed and then told me that they'd gone to church a few years ago. 'We wanted to expose our kids to it' they said, 'but we never went any deeper than that. We never made it a regular part of our lives.'

I didn't really say anything. Then Chad's father added: 'We believe in God though. We're good people. That's enough isn't it?'

And because of where we were and the situation they were in, I said yes. Even though I knew it wasn't true.

I spoke with Chad and his family many times after that first afternoon. Every time I tried to do what a pastor supposed to do. I tried to model the presence of Christ. I tried to get them to articulate their feelings and name their fears. I encouraged them to affirm their faith and to identify where they felt God was in their struggle.

I tried, but I could never get past the surface things with them. And I think it's because they never let their faith get any deeper than the surface of their lives.

One of the last conversations I had with Chad's parents happened one winter morning. They'd just been given some bad news, a setback in Chad's treatment.

We talked about it for a while and when I asked if I could pray with them, they said: 'No. We've lost our faith.'

Now, it's not that I don't understand their feelings or empathize with them. And it's not like seeing one of my own boys in Chad's place wouldn't stretch my faith to the breaking point.

And I would never dream to say it to them, but the fact is that had their faith been a deeper part of their lives it might not have been so easily blown away.

The fact is they never let their faith take root in their lives. And when they got to a point in their lives when they needed a faith to grab onto, it wouldn't hold them.

Listen.

There was a man I knew in the first church I ever served. In New Jersey. Sheldon.

Sheldon reminded me a lot of the fastidious character in the Odd Couple.

He'd been a teacher, a principal and a professor. He'd served on township boards and city councils and task forces. He'd coached sport teams and led Boy Scout troops. He'd traveled all over the world. He had a family.

His life was a thicket of activity.

In the short time I served as his pastor, Sheldon was always asking me questions: What does the bible say about X? Is it true that Jesus…Y? I've always wondered…. Z, what do you think?

Initially I thought the barrage of questions was because he was an educator and, thus, naturally curious. But that was only part of it.

One Sunday morning, well before worship began, I met Sheldon for breakfast. It was the Advent season and Sheldon was the scripture reader that day.

The passage that Sunday was from the beginning of John's Gospel: 'In the beginning was the Word and the Word was with God and the Word was God.'

Sheldon commented on the philosophic language. 'What the heck does it mean?' he asked.

And I just said that it's John's poetic way of saying that Jesus is God.

Now that's a pretty basic concept, I thought, so I just said it kind of quickly, matter-of-factly.

But Sheldon said: 'What?' like he'd missed the punchline.

I just repeated it again: 'In the beginning was the Word and the Word was with God and the Word was God. It's just a pretentious way of saying that Jesus is God.'

Sheldon sipped his tea and he said, softly: 'I don't know why I've never heard that before.'

By the time he set his tea back down on the table, he was crying.

And I had no idea why.

I waited for him to say something. After a moment he told me how he had a PhD after his name, how he could point to schools he'd built, how he could rattle off the names of children he'd taught—teachers he'd taught, how his savings was flush with the fruit of his life's work and how his home was filled with pictures and trinkets from all the places he'd been.

And then he confessed to me:

'I've never given my faith a fraction of the time I've given to other things.

I've been a Christian all my life, but I don't know any more about my faith than I did when I was twelve years old.

I tell people all the time 'You'll be in my prayers' and that would be true, if I did. But I've never learned how to pray, not really.

I've been a Christian all my life, but my faith is the one thing in my life I don't have anything to show for.

I can point to kids who know math because of me, but I can't point to anyone who knows God more deeply because of me.'

The frankness of what he'd said winded him.

A moment passed. He patted my hand and said:

'It's not that my faith wasn't important to me.

It's that so many other things were important too.'

Listen.

I've known other people. I know some here.

People in whom the faith has grown and flowered; people whose lives are beautiful. And I don't understand them. It's like their lives are fertile soil for the Gospel.

I mean…Andy, I get. I meet people like Chad's parents all the time. Sheldon is me all over.

But genuine, truly humble, serving Christians—they are a mystery to me.

I mean—they live in the same world as Andy. They work in the same places as Chad's parents, and they have the same sorts of friends as Sheldon does.

But there is something different about them.

They love. They care. They go. They do. They give. They serve. They share. They embody. And if you were to recite all the fruit of their faithfulness they would be embarrassed.

I've known people like that. I know some here.

When the crowds press in on Jesus to hear him preach, I'm sure there were plenty by the lake shore who wanted to hear clear-cut, practical kinds of teaching: Do This, Don't Do That, Follow These Three Steps.

What Jesus gives them is stories. And Jesus never says it, but what he's doing is inviting them to consider who they are in the stories and who God is inviting them to become.

Let anyone with ears to hear: listen.

Scandalous

Luke 15:11

Taylor Mertins

The Bible is scandalous.

I mean, the first two human characters in it, Adam and Eve, spend most of their time completely naked until they decide to cover themselves with a handful of fig leaves.

The patriarch of the faith, Abraham, passes off his wife as his sister on more than one occasion to save his own behind.

And David, the one who brought down the mighty Goliath, killed 200 Philistine men just to procure their foreskins in order to present them as a dowry so that he could marry the daughter of King Saul.

Scandalous.

And that's just three examples from the Old Testament.

When Jesus shows up on the scene it gets even crazier.

He eats with all the wrong people, he heals all the wrong people, and he makes promises to all the wrong people.

For a while, in the midst of his ministry, he attracts all kinds of people. The good and the bad, the rich and the poor, the holy and the sinful, the first and the last. But at some point, the crowds begin to change; they start leaning in a direction we might call undesirable.

All the tax collectors and the sinners were coming near to listen to him. The tax collectors were Jews who profited off of their fellow Jews. They took from the top and made little nest-eggs for themselves while their fellow countrymen suffered under the dictatorial rule of Rome. And the sinners, well, just imagine your favorite sinful behavior and you know who those people were.

And they are the ones gathering near.

Not the respectable Sunday morning crowd we have here at church. Not the folks who sleep comfortably at night knowing their padded bank accounts are safe. Not the people who jockey to the highest positions in the community.

No, Jesus attracts the very people we would repel.

223

And the Pharisees and the scribes, the good religious folk, (people like us), they were grumbling among themselves and saying, "This Jesus is bad news. He not only welcomes sinners into his midst, but he has the audacity to eat with them!"

So, Jesus told them a story.

If you don't know this by now, well then let me tell you yet again, Jesus loves to tell stories. Everywhere he went, among all the different people, with all their different problems, he would bring his hand to his chin and triumphantly declare: "I've got a story for that."

And this story, the one he tells the grumbling religious authorities, the story that is probably best known among all the parables, is through which the whole of the gospel comes to light.

It is not an exaggeration to say that this is the most important parable Jesus ever told, and just about every time we retell it, we ruin it.

And it's scandalous.

Listen: A man had two sons. And one day the younger son gets the bright idea to ask for his inheritance right then and there. He didn't have the patience to wait for his old man to die before he received his due. And the father, inexplicably, agrees. He splits himself, turns it all over to his boys, he effectively ends his own life so that they can have what they would have had at his death.

To the older son, he gave the family business.

To the younger son, he cashed out his retirement package.

The older son remains at home, taking care of that which was entrusted to him, and the younger son, the one who demanded the inheritance, runs off in a fit of joy with his now deep deep deep pockets.

But it's only a matter of time before the younger son has squandered his early inheritance. Maybe he blew it at the blackjack table, maybe he threw it away in empty bottle after empty bottle, or maybe he spent it on women. Regardless it gets to the point that he is now far worse off than he was before he asked for the money— he steals food out of garbage cans at night, he sleeps under a tarp off in the woods, and he showers in the sinks at gas stations.

224

And then, one day, he arrives back to himself and realizes that he could return to his father and his brother, that they could give him a job and he could start over. So, he begins to practice his confession and contrition: "Dad, I'm so sorry for what I did. I'm no longer worthy to be called your son. Would you please help me?"

He hitch-hikes home, all the while practicing his little speech under his breath, wondering if his father will buy it and welcome him home or slam the door in his face. He even practices making his face look properly repentant to help him with his cause.

The day of his hopeful reunion arrives, and he paces around the block worrying about his words when all of the sudden someone tackles him from behind and it takes him a moment to realize that someone is kissing his hair and head and neck.

The younger son rolls his assailant over only to discover that it's his father, crying profusely, with a giant smile on his face.

The son opens his mouth to begin his practiced speech and his father interrupts him: "I don't want to hear a word of what you have to say. We need to throw a party."

And with that the old man grabs his son by the collar yanks him up off the ground, and starts singing at the top his lungs out in the middle of the street. They stop by every convenience store on their way home picking up all the cold beer, ice, and hot dogs they can carry. And by the time they make it to the house a slew of text messages, emails, and tweets have gone out inviting the whole of the neighborhood over to celebrate the lost being found.

Meanwhile, the older son (remember the older son), he's out mowing the backyard at his Dad's house. He's got sweat dripping everywhere, and his mind is running over the list of all the other stuff he's supposed to do, when he looks up and sees countless figures moving past the windows inside. And when he turns off the mower he can hear the music bumping and the people singing.

He quickly makes his way up to the closest window, peers inside, and sees his father with his arms around his good-for-nothing younger brother, and the older son shuffles off it a fit of rage.

Hours pass before the father realizes his other son is missing the party. So he tries to call him, no answer. He tries to text him, no response. It gets to the point that the Dad gets in his car and shows up at his older son's house and starts banging on the front door.

"Where have you been? You're missing the party!"

"I'm missing the party? When did you ever throw me a party? I've been like a slave for you all these years, taking over your business, driving you to your doctor's appointments, heck I was even mowing your yard this afternoon, and you've never done a thing for me. And yet my brother shows up, and you throw him a party and you invite the whole neighborhood?"

And before he can continue his litany of complaints the father smacks his older son across the face and shouts, "You idiot! I gave you all that you have. And what do you spend all your free time doing? Taking care of an old man like me and I never asked you to do any of that."

"But Dad..."

"Don't you interrupt me right now, this is important. All that matters is that your brother is finally alive again. And you, you're hardly alive at all. The only reason you didn't come into the party after mowing the lawn is because you refuse to die to all of these dumb expectations that you've placed on yourself. We're all dead and having a great time and you, you're alive and miserable. So do yourself a favor, son of mine, and just drop dead. Forget about your life and come have fun with us."

The End. That's the whole story right there.

And we know what we're supposed to make of it.

We know we've been like the younger brother, venturing off into the unknown world only to make stupid choices and hope that we will be received in our repentance.

We know we've been like the older brother, disgusted with how some people get all the good stuff even though they don't deserve it.

226

Or we know we've been like the father, praying for a wayward child, or spouse, or family member, or friend to come to their senses and return home.

And just about every time we encounter this story, whether in a sermon, or Sunday school, or even in a book or movie, the same point is made—see yourself in the story and then act accordingly.

But that ruins the story. It ruins the story because it makes the entire thing about us when the entire thing is really about Jesus.

If the story we're about us then we would hear a fuller ending. We would learn whether or not the elder brother decided to ditch his self-righteousness and join the party. We would discover whether or not the younger brother truly repented and left his foolish life behind forever. We would even discover how the father attempted to reconcile his sons back together.

But Jesus doesn't give us the ending we might be hoping for. We don't get to know what happens and to whom because that's not the point.

Do you see it now? This is about as scandalous as it gets in the Bible because no one gets what they deserve, and the people who don't deserve anything get everything!

The father loses everything for his sons. He gives up his life simply to meet the demand of his younger son.

The older son loses out on all that he hopes for by doing all of the right things only to never be rewarded for it.

The younger son dies to his ridiculous extravagance and is thrown the party of all parties just for coming home.

In this story, straight from the lips of the Lord, we catch a glimpse of the great scandal of the gospel: Jesus dies for us whether we deserve it or not. Like the younger son we don't even have to apologize before our heavenly Father is tackling us in the streets of life to shower us with love. Like the older son, we don't have to do anything to earn an invitation to the great party, save for ditching our snobbery.

This story, whether we like to admit it or not, ends before we want it to. We want to know what happens next, we want to know if the older brother goes into the party. We want to know if the younger brother stays on the right path. We want to see the father relaxing in his lazy boy knowing both of his kids are home.

But the fact that Jesus ends the story without an end shows that what's most important has already happened. The fatted calf has been sacrificed so that the party can begin. Jesus has already mounted the hard wood of the cross so that we can let our hair down, and take off our shoes, and start dancing.

We were lost and we've been found. That's the only thing that matters. Amen.

Even a Camel Like You
Mark 10:17-30
Jason Micheli

Last June I had the dubious honor of being invited to serve as the guest preacher for the high school's Baccalaureate service.

There's nothing quite like preaching to a congregation full of teenagers who are all there because their parents made them. It's kind of like being a comedian in front of a completely sober crowd.

When the invitation came, I tried to pass it off to the senior pastor, but I was told that he is much too old to relate to high school students. Because it was an interfaith ceremony the program didn't even refer to me as a preacher. Instead it called me an "inspirational speaker."

Now I warned them how I felt about that title; I told them how 'inspirational speaker' makes me think of guys on TV with capped teeth, hair plugs and seven steps to something. This scripture about Jesus and the rich man—this is the passage I chose to preach on for the Baccalaureate.

Now, I admit it's possible I was in a contrary mood. It's possible I wanted to subvert people's expectations of sentimentality. It's possible I didn't anyone confusing me for an inspirational speaker.

But it's also true that in Matthew's version of this scripture the rich man is said to be 'young,' which makes this rich man the only young person mentioned in all of the Gospels. So it was more than just me feeling contrary, I thought it was an appropriate scripture given my audience.

To all of those seniors setting off for college and the American dream, to all of their parents who had just as many ambitions for their children if not more—I told them about this rich, young, religious high-achiever who asks Jesus about eternal life.

And in telling them about the rich young man, I also told them about a young woman I knew in my previous church. A young woman who was a straight-A student at an Ivy league school, who was nearing graduation, whose parents were anticipating her career and six-figure salary.

I told them how Ann, that young woman, threw them all for a loop one day and announced that rather than doing anything they had hoped she was going to work in a clinic in some poor village in South America.

All because Jesus 'loved' her.

I *thought* the sermon went alright. I got a few laughs, mostly at Dennis' expense. I saw a couple of heads nodding in affirmation. I didn't notice any one sleeping or scowling. All in all, it seemed like it went okay.

Then I made the mistake of walking into Wesley Hall for the reception.

All I wanted was a cup of lemonade.

At first, I didn't even make it through the double doors.

"Do you always preach like that?"

The question was barked at me in a hushed, let's-not-a-make-a-scene tone of voice. He was wearing an expensive-looking suit with an American flag pinned to his lapel, and his bald head was flushed red with bulging out everywhere.

"Do you always preach like that?" he questioned me.

"I guess you don't go to church here?" I said.

"No, and we never will."

"I guess I don't understand."

"My daughter has worked hard and I've saved so she can go to the best college and law school. And you're telling her she should just throw all her ambition away to go help the poor? That's irresponsible. You call yourself inspirational speaker?"

And, okay, maybe I was in a contrary mood that day.

"Look," I said, "it sounds like your problem's with Jesus not with me. Maybe you should take it up with him."

He stormed off with his family in tow.

Next, I tiptoed up to the punchbowl hoping nobody would notice me, and thought I was in the clear. But then a different Dad, this one in a yellow polo shirt and khakis came up to me.

He had a gold chain and cross around his neck. He smiled and shook my hand and said: "Jesus didn't really mean sell EVERYTHING and give it to the poor."

"He didn't?" I asked.

And he smiled at me like I was no older than the high schoolers and he said: "Of course not. Don't you see he just meant we should keep things in their proper perspective? That money and possessions aren't problems so long as we put God first in our lives?"

And like I told you—it's possible I was just feeling contrary.

I took a sip of lemonade and replied: "Proper perspective, huh? I like that. That sounds good. That sounds a lot more manageable. I don't know why Jesus didn't say that, but I like that a lot better."

I left him there at the punch bowl not sure whether I'd just agreed with me or not.

I almost escaped to the fellowship hall. I made it to the door by the kitchen, when a Dad, a church member here, stopped me.

He shook my hand and said: "Jesus just told that one man to sell everything and give it to the poor, right?"

"What do you mean?" I asked.

"Jesus didn't ask anyone else to do that did he?"

And I thought about it and replied: "Well, the disciples weren't rich but, yeah, they gave up everything too when Jesus called."

I didn't wait for a follow-up question.

I walked down to my office to take off my robe and go home but lingering outside my office door was a mother with three embarrassed-looking kids loitering near her.

"Can I help you? The ladies' room is right there if that's what you're looking for."

She blushed but didn't smile. "I was just confused by your message" she said.

"Oh, well, don't worry. That's how my congregation feels most of the time."

She shot me a perplexed look and motioned to her tallest girl standing to her left: "My daughter invited Jesus into her heart when she was fifteen. She's saved. She doesn't have to change her plans, give up her dreams or DO anything."

"You must be Baptist," I said.

She nodded but she didn't laugh.

And I might've mentioned I was kind of feeling contrary that day.

"Lady, I'm a Methodist. We're the ones who notice how whenever Jesus talks about salvation he seems to want a lot more from us than just our hearts."

"Good Teacher, what do I have to do to inherit eternal life?"

Jesus is on his way to the nation's capital when this rich guy from the suburbs comes up to him with a question.

And Jesus doesn't appear all that interested in the spiritual questions of these well-to-do, upwardly mobile types. Jesus just tries to blow him off with a conventional answer about obeying the commandments.

"I do all those things already. What else? What else must I do to inherit eternal life?"

Then St. Mark says: "Jesus, looking at him, loved him..."

This is the only place in all of the Gospels where it says Jesus "loved" somebody. Jesus talks about love but this is the only place in the Gospels where Jesus loved an individual.

"Teacher, I've kept all the commandments since I was a kid. What else must I do to inherit eternal life?"

And Jesus looks at him. And Jesus says: "Because I love you...there is one thing you can do...just because I love you...go, sell everything you possess, give it to the poor and then come follow me."

232

He's the only one Jesus loved, and Jesus asks everything from him.

They watch the rich man walk away, depressed and grieving.

And Jesus looks at the disciples and says: "You know— you just can't save rich people. It's hard. It's just about impossible."

Near as I can tell, this is the only place in the bible where Jesus invites someone to become a disciple and the person refuses.

And yet we call this story Gospel, good news.

I left that Baptist mother looking confused outside my office. I actually made it to the parking lot. I'd almost made it to my car when this student with floppy hair and a wrinkled dress shirt said to me: "Did you choose that bible story yourself?"

I turned around, took a deep breath and said, in love: *Look kid, I might have to take that crap off your parents, but I don't need to take it from you.*

"Yeah, I chose it. Why?"

"I thought it was inspiring," he said.

And I did a double-take and squinted at him: "Are you jerking me around?"

"No seriously. It's inspiring to think that Jesus believed in that rich man enough to ask him to give up everything. Jesus wouldn't have asked if he couldn't do it, right? Jesus must've thought he was capable of great things."

He was about to get in his car when I said: "Hey, would you mind going back inside? There's an angry looking bald guy in there. He's wearing a nice suit and he's got his boxers in a twist. He didn't get that scripture. But you did. Why don't you explain it to him."

We hear this story as bad news.

We feel the need to explain it, excuse ourselves from it, suck the urgency out of it with a thousand qualifications. As a preacher, I know I've thought it's my job to clean up after Jesus, to say things more delicately than he said them.

But maybe this scripture really is good news.

Maybe Jesus has more faith in you than you have in yourself.

Maybe Jesus believes in you enough to say to you that you were made for more than just checking-off the boxes of religious obligation. Maybe Jesus loves you enough not to leave you as you are right now. Maybe Jesus thinks you're capable of more than just a successful life. Maybe he thinks your life can be significant.

Maybe—maybe the point of this story isn't that Jesus asks EVERYTHING from you. Maybe the point of this story is that Jesus believes you're CAPABLE of giving him everything.

I mean—isn't interesting how the rich man asks about his eternal life, but Jesus responds instead by talking about the Kingdom? As in... *thy Kingdom come, on earth as it is in heaven.*

Isn't it interesting that we speak in the passive voice of "being saved" but Jesus speaks of salvation with active verbs: GO, SELL, GIVE, COME, FOLLOW.

Let me make it plain.

There is no salvation apart from following Jesus.

The Gospel is not "Jesus died for me now I might think about following Jesus."

Following Jesus isn't an afterthought.

Following Jesus *is* salvation.

Giving him your whole life, this life, in this life, is salvation.

Following him now is participating now in the salvation God is working for the world.

Because God's plan wasn't just to come in the flesh and die on a cross.

God's plan was to change the world, to remake the world.

And he chose his followers to be that change.

That's what it means to be loved by Jesus.

In his book, *The Hole in Our Gospel* Richard Stearns says: "....In a broken, fallen world, in a world of poverty and injustice, as followers of Jesus you and I are God's plan A....he doesn't have a plan B."

This wouldn't be my plan. This isn't how I would do things.

I wouldn't have this much riding on you. I wouldn't ask so much of you.

Frankly, I know a lot of you and I'd never imagine you'd be capable of giving your whole lives to the Kingdom. I mean that just sounds... impossible. But I suppose nothing's impossible with God.

The Dinner Party
Luke 14.7-14

Taylor Mertins

When he was invited to the dinner party, he knew it was a mistake. To begin with, he had never been to a dinner party before and this one was being hosted by all the religious bigwigs in the area.

But the invitation had come nonetheless, and the host wanted him to be there.

He mulled over the possibility of going for a few days, weighing out the pros and cons. From what he could tell, it would be a boring evening. These weren't really the type of people known for being fun. But they were *the* people with power, and he apparently had a place at the table. So, he decided to go.

When he got to the house he was immediately overwhelmed with the opulence. It was as if it had been taken right out of a Better Homes & Gardens magazine, and he was worried about touching anything and everything.

He had spent hours fretting over what to wear, and even though he settled on jeans and a button up shirt, he was clearly underdressed. The men were in suits and the women were in long flowing dresses.

Nevertheless, he politely tiptoed through room after room, with the occasional nod toward one of the other guests until he heard a simple bell ringing from the other side of the house and assumed the time had come for the dinner party to begin.

He entered the dining room and was bombarded by the bartender who wanted to know his order.

"Got any wine?" He asked.

"Why sir, we have the cave filled to the brim with a great variety of years and regions! Shall I make a recommendation?"

"How about you bring me a glass of the stuff that you can't get rid of, that'll be fine."

And with that the bartender started off in a fit of rage.

The man then turned toward the dining room table and took in its perfection. The settings were beautiful, and the napkins looked as if a professional origami artist had spent hours creating unique folds for each plate. He felt all of the eyes in the room on him as he made his way over to the table, but before he could pull out a chair, the man next to him winced and reached for his lower back.

"Something wrong?" he asked.

The man was doubled over now and said, "I threw my back out this morning and I thought I had worked it out but now I feel like I can't move."

So, he took the man by the hand, led him over to the table, pushed some of the plates and cups and cutlery out of the way, and laid the man down. He fussed around for a few minutes poking here and there while muttering a few things under his breath and immediately everyone gathered around in a tight circle with their jaws on the floor.

"Has he no decency?

"Where are his manners?"

And finally, the host entered only to exclaim, "What in the world do you think you're doing?"

The man looked up from his makeshift examining table and simply shrugged his shoulders and said, "If it was your kid, or your spouse, who was hurting, wouldn't you drop everything to do something about it?"

And no one said a word.

The man with the back problem promptly got off the table, now fit as a fiddle, and the hired help rushed in to put everything back in its proper place.

With a wave of the hand the host encouraged everyone to find their seats so the feast could begin.

And yet the man, who had already offended everyone in the room, noticed that all the guests rushed to get to the seats as close to the host as possible.

He stood there in silence, observing the frantic frenzy of power dynamics, and contended himself to remain silent until they noticed that he had not taken the remaining seat.

And so it was in the midst of a profoundly uncomfortable silence that all the eyes fell upon him once again.

"Hey, the next time any of you go to a party, don't sit in the best places. Someone more important than you might've been invited, and then you're going to have to give up your seat to go sit in the last place. So, don't you think it would be better to start off at the end, and that way the host can come and raise you up to a better place?"

Again, no one said a word.

The man took it as a sign that he should keep going.

"Where has all the humility gone? There is a great and wonderful joy, known only to a few, that comes with humility. It comes not because humility earns you anything, but it brings a newfound sense of joy from not having to be in control of every little thing. You can finally enjoy the party instead of trying to be responsible for it."

The other guests started to fidget uncomfortably in the chairs.

"Look at yourselves. If you keep showing up at these things and only choose the best seats, you're going to cut yourselves off from all the other places and all the other people at the table, who, in my experience, are the ones who have the most fun. I know some of you would rather die that have sit in the back, but dying to all of this is the best thing you could ever do."

The man started to really feel the words bubbling up within him and he began swinging his arms with ferocity spilling wine all over the oriental rug.

He stared deeply into the eyes of everyone around the table, all of the winners of the community, people who were so self-satisfied with all they had done and earned, and he began to pity them. He instantly knew that, to them, this was the most important moment of their week—sitting around a table, jockeying for power, doing everything they could to impress the person to their left and right.

So he continued, "Just go ahead and die to everything you think you've done and earned for yourself. None of you are as good as you think you are anyway. And if, only if, you're able to die to that, maybe you can actually start enjoying yourself."

And he sat down.

Over the next hour the guests ate in silence as the courses of food were brought out in proper order. They were either so moved by his words or infuriated by them that they did not know what to do or what to say.

The evening quickly came to its inevitable conclusion and the guests began to express their gratitude to the host, promising to return the favor by having the host come to their respective places, and the man felt another rally coming.

"You need to throw away the book."

"What did you say?"

"You need to toss it out to the trash and leave it there forever."

"What book?"

"The one you've been keeping in your head about who owes you what. You're so stupidly stuck in your bookkeeping that you're trying to keep the world together and you can't even see how quickly its ripping at the seams. Why don't you just let it all go? I mean, what good does it do you to climb the social ladder by inviting people just to have them invite you back. You already have all of this. Next time try inviting the wrong people. Think about how much fun you could have at the table surrounded by the last, least, lost, little, and dead. I promise you this: you will never really be happy until the bookkeeping stops, until you learn how to let go of your clenched hand, so that someone else can grab hold and bring you onto the dance floor of life."

The guests, again, looked upon the scene with disbelief at a man with no sense of manners at all and they, along with the host, fumed.

"Anyway," he began, "Thanks for the evening, I guess. The wine was okay, the food was good, and the conversation was to die for." And with that he left.

It was only then that one of the guests worked up the courage to ask the host a question: "Who was that guy?"

And the host replied, "His name is Jesus. And I could just kill him for everything he did and said tonight."

Friends, if we want to take Jesus' words from the parable at the dinner party literally, that's fine, but it's a quick recipe for a ruined evening. If we invite the wrong people over, they're not going to invite us to their houses, nor would we really want to go to theirs in the first place. But, again, these parables aren't here for us to understand how we are supposed to be living, but they function to show how God lives for us.

Jesus destroys the exceptions of the dinner party crowd and he does it throughout his ministry. He is a critical Lord, though we often forget that part of him. He's critical because he wants to destroy all of our favorite and foolish expectations. Being first, found, big, important, and alive matter little in the kingdom of God. They matter little because Jesus didn't come to make the first firster, or the found founder, or the important importanter, or the alive aliver. He came to raise the dead.

And we can die, we can die to the desire to sit at the best places, we can die to the bookkeeping that keeps us awake at night. We really can die to all of that because Jesus already has.

Look: It's as if Jesus is sneaking into the dinner parties of our lives, seeing our jockeying and our comparing and our bookkeeping, just to whisper into our ears: "Why are you doing all of this when I already threw out the book on you? Why are you keeping score when God doesn't? God already nailed all of your sins to my cross, past-present-future. Go ahead and die to all of that so you can finally start having some fun."

So hear Jesus today, hear him through scripture and song and silence and sermon, hear him through the sacrament to which we are invited at the table. For as much as we would like to argue against it, we are the poor, the cripple, the lame, and the blind. We are the ones invited to Christ's dinner party, an invitation we cannot repay, and he wants us to have fun. Amen.

Extracting the Truth
Luke 16.19-31
David King

In the town of Bakersfield, there are two McDonalds, one downtown and one just on the town's borders. Bakersfield is a small, formerly industrial town that now sits on the backrow of America. Sandwiched between the two McDonalds on the now vacant streets are several churches, many in buildings never initially designed for worship. Besides the McDonalds, the only gathering place for the people left out of America's innovation are the churches there. The churches sustain the memory of their lives, a project very important when there is no one else to remember them and give them the hope of a different life.

Jeanette is a native of Bakersfield, the child of immigrants from Mexico. She runs a church by the name of Full Gospel Lighthouse. On Sundays, they offer two services, one in English and one in Spanish. On one particular Sunday, Jeanette had invited a photographer by the name of Chris Arnade to come to Full Gospel Lighthouse. He was working on a book called "Dignity: Finding Respect in Back Row America," and he wanted to interview Jeanette about her work with the church.

The English service was small and quick, but the Spanish service gathered a larger crowd in the oppressively hot building. After an hour, Chris leaves.

Once the service is over, Chris gets a text from Jeanette that asks to meet at the McDonalds down the street from the church. It is there that Chris asks her about her work in the church.

After hearing the story of Jeanette's former husband, who drank so much that he left the family and became homeless, Chris asks the question he came to ask: "What does your religion mean to you?"

Jeanette waits a moment, almost confused by what she considers the obvious answer. She tells him without God, she would be lost. Without God, she wouldn't have peace. Without God, she tells Chris, she would be dead.

I think it is fair to say that the condition of Lazarus that Jesus starts the parable with is not one of peace. Like Jeanette, Lazarus has found himself on the back row of society, totally cast aside from the consideration of the high-powered tellers of Wall Street and Rome. There is no avoiding the fact that Lazarus, for all intents and purposes, is dead to the world.

The rich man, on the other hand, wears fine linen made of purple and feasts sumptuously every day. Not only that, but he is secure in his life. He goes to and from work, in and out of the gate, with the surety that he matters in the world, that the world needs him. He is, after all, wealthy. The rich man has learned to live his life from the safety of the world; he has learned to live as though God does not exist. In Jesus' time, there was a strong association between wealth and the mark of God's blessings. The dominant theology of the time was one of prosperity, one in which the gaining of wealth was both an indicator of the presence of God and an entrance to the life of God.

You see, the rich man's wealth gives him access to the temple, to the priests, to God. The rich man was so wealthy that he could buy a goat for every sin he committed, and given the picture Jesus is painting, that's a lot of goats. The rich man is capable of being clean, of maintaining ritual purity in the eyes of the law.

Lazarus, on the other hand, couldn't even get up to walk to the temple. And in fact, if he had, he wouldn't have been allowed to enter. The Law would have precluded him from entering the presence of God because he had been made unclean by the dogs who licked his sores. Not only was Lazarus down and out, but he was quite literally precluded from the presence of God. Not only was he ritually unclean, but he could do nothing about his condition. In the rich man's eyes, Lazarus is hardly even recognizably human.

Enter death. Despite the rich man's best efforts at replicating the immortal banquet, death comes for both of them. The great equalizer comes onto the scene in a flurry of immediacy, and boom, we're in the afterlife. Lazarus is whisked away into the bosom of Abraham, and the rich man, having had what we can infer to be a funeral of opulence, finds himself in torment.

The rich man dies, and when he does so he is not one whit less dead than Lazarus.

That's it. That's all we are told. Lazarus and the Rich man simply end up where they are. When the rich man cries out in anguish to Abraham, Abraham reminds him that…well, he reminds the rich man that this is simply how it is. Abraham does not list off the times the rich man ignored Lazarus. Abraham notes Lazarus only as a foil for the rich man's experience. There is nothing of moralism in Abraham's description, because it is precisely that: a description, not a proscription. In the eyes of the rich man, there is no rhyme or reason for his anguish.

That's the rich man's rub. The distinction between them doesn't come through. Neither Lazarus nor he got what they deserved. Both are sinners. For all the rich man's gestures towards purity, he ends up in Hades. For all of Lazarus' impurity, he ends up in bliss with Abraham. The state of affairs after death is nothing but a reversal of their earthly existence.

That's the thing – the difference between the two figures is that Lazarus doesn't do anything. Lazarus doesn't speak a word, he doesn't make any motions. He, like the unjust steward from last week's scripture, banks on God's work, not his own. What we so often miss in this parable is the fact that its main character *isn't* the story's main character. The circumstances that make Lazarus' life a version of death also make it so that he is absolutely inadequate to the task of doing anything for himself, much less for God. Lazarus' condition makes him entirely dependent on grace. And before anyone assumes that I am worshipping poverty, we ought to note that Lazarus' life is a living hell that I would not wish on anybody.

By the world's standards, Lazarus' life makes him so *un*deserving of God's grace. By the world's standards, Lazarus does not need to be saved – he is dispensable and expendable, a sinner caught in a net he has no hope of getting out of. And yet, Lazarus is raised into the bosom of Abraham.

This is a parable about resurrection and undeserving grace. The rich man in the story has not understood that. Even in death, he cannot accept his position: to him, Lazarus is still a tool to be used. The grace offered and on display here is so offensive to the rich man – a grace that does not have favour that can be gained, but that is offered to even the most impure and destitute.

The God who condescends in the flesh of Jesus Christ holds no regard for status. Or, if he does, it is the status of the poor. The morals of this story, the reversal of fortune for the poor and the rich, it stands true *only if* the poor man named Jesus is raised from the dead. The resurrection is not incidental to the ethics of the story. The resurrection is what makes the ethics intelligible, for it reveals the kind of God we worship.

That's why Abraham won't send Lazarus to the rich man's brothers. They are so set in living without God that even the resurrection will be explained away. The God who makes the dead live again with an unabashed grace simply does not make sense. But God abandons no one, not even the rich man in Hades. The word for "torment" used in verse 23 in the Greek means "the extraction of the truth." The rich man's torment is being confronted with the truth revealed by grace in the cross: the utter truth that we are dependent on God, not us, for our salvation. No one is outside the realm of such grace.

This is a parable that teaches us that such things as a resurrection, such things as underserving grace matter to our lives. If Jesus is not raised from the dead, and if he does not raise up the undeserving like Lazarus, then our faith is in vain.

When Jeanette told Chris in the McDonald's in Bakersfield that without God, she would be dead, Chris writes that he was cured of his atheism. He is not a Christian, but he no longer thought that faith was a thing used to explain away the world.

Chris tells Jeanette that the kind of community he saw in the church and in the McDonalds is something that he has seen in much of America's back row. He asks her if she goes to the McDonald's often. She pauses and thinks.

"Our lives used to be centered around work and church," she says. "Now, it is centered around McDonald's and Church."

McDonald's is not where we expect to find God – but neither do we expect to find God in Lazarus. But the fact that we do should come as no surprise. We worship a God who has condescended to us in our own flesh, who rose from the death we proscribed, and who makes his presence known to us through bread and wine. When we gather around the altar to remember and celebrate the mystery of Good Friday, we are being gathered by a God who can make a church out of such bad Christians as ourselves. We are being gathered by a God whose grace can lift up someone like Lazarus. Our God is a God of surprises. May our lives celebrate such a truth.

The Game Is Over
Luke 16:19-31
Taylor Mertins

The man was running out of room in his garage for all of his stuff. His wife thought it was extravagant for them to have five cars to begin with, but now the jet skis and the boat were simply making things unmanageable. And though he was supposed to figure out whether or not they could grease the hands of the local government enough for another building permit to let him but yet another addition to the back of his house, his mind was consumed by a far more stressful matter.

Larry.

Larry stood outside his house every day, walking back and forth over his grass—the grass he paid a small fortune to keep maintained. Larry had his little cardboard sign asking for money or for food and people would slow down and pass him a few dollars, or a spare muffin. And every day, Larry would return from sunup till sundown, and it was driving the rich man crazy.

He had done everything he could think of—he called the police, but they explained the property upon which Larry walked actually belonged to the city and there was nothing they could do about it—he proposed a new city ordinance banning the panhandlers like Larry from asking for money within the local municipality but all the local churches fought against it—he even tried playing extremely loud and annoying music through his expensive stereo system to try to drive him off.

But nothing worked.

Day after day Larry showed up and the rich man couldn't stand it.

And yet, one day, the man woke up and began his normal routine only to discover that Larry, the nearly permanent fixture out his window was gone. The man danced around in his kitchen sliding across the marble floors. He drank his imported coffee and was thrilled to discover that Larry's obituary was in the newspaper.

The rich man's problems were over!

He was so excited that he ran through the kitchen to share the good news with his wife, but as he rounded the corner into his indoor movie theater he felt a stabbing pain in his chest and he fell to the ground dead.

Sometime later the rich man realized he was in hell with flames of fire lapping all around him constantly. He even had to admit to himself that this torment was worse than seeing Larry outside all day. But then he strained his eyes and he saw Larry just on the other side of the fire, and he was standing there with what looked like an angel.

"Hey!" He shouted, "Send Larry over here with a Campari on the rocks—it's getting hot in here."

To which the angel replied, "You had good things your whole life, and Larry here, Larry had nothing. Here he is comforted and you are in agony. Also, notice—you can't come over to us and neither can we come over to you."

The rich man promptly fell to his knees, "Please! Send Larry to my brothers, that he might warn them about this place so they don't have to suffer with me in agony."

The angel said, "They have the scriptures, they need only trust what they read."

"No," he said, "You don't understand. That's not enough. They need someone to return to them from the dead for them to believe."

And the angel finally said, "If they don't already trust, neither will they be convinced even if someone rises from the dead."

Thanks for this one Jesus.

The wealthy and powerful in this life will burn in torment forever and ever, and those who are weak, and poor might suffer now but will be comforted in the beyond. Therefore, do what you can people—give away your wealth and life like Larry/Lazarus such that your reward really will be a reward.

It's easy for this scripture to become a lambasting sermon about the poverty of wealth and the riches of near-destitution. Plenty of pastors have stood in their pulpits and held this one over the heads of their people in order to pad the offering plates, or guilt people into signing up for different ministries, or embarrass the well to do for their ignorance about their impending flames.

And there's some truth to it. It's a challenge to read the whole of the gospel and not read it as an indictment against the wealthy. But, as usual, there's more to the parable than the parable itself.

Living well and accumulating lots of possessions and deep bank accounts might be the world's most overpowering ideal lifestyle, but in the kingdom of God they matter little. We, wrongly, use those categories to describe both the saved and the lost, the winners and the losers.

Winning equates to wealth and losing equates to poverty.

And yet in Jesus' eyes its living badly—being poor, hungry, and covered in sores—that turns out to be the mechanism by which people are apparently saved.

We can hardly blame ourselves for missing this divine reversal—we have it so repeated into our brains from our infancy even until this very moment that who we are is based on what we have earned. One need not flip through the channels on the television, or see the billboards covered in potential lottery earnings to have this proved over and over again.

We elevate the powerful and the wealthy both purposefully and subconsciously. We like to elect politicians who have done well for themselves, we read the books from the self-made millionaires, and we look up to our wealthiest family members.

And here's the kicker—for all of our fascination and worship of those with money, they've done little good with it. Think about it: if the world could've been fixed by what we might call good living and good earning—then we would've fixed everything by now.

But we haven't.

Instead, it's the winners of this world who, more often than not, achieve their earnings off the backs of the least, last, lost, little, and dead.

They are the ones thrown to the curb while new homes, with new families, and new cars fill the neighborhoods.

But because we admire the wealthy and want to be like them, we blind ourselves from seeing how the ones with all the stuff use Jesus' favorite people as the mechanisms through which they achieve and maintain all that they have. It has been their ignorance of the poor, their locking up of the marginalized, their segregating by skin tone, that has brought about a very particular end in which it sounds like good news to those on the top, to those who actually have something to lose.

And still, even with all their earning, and trying, and striving, and politicking, and maneuvering, the world is still a mess! The rich just keep getting rich and the poor keep getting poorer.

Here is where the parable stings the most—the rich man, with all that he has, his being first, most, found, big, and alive, he is not able to delay or avoid his death any more than Larry is with his lastness, leastness, lostness, littleness, and deadness.

The bell tolls for us all.

Do you see it now? When it comes to the Good News, success defined by the world merits us not one thing.

The rich man might start out and seem like a real winner. But he can't even see the truth in his death—he refuses to accept that he has died! He bargains with father Abraham to make the most of his situation and he loses.

It is because he was so convinced that good living, having all the right things, was the instrument of salvation that his death is simply unacceptable. And, to make matters worse, Father Abraham frightens all of us to death, pun intended, with his final declaration—not even seeing a dead person rise from the grave can change our minds.

We are quite stuck in this worldly worldview of ours.

However, lest we hear this story today and leave with the impression that we are being called to go out and live like Larry—hanging out by the gates of the rich until we develop sores all over our body—that's not quite what Jesus is saying.

This is not a story of imitation. It's not a "go and do likewise."

It is just a story of the truth.

And the truth is this: The game is over.

No one, certainly not God, is keeping score and tallying up all of our good works against our bad. There is not a divine ledger with little tallies every time we misstep or we bring about something good in the world. And there is definitely not a test by which the accumulation of our wealth will determine whether or not salvation is in fact ours.

The truth is a much harder pill to swallow precisely because everything else in the world tells us the contrary.

Do all you can, earn all you can, achieve all you can, save all you can, invest all you can, those are all slogans of the world.

But the truth is that the game is over. We have nothing left to earn, really, because the cross comes to all of us and all of us die.

And if we can accept that we are already dead, right here and right now, because of our baptisms, well then we can actually start living because we already have all we need.

Jesus came to raise the dead—nothing more, less, or else. He did not come to reward the rewardable, or to improve the improvable, or even convert the convertible. He came to raise the dead.

Heaven, whatever it may be, is not the home of the good, or the wealthy, or the powerful. It is simply the home of forgiven forgivers.

Hell, whatever it may be, contains only unpardoned unpardoners.

Everyone in heaven has decided to die to the question of who's wrong, whereas nobody in hell can even shut up about who's right.

And that's precisely the rich man's problem—he has been so conditioned and convinced that his earning should have earned him something that he can't stop thinking about how he did everything right.

But who gets to define what, in fact, is right?

Notice, Jesus does not begin his story with a disclaimer that this is precisely what will happen to the rich and to the poor when they die, nor does he command the listeners to go and be like Lazarus in their living until the day they die.

He simply tells a story—and a frightening one at that.

But in the end the parable tells us one thing—The game is over.

Whatever we think we need to do to get God to love us or forgive us or save us, it's already been done. All of our sins, those of the past, present, and future, are nailed to Jesus' cross.

The question isn't "What do we need to do to get saved?"

The question is, "How are we going to start living knowing that we are already saved?" Amen.

Unfair
Luke 18.9-14
Taylor Mertins

60 years.

That's a long time.

Basically, double my life.

It is a really remarkable thing that this church is celebrating its 60th anniversary. And yet, the entire Christian tradition is 2,000 years old. 60 out of 2,000 sounds a little less impressive.

However, to live, and survive, in a time such as this is truly worth celebrating. The last 60 years have been marked, much to our chagrin and disappointment, with the decline of the church in America.

But here we are!

And not only are we here, but we are celebrating our being here! We have much to celebrate—not just the anniversary of the church, but also the gospel being made manifest in a place like Woodbridge to those with eyes to see and ears to hear.

Seeing as its the church's anniversary, we can't really know who we are without knowing where we've been.

Cokesbury began in that strange and picturesque time we call the 50's. In the 50's everything felt right—we were on the other side of the greatest war ever waged on the earth, and we won. Hawaii and Alaska were added to the union. The Barbie Doll was first introduced.

A gallon of gas only cost 25 cents!

We are inherently a nostalgic people and it is very easy to look back and remember what we might call good. We can turn on an old movie, or remember a particular politician, or even a fashion trend from the past and think fondly of each of them.

However, the 50's, for whatever good they might've introduced, there was an equal number, if not more, of what we could certainly call the bad.

In the late 50's the first Americans were killed in Vietnam. The Civil Rights movement was spreading across the country and black churches were being regularly bombed on Sunday mornings. And the scapegoat of Communism was causing us to ostracize and at times imprison some of our own citizens.

I once heard someone describe the fifties as a time when everything was black and white, and everyone knew right from wrong. And yet, if you just look at a list of major events that took place the year this church started it feels more like a time of gray, when everything was confused.

60 years ago, a handful of people from our community started meeting and called themselves Cokesbury Church. To those individuals, the time was ripe for the gospel and the sharing of the Good News, so they did.

But then something changed. It's not possible to pinpoint exactly what happened, but we all know that we live in a very different world than the world of 1959. In 1959 everyone assumed that you would grow up, get married, have 2.5 children, pay your taxes, and go to church. Business were closed on Sundays because everyone had a church to go to and it was a major moment of the week for all sorts of communities.

That world is long gone.

Which leads us to the parable of the Publican and the Pharisee.

I know this seems a strange text to be read and preached upon as we celebrate 50 years as a church, and I will plainly admit that perhaps it wasn't such a good idea, but we might as well listen to what God has to say to us today, even as we celebrate.

The parable ends rather disconcertingly: Those who exalt themselves will be humbled and those who humble themselves will be exalted. Which seems like I should stand in a place like this and tell people like you to be more humble. But this parable isn't really about humility at all. If anything, it's about our futility. It's about the foolish notion that we can do anything to get ourselves right with God.

Listen: There's a man who is good and faithful. He's not a crook, or a womanizer, or an alcoholic. He loves his wife and plays on the floor with his kids when he gets home from work. He evens tithes when the offering plate comes around. He is exactly unlike the tax collector.

The tax collector is a legal crook who steals from his fellow people and bleeds all the money out of them that he possibly can. He's like a mid-level mafia boss who skims from the top before sending the money up the chain. He's got enough cars and boats that he can never drive all of them.

They both show up for worship. The good faithful man thanks God that he's not like the tax-collector and the tax collector asks for God to have mercy on him, a sinner.

And Jesus presents these two men as the means by which God's grace is communicated in a completely unfair way because it's the tax collector who gives home justified.

Let's think about it this way: Which of the two men would we like to have sitting next to us in the pews on Sunday morning? What would we do if the tax collector was here in our midst? How would we respond if he took a little money out of the offering plate and showed up with a new woman every Sunday?

It's all wrong, right?

This parable is one of Jesus' final declarations about the business of grace. Grace—the totally unmerited and undeserved gift from God. And here, with resounding convictions, Jesus tells the disciples for the thousandth time that the whole game is unfair.

Grace is completely unfair because what we think is good and right and true matters little to God. Ultimately, not one of us matches up to the goodness of God and instead of kicking us out of the party for being unworthy, God says, "I will make you worthy."

Do you see what that means? It means that the good religious work of the Pharisee is not able to justify him any more than the crazy sins of the tax collector can kick him out. The whole point of this parable, of almost all the parables, is that these two are both dead in the eyes of God, their good deeds and their sins can't earn them or prevent them from salvation—they have no hope in the world unless there is someone who can raise the dead.

And even here knowing the condition of their condition, which is also ours, even in the midst of celebrating 60 years as a worshipping community, perhaps we understand what Jesus' is saying in our minds but our hearts are desperate to believe the opposite.

We might not like to admit it, but we all establish our identities by seeing how we look through other people's eyes. We spend our days fixing our words and our looks in front of the mirror's of other people's opinions so that we will never have to think about the nightmare of being who we really are.

And that's where this parables stings the hardest. This parable, more than most, is so resoundingly unfair that we can't bring ourselves to admit the truth: We're not good enough.

And we fear the tax collector's acceptance not because it means we need to accept those derelicts around us, though it certainly wouldn't hurt. We fear his acceptance because it means that none of us will ever really be free until we stop trying to save ourselves and justify ourselves all the time. And that's all we do all the time!

We do it in ways both big and small. We purchase things we shouldn't all with the hope that those thing will bring us more approval in the eyes of the people we want approval from the most.

We posture bits of morality and ethics and even politics with some vague hope that it will put us in better standing with God.

And as long as we struggle, like the Pharisee, to do everything perfectly perfect all the time, we will resent the unfairness of God to all of our struggling.

God is unfair—It's true.

But God's unfairness is Good News. For if God were really fair, fair according to the terms set by the world, then God would've closed to the door to the party a long long time ago.

Which leads us back to what we are celebrating today. No matter who we identify with in the story—the good religious liar or the honest tax collector—there is a really strong temptation to thank God that we are not like other people. We pass someone on the street or we see the name on a particular bumper sticker on someone's car or we read someone's facebook status and we measure our lives against theirs and we come out on the other side grateful. It's even present in an anniversary like this, because isn't surviving in the current marketplace of ideas a subtle form of thanking God we're not like everyone else?

Christians, at least in the last few decades, have tried to avoid being seen as different from other people. We have done so out of fear of seeming too strange, or too fundamentalist, or too evangelical. We've been content with letting our faith become privatized and something we do on Sundays. But because we have tried so hard to not seem different, it has been unclear why anyone would want to be like us, much less join a church that started in 1959.

Or, to make things worse, we've established a Christian identity such that only perfect people can be present in the pews.

It's no wonder people don't want to come to church.

The truth of the matter is that being Christian means being different. But unlike how we so often present this in worship or in

256

the greater cultural ethos, it doesn't mean being like the good religious man, it means admitting that we are all like the tax collector.

You see, following Jesus means admitting the condition of our condition—its falling to the floor Sunday after Sunday with the same confession on our lips, "God, be merciful to me, a sinner!" And it's knowing that before we can even bring those words to our lips God has forgiven every last one of our sins through the cross of his Son.

That's what makes us different. Not being able to keep a religious roof over our heads for 60 years, but 60 years of rediscovering week after week how good the Good News really is. It's why we come to this table over and over again to be made one with the one whose humility on the cross turned out to be a victory that defeated sin and death.

In the bread and the cup we see how unfair God is. Because, if grace were fair, then none of us would be worthy to come to the table, whether we're a publican or a pharisee. But thanks be to God that grace is unfair, making room for each and every single one of us. Amen.

We're in the Ditch
Luke 10:25-37
Teer Hardy

It feels like I am still drying out from the storms of Monday morning. Monday was Camden's first day of baseball camp and together we braved the rain falling at the rate of five inches per hour to make the trek to Yorktown High School. Along the way, yelling over the sound of the rain beating down on our Toyota, I explained how on Earth Camden would be able to play baseball inside because the rules on his side of 16th Street suggested he would be in for a day of disappointment.

The trip home from Yorktown required three detours as the roads in the area began to flood quickly. Later Monday evening, as many were pulling up the water-soaked carpet in their basements and dragging it to the curb, I turned on the evening news and saw story after story of people who did not heed the "turnaround and don't drown warnings," finding themselves in the creek without a paddle. Each of the News 4 reporters highlighted the actions of "Good Samaritans." According to the news reporters who had obviously not braved the storms themselves as their hair was perfectly in place, the Good Samaritans of Monday morning's storm provided rides to stranded commuters when the commuters found themselves unable to help themselves along the road from home to work.

The title "Good Samaritan" is a churchy title but the story of how this person earned the title is almost as well-known as the Nativity story to those who count themselves as unchurched. The Good Samaritan in Jesus' parable has become a secularized saint that the Vatican has yet to canonize. Simply known as the Good Samaritan, this fictional character created by Jesus has become modern-day shorthand for a do-gooder doing good things for strangers.

Someone changing a stranger's flat tire along the Beltway is as labeled a Good Samaritan. The secularized saint lends their title to people who give a bottle of water to someone holding a cardboard sign along Glebe Road.

But the secularized sainthood of this story causes us to miss the bite of the story. We (think) we know the parable so well that we miss the point of Jesus' words and, in turn, the parable is turned into a "Biblical example" of good morals instead of being an earthly example of heavenly truth.

The encounter begins with a lawyer doing what lawyers do best—asking questions they already know the answer to. The lawyer asked Jesus, "what must I do to inherit eternal life?" Knowing this lawyer was an expert of the Law, Jesus tossed the question back to him, "What is written in the law? What do you read there?" Jesus essentially said, "You are the expert, why don't you tell me." And like the law professor's pet student, showing off for his other lawyer friends to see, the lawyer responded by quoting the Law, Deuteronomy 6 and Leviticus 19.

> "You shall love the Lord your God with all your heart, and with all your soul, and with all your might"—Deuteronomy 6:5

"You shall love your neighbor as yourself"—Leviticus 19:18

To justify himself—to prove he know what he knew and to push Jesus—the lawyer asked the question we today love to ask our kids or use to prove we know who to love when the headlines show despair and hopelessness: "who is my neighbor?"

"Who is my neighbor" was not an earnest question from the lawyer; remember he is an expert of the Law. Rather, this question was an attempt by the lawyer to determine what the bare minimum was to be done so that he and those listening could "inherit eternal life." But the lawyer, a professional asker of questions, asked the wrong question. To inherit something, whether it is eternal life or a toaster, is to have something given to you. Inheriting something is not the same as earning something. So, the lawyer continued asking the wrong questions and instead of throwing another question back to the counselor, Jesus tells his parable.

In 2019, we miss the details that made this parable so good to Jesus' original audience. The Gospel writer assumes the reader knows the road between Jerusalem and Jericho was dangerous. For someone to travel this road by themselves would be as foolish as someone trying to drive their Prius through a flooded section of Canal Road. The journey from Jerusalem to Jericho was not a journey many would take on their own because more often than not they would end up in a ditch, left for dead after being attacked and robbed.

The secularization of the Good Samaritan misses this detail as we focus in on the lack of action taken by the two priestly characters making the same treacherous trip. Remember, the Gospel writer assumes we know Jesus' audience, the lawyer and bystanders, were Jewish. After hearing the lack of action taken by the priest and the Levite there is no record of disgust from either the lawyer or others listening to Jesus' story. It is not that the lawyer is heartless (shocker) instead it is that we miss the Jewishness of the parable. If the priest or the Levite were to render aid to the man in the ditch, they would become ritually unclean and thus unable to fulfill the religious obligations of the community. The priest and the Levite are not the bad guys and the lawyers knew as much because they, the priest and the Levite, were following the Law as the lawyer.

On top of their religious obligations, not stopping was not unreasonable as an injured person was commonly used as a trap, intended to lower the guard of a would-be robbery victim.

For the original hearers of this parable, the phrase Good Samaritan would have been an oxymoron. Jews and Samaritans were the ancient versions of the Hatfields and McCoys. A Good Samaritan would have been an offensive title for the ancient Jewish listener of Jesus' story.

Samaritans and Jews worshiped the same Hebrew God yet had different scriptures, Temples, and practices. The Samaritans traveled the Jewish city of David during Jesus' day, to the Temple, and ransacked it. The Samaritans dug up bodies and placed them in the Temple, an act that defiled the Holy dwelling place of God and mocked God's Laws. The priest and the Levite would not touch the body of the man in the ditch out of deference to the Law, but the Samaritans mocked this Law by vandalizing the dwelling place of God with bodies removed from a ditch.

To the lawyer and those within earshot of Jesus' words, there was no such thing as a Good Samaritan. The Samaritan hero was the ultimate turning of the tables, so much so that the lawyer could not bring himself to say to words good and Samaritan together when he answered Jesus' final question, "Which of these three, do you think, was a neighbor to the man who fell into the hands of the robbers?" The lawyer said, "The one who showed him mercy."

The lawyer could only acknowledge the mercy shown by the person he considered to be the other.

Then Jesus gave the lawyer an impossible task, the part of the parable we turn into teaching moments for our children and ignore for ourselves: "Go and do likewise."

Go and care for the person in the ditch.

Go and care for the person, the group of people you despise.

Go and care for the person wearing the MAGA hat.

Go and care for the person wearing the Black Lives Matter shirt

Go and care for the person who has wronged you.

Help every single person that comes across your path without first wondering if they are "just going to buy booze" with the fist-full of money you are going to give them.

Go and care for every single person who you believe has gotten what they deserved. Care for them without reservation and instead with extravagance.

The Good Samaritan we all like to identify with paid for the stranger he found in the ditch along the dangerous road to stay in an inn, a hotel, for three weeks. Two Denarii was the equivalent of two days of wages.

Go and care for the stranger, the one you despise, with the extravagance of two days earnings. Two day's earnings before taxes.

Jesus's parable moves the focus from what was or what was not done by the priest and Levite to the one who was viewed as the other who responded with mercy.

The lawyer learned eternal life begins with extravagant mercy and now just knowledge of legal loopholes and definitions.

The problem, exposed by the lawyer's inability to even say the words good and Samaritan together, is that this much extravagance is beyond us. Our inability to respond with the extravagance of the Good Samaritan when we see someone lying in a ditch along the road is the reason we look to the priest and Levite in the story with disgust. We deflect and we place ourselves in the role of the Good Samaritan and justify the role by counting up the stranded drivers we have rescued but to be the Good Samaritan we must show extravagant mercy to the one(s) we believe deserve extravagant mercy the least.

Simply put ... we are the ones in the ditch.

We cannot fully understand or recognize the extravagant mercy of the Good Samaritan until we ourselves have been pulled from the ditch by Christ.

Christ, the true Good Samaritan.

The one whose Good News was and continues to be so offensive that he was despised, rejected, and crucified.

We cannot recognize extravagant grace and mercy until we have been saved by the other.

Save by the despised.

Saved by the rejected.

Saved by the crucified.

The late Episcopal priest Robert Capon put it like this— once we see ourselves in the ditch, we can begin to see Christ in the other.

Jesus will reveal our neighbor to us, and like the lawyer, more likely than not it will offend our secularized-Good Samaritan sensibilities.

The Good News is that like the lawyer, our own justification—our enoughness—has already been determined by Christ's extravagant grace and mercy and not by our ability to love our neighbors. Christ will pull us out of the ditch, providing aid and care, regardless of our ability to go and do likewise.

Won't You Be My Neighbor?
Luke 10:25-30a
Taylor Mertins

I drove into the church parking lot on the 5th of July, got out of my car, and walked across the asphalt toward the sanctuary. The light of the early morning sun was shining through one of the stained-glass windows, and everything looked beautiful. It was peacefully quiet, so I knelt down by the altar and prayed for God's will to be done.

And then I got up and walked to my office to get working. I checked some emails, made a few phones calls, and eventually opened up my bible to start working on the Sunday sermon. Some time passed before the phone started ringing, my caller ID said that it was the church secretary calling for the other side of the building.

"What is it?" I answered.

"Umm," she began. "I'm not sure how to quite put this, but did you happen to see the woman in the bikini lying down in one of the church parking spaces on your way in?"

And that's how it began.

A man was going down from Jerusalem to Jericho and fell into the hands of robbers, who stripped him, beat him, and went away, leaving him half dead.

From the safety of the secretary's office we peered through the blinds and assessed the situation. All the way in the furthest spot away from the building, the one closest to the main road, was a young woman on her back, wearing nothing but a bikini, and she wasn't moving.

The secretary promptly elbowed me in the ribs, "You're a pastor, aren't you supposed to do something?"

"Of course, I'm supposed to do something." I said as I waited for someone else driving by the church to do something.

Now by chance a priest was going down the road; and when he saw him, he passed by on the other side. So likewise, a Levite, when he came to the place and saw him, passed by on the other side. But a Samaritan while traveling came near him; and when he saw him, he was moved with pity.

I felt pitiful as I reluctantly made my way across the parking lot, unsure of what was about to happen. Car after car came flying down the road while the woman was curled up on the asphalt, and not one of them so much as slowed down to see the scandalous scene.

As I got closer, I thought about picking up a stick, in order to poke her to make sure she was still of this world, but then she slowly rolled over on to her side and looked me right in the eye. She smelled like the basement of a fraternity house, the little clothing she had on had tiny little rips and tears in it, and she looked utterly perplexed.

For a time neither of us spoke, and then I remembered that I'm a pastor so I said, "Can I help you?"

"Honey, I could use a ride," she said with a hiccup and a twinkle in her eye.

I slowly offered her my hand, and as I picked her up from the ground she said, "You're wondering how I got here. Well so am I. The last thing I remember is being at the park for the 4th of July, partying, having a lot to drink, and then I woke up in someone's yard over there. I tried to walk home, but I lost my phone, my wallet, and I think I'm still drunk, so I decided to take a nap here in this nice parking spot."

"Okay" I said, "I'll drive you home."

The Samaritan went to him and bandaged his wounds, having poured oil and wine on them. Then he put him on his own animal, brought him to an inn, and took care of him.

We wobbled across the lot arm in arm and I could feel the eyeballs of everyone in their cars silently judging me as they drove by. It took an inordinate amount of time to make it from her napping location to my car, and we had to stop no less than three times for fear that she was going to empty out what she had put in the night before.

Eventually, I struggled to get her buckled safely in and asked if she would be able to guide me to her house. To which she replied, "You should have been there last night! The lights and colors were just like illuminating."

So I asked again, and she responded by pointing with her index finger toward the main road.

"Wonderful," I thought, "directions by charades."

We reversed out of the parking lot and I followed her finger across town.

At one point, as we neared the top of a hill, she slowly raised her hands up above her head and shouted, "Woooooo I love this part of the ride!"

When we passed by the police station, she sank as deep as possible into the seat until her feet were up on the dashboard and she let forth a burp that smelled of stale beer, hotdogs, and regret.

When we came to one of the stop lights on the journey, I looked across at my cargo and saw that she had fallen asleep so I gave a little tap on the horn to wake her back up.

We had a time finding her house as we went up and down streets which she either could not read or remember. But eventually, we pulled up in front of a nondescript house and she let out a sigh of acceptance.

The next day he took out two denarii, gave them to the innkeeper, and said, "Take care of him; and when I come back, I will repay you what more you spend."

We sat in the car in uncomfortable silence while she looked out the window at her future with a strange and detached look on her face.

"So, are you a pastor or something?"

"That's what they call me on Sundays."

"Do you do this kind of stuff a lot?"

"Honestly, not enough. What about you?"

"All the time."

And with that she opened up the door and fell out of my car. She promptly picked herself up and staggered across the lawn and up to the front door all the while whistling a strange rendition of what I only realized later was the Star Spangled Banner.

She made it to the front door, and patted down on her non-existent pockets for her keys that she didn't have, and began banging on the door until someone let her in.

And then I drove back to the church.

Which of these three, do you think, was a neighbor to the man who fell into the hands of the robbers" He said, "The one who showed him mercy." Jesus said to him, "Go and do likewise."

Jesus ends his parabolic encounter with this great question, "Which of these three, do you think, was a neighbor to the man who fell into the hands of the robbers?"

And immediately we know how this story is supposed to work. The Samaritan is the good neighbor, and we are supposed to be the good neighbor to our neighbors. But, who really wants to be like that?

The Samaritan is not a very good example, at least he's one that we should be careful of imitation. He's a fool! He wastes his good money on a no good stranger in a ditch, gives him his own ride, and then has the gall to put him up in a swanky hotel without receiving anything in return.

Moreover, Samaritans were outcasts. He is a loser who comes to deal with another loser. His actions are crazy and reprehensible. He lays down whatever his life might've been for someone he doesn't even know, simply because he, as an outcast, has found solidarity with another in the dump that life has offered him.

The loser has found his truest neighbor, another loser.

Which, incidentally, is what the whole gospel is about— Jesus came to save a lost and losing world, by becoming lost and defeated. But in this world of ours, populated by losers, all of us are hopelessly committed to a version of the world dictated by winning, by being the best, by looking out for ourselves.

It would be funny if it wasn't so tragic. But it is tragic, because grace works only in the midst of being able to recognize how badly we need it.

Or, to put it another way, if Jesus wanted to be a better motivational speaker he would've ended the parable thusly: Don't be like the Samaritan; it will ruin your life. You will become a mockery among your friends, you will be a loser.

But Jesus isn't a motivational speaker, he is the Lord.

Which bring us back to the question posed at the end of the parable: Which person was the neighbor to the man in the ditch? But what if there's a better question… and what if that better question is this: Which person in the story is Jesus?

As we have said again and again the parables are primarily about Jesus and only secondarily about us, much to our disappointment.

The central figure, contrary to just about every version of this story ever told or ever preached is not the Good Samaritan. He is simply one of three people who actually figures out what it means to be a properly good neighbor.

Jesus in the story, the one who demands all of our focus and attention, the one to whom the three are either neighborly or not, is the one down in the ditch.

Jesus is free among the dead—He is the one who, again and again, is with the last, the least, the lost, the little, and the dead.

If we want the parable to tell us to imitate the Good Samaritan, which it certainly does, then that's fine.

But if that's all the Good Samaritan is good for, then it isn't very good.

Instead it leaves people like you and me feeling fine and guilty. We feel fine in terms of thinking about times we have been neighborly toward our neighbors, or it can leave us feeling guilty about the many times we haven't.

When, in fact, the whole story is about how Jesus is the one down in the ditch. That he, the Lord of lords, has condescended himself to our miserable existence and can be found in the place of our own ditch-ness and suffering.

This story is but another resounding reminder that we don't have to go looking for Jesus, or even that we have to be like the Good Samaritan to earn Jesus.

It's that Jesus was willing to do for us what we could not, and would not, do for ourselves or our neighbors.

Jesus has moved in next door knowing that we, his neighbors, are a bunch of losers.

And that's good news. Amen.

Meet the Team

Crackers and Grape Juice began in the spring of 2016 with a conversation between Jason Micheli and Teer Hardy. In the years since, two shows have been added to the podcast lineup, Strangely Warmed and You're Not Accepted [formerly (Her)Men*You*Tics], but the goal has remained the same: talking about faith without using stained-glass language.

Jason Micheli is a United Methodist pastor in Annandale, Virginia, having earned degrees from the University of Virginia and Princeton Theological Seminary. He writes the Tamed Cynic blog (tamedcynic.org) and is the author of *Living in Sin* and *Cancer is Funny: Keeping Faith in Stage Serious Chemo*. He lives in the Washington, D.C., area with his wife and two sons. Jason is the co-founder and c of Crackers & Grape Juice.

Teer Hardy is husband, father, and brewery theologian. He lives in Washington D.C. area and is a United Methodist Pastor. Teer has received degrees from West Virginia Wesleyan College and Wesley Theological Seminary. Keep up with his sermons and thoughts on his blog (teerhardy.com) or on Twitter @teerhardy. Teer is the co-founder and c of Crackers & Grape Juice.

Taylor Mertins is a United Methodist pastor in Woodbridge, Virginia, having earned degrees from James Madison University and Duke Divinity School. He regularly posts sermons, devotionals, and other theological reflections at his blog (ThinkandLetThink.com) and you can follow him on Twitter @tcmertins. Taylor is the host of Strangely Warmed.

Dr. Johanna Hartelius is a message expert and founder of VDF Consulting and Professor of Rhetoric at the University of Texas,

Austin. She works with clients at all stages from conceptual invention of ideas and products to the creation of audience strategies. With extensive experience as a professor and award-winning scholar, she leverages her expertise to assess and develop clients' internal communication as well as public image. Johanna is the host of You're Not Accepted.

Tommie Marshell is the editor and producer for Crackers and Grape Juice. A professional photographer in Oklahoma City, Tommie is a lover of chickens, wayward goats, and her two boys. A fan of MMA, when she's not watching UFC she's kicking her Jason and the other Jason in the ass. You can find her work here - https://www.facebook.com/marshellphotography/.

David King is a senior at Haverford College studying Religion and Philosophy. His academic interests are in theology, ethics, and language. Outside of the classroom, David loves to read, sing, bike, and run.

Made in the USA
Middletown, DE
11 January 2020